Instructor's Resource Manual
to accompany

Adler and Proctor's

LOOKING OUT/LOOKING IN

TWELFTH EDITION

Heidi Murphy
Central New Mexico Community College

Ronald B. Adler
Santa Barbara City College

Russell F. Proctor II
Northern Kentucky University

D1416392

THOMSON

WADSWORTH

Australia • Brazil • Canada • Mexico • Singapore • South Africa • Spain • United Kingdom • United States

THOMSON

WADSWORTH

Instructor's Resource Manual for Looking Out, Looking In

Twelfth Edition
Ronald B. Adler · Russell F. Proctor II

Thomson Higher Education
25 Thomson Place
Boston, MA 02210-1202
USA

For more information about our products, contact us at:
Thomson Learning Academic Resource Center
1-800-423-0563

For permission to use material from this text or product, submit a request online at **http://www.thomsonrights.com**

Any additional questions about permissions can be submitted by e-mail to **thomsonrights@thomson.com**

Printed in the United States of America
1 2 3 4 5 09 08 07

ISBN-13: 978-0-495-10128-4
ISBN-10: 0-495-10128-1

CONTENTS

INTRODUCTION

Any successful course is a special mixture of the instructor's teaching style and competencies, the students' interests and abilities, course requirements, time strictures, and choice of text. This Instructor's Resource Manual for *Looking Out/Looking In* is a compilation of various materials we have found useful in teaching our basic interpersonal communication courses. We offer these suggestions with the hope that they will help you develop your own successful blend of ingredients.

You might use the teaching strategies given here in the way a good chef uses recipes. Although they're a starting point, your own special talents and the needs of the specific classroom may call for an adaptation of the basic formula—or even the creation of a new approach. You'll find that the format of *Looking Out/Looking In* will allow this kind of flexibility. The text is organized into eleven chapters, each covering material available for one unit in a course. Chapters 2 through 7 are written so that they may be arranged in any sequence that suits your needs.

This Instructor's Resource Manual, the separate Student Activities Manual, and the text itself provide more exercises and activities than you can probably use in a one-semester course. Once again, we have offered this abundance so that you may pick and choose from among the exercises the ones that will work best for you. We're sure you have many of your own favorite exercises to add to the blend as well.

The Instructor's Resource Manual is organized into three parts as follows:

Part I provides general suggestions concerning course format and grading options. A detailed course syllabus is included to illustrate how to organize a course using the text, the Student Activities Manual, and the Instructor's Resource Manual. This section also contains lists of internet sites that relate to chapter material, including links to journals, publications, collections, bibliographies, teaching strategies, and other course-related materials such as audiotapes and videotapes. The section ends with an extensive list of films and television shows that can be used in class as material for description and analysis, to model desirable interpersonal behavior, and to illustrate effective communication.

Part II contains chapter objectives, and notes for class and student activities in each chapter are found here. Exercises found in the text are listed in boldface type by title in the index of *Looking Out/Looking In*. Activities from the Student Activities Manual are listed by number (e.g., 1.4 for the fourth activity in Chapter 1).

Part III is a test bank of over 1,000 questions and answers keyed to each chapter. They are organized by chapter and then by question type (T = true/false, M = multiple choice, Matching = matching, and E = essay). In addition, you will find that each question is referenced to the text page(s) on which it can be found and by cognitive type. Thus, each question looks like this:

How many parts are there in this *Instructor's Resource Manual*?

a. four
b. three
c. two
d. one
e. This *Instructor's Resource Manual* is not divided into parts.

Answer: b   **Type: M**   **Page 123**   **Knowledge**

Please note that the cognitive type identifiers will help you construct quizzes or exams that are easier or more difficult, depending on your purpose. The cognitive types are:

Knowledge (remembering terms, facts, or theories)

Comprehension (understanding, summarizing material)

Application (use of learned material in new and concrete situations)

Analysis (understanding content and structural form by differentiating, inferring, or outlining)

Synthesis (categorizing, combining, or organizing parts to form a new whole)

Evaluation (judging, comparing, or contrasting the value of material for a given purpose)

Recall (simple recall of reading--no course content)

We include this last category for instructors who like to give simple quizzes on the chapters to check that their students are keeping up with the reading. Other instructors prefer not to use these types of questions because they do not test course concepts. By separating out this category, and grouping the questions together at the beginning of the true/false and the multiple choice sections, instructors who want these questions can find them easily and those who don't want to use them can skip over them quickly.

The test bank is available on computer disk for adopters of *Looking Out/Looking In*.

Part 1

General Suggestions

THE INSTRUCTOR IS THE MAIN INGREDIENT

It is our belief that instructors of interpersonal communication have a particularly rewarding but difficult job. In addition to dealing with the problems faced by all instructors in the classroom, the interpersonal communication teacher faces the challenge of being the model interpersonal communicator in the classroom. In recognition of this role, we strongly suggest that as instructor you actively participate in class exercises. Although there will be many times when you must play a specialized role to facilitate an exercise, we encourage you to interact with the student whenever you can. Our involvement has paid dividends in three ways.

1. It encourages participation from our students. When they see that we are willing to discuss our own experiences, they seem to be encouraged to do the same. Student comments support this assertion.

2. Giving something of ourselves seems to increase our interaction with the group. Although it may sound paradoxical, we've found that we have been most successful when we've taken the risk of participating and making mistakes.

3. Our participation gives us a good perspective on the student's experience in the class. We sometimes discover that what appears to be a simple exercise to us is actually quite challenging; and on the other hand, activities that appear valuable in theory may prove to be dismal failures in practice.

STUDENT FEEDBACK

So that you may discover how students perceive the class, we suggest that you ask your students to make periodic formal evaluations of the course. We found that using a form encourages more specific responses that are the most useful to us. You will probably find that allowing students to respond anonymously works best, although you might allow students to sign their names if they wish. You can design the form to fit your particular situation.

Here is a sample form we have found useful:

1. What expectations did you have for this course (unit)? Has the course (unit) met your expectations? If not, why not?

2. Do you find the workload too light, too heavy, or just right? Were there any specific assignments on which you'd like to comment?

3. Do you think that the grading has been fair? If not, why not?

4. What do you think of the classroom atmosphere? How would you like to see it change?

5. Have the readings (text and outside) been satisfactory? Please give specific examples.

6. Is the teaching style satisfactory? What do you like about your instructor's style? What do you think should be changed?

7. Please make any other comments you feel might be helpful. Do you have any suggestions for improvements? Is there anything you feel we ought to continue doing?

8. What was one thing you learned today?

9. What thing(s) were unclear?

10. What question(s) do you have?

11. What would you like to discuss next time?

12. Do you have any relevant examples or experiences you'd like to share?

THE IMPORTANCE OF EXERCISES

Our unshakable belief is that complete learning takes place only when the student understands a concept on an affective as well as a cognitive level. For example, we consider ourselves to have failed if by the end of the semester a student can list all the factors necessary for effective listening but cares no more about being attentive or understanding than when he or she began our class.

This commitment to encouraging our readers to examine everyday behavior explains the number of exercises you find in *Looking Out/Looking In* and the *Student Activities Manual*. We have purposely supplied more than you'll need for a one-semester course. Our hope is that you can find exercises that work for you for each unit you cover in your interpersonal communication course. We've taken this extra step because we expect that participating in exercises, both group and individual, will make a personal application of the subject almost inevitable. Each activity is designed to lead the reader beyond talking about how people communicate and to ask the question "How do I communicate?"—and further, "How can *I* make my communication more satisfying?"

This emphasis on self-examination necessarily involves asking your class to examine (individually and as a group) feelings and behaviors that often aren't revealed in academic settings. Although we've found that very little growth comes without this kind of examination, it's absolutely essential not to push too hard, not to demand more self-disclosure or risk than the group is ready to volunteer. And always, we respect a student's right to pass or to carry out an alternate task in place of a given exercise. Despite our best efforts, we are often unaware of the personal anguish that some of our students suffer that they would prefer to keep private.

You'll find that the text exercises start by asking for very simple contributions and progress gradually to relatively greater amounts of self-disclosure. We hope that this pacing will prevent any anxiety on the part of your students; but in any doubtful cases, we urge you to move at whatever pace seems right for your situation.

STUDENT ACTIVITIES MANUAL USE

The *Student Activities Manual* is a valuable student aid for the course.

Student Activities

In addition to the many exercises in the text, the *Student Activities Manual* for the twelfth edition has 50 individual and group Skill Builder and Invitations to Insight activities that focus on written and oral interpersonal communication skills. Additional features of the *Student Activities Manual* are the *Your Call case studies* that focus on ethics, competence, and adaptation to situations; *Mediated Messages activities,* which invite students to adapt their knowledge of interpersonal communication to mediated situations; *oral skill* activities designed to allow students to exhibit communication behaviors they have studied; and *group discussion topics and activities* designed to encourage collaborative learning, listening skills, affective and cognitive development, and cognitive complexity.

Study Guide

The Study Guide section contains over 500 puzzles and test questions with answers that enable students to test themselves on the many concepts and skills contained in the text. In addition, extensive outlines help students check their reading or follow classroom lectures. Students using the Study Guide aids in the *Student Activities Manual* should understand class material more readily, guide themselves through skill development more easily, and score higher on exams.

CLASSROOM ENVIRONMENT

Although many of the exercises and activities in this book suggest particular arrangements, we feel that some general notes on the design of the classroom may be in order. If we expect our students to interact with each other, it becomes very important to create the best environment possible to promote this development. Knowing that we all work within certain limitations, we'd like to mention some of the items we have found helpful. Chapter 6 speaks directly to this subject.

1. Arrange the classroom seating so that all members of the group can see each other. If the room plan will allow it, a circle is the most useful arrangement.

2. If possible, choose comfortable chairs or small table-armed desks that can be easily rearranged into large groups, small groups, and dyads. Vary the arrangement of the classroom to meet the needs of lecture, discussion and group work.

3. Regroup students frequently. This allows them to get to know many more people and to get new perspectives on communication behavior.

Another way to set up a good classroom environment is to set up expectations about attitude and behavior in one of the first classes. Two methods that address this are the "contract" and the "standards for student success."

Bill Edwards of Columbus State University in Georgia offers this version of an instructor/student "contract" that he and his students adapted from Melanie Booth-Butterfield at West Virginia University.

I divide my class into two groups. One group will re-write the contract for the professor and the other group will re-write the contract for the students by accepting, revising, adding, and omitting contract items.

Instructions: Read the following contracts. Revise the contracts in any way you see fit. Your goal is to design a good contract that each party will sign. You can omit, revise, or accept any item. You can create new items.

INTERPERSONAL COMMUNICATION *PROFESSOR'S OATH*

As your professor I pledge that I will do the following appropriate teacher behaviors:

I will strive to be on time for class and to dismiss the class in a timely fashion when I have finished, so that you don't have your time wasted.

I will offer you an opportunity to ask questions and make observations.

I will respect you and treat you as an adult.

I will try to always be fully prepared and well-organized in class.

My material will be up-to-date and contemporary in hopes that it will apply to your life.

I will attempt to be unbiased and reasonable in my approach to the material.

I will always be available to talk to you during my office hours.

I will try to be energetic, encouraging, and enthusiastic, because I like the material and I hope you do too.

None of the assignments will be busy work. Each will have direct relation to class goals.

I will prepare you for assignments and exams.

I will provide quick feedback on written assignments and exams.

I will put forth effort in teaching this class.

Signature: _____

INTERPERSONAL COMMUNICATION *STUDENT'S OATH*

As a student in this course I pledge to do these appropriate student behaviors:

I will be actively involved with the class and its activities, asking questions, providing examples, etc.

I will smile and nod at my professor at lot, because I know this encourages the teacher to do his/her best.

I will not read newspapers, have side conversations, wear my headset, have my beeper turned on, pack up early during class because I know that it hurts my learning and my teacher's feelings.

I will be on time for class on a regular basis.

I will not attempt to cheat on exams, copy others' assignments, turn in others' work as my own, etc. All work that I do in this class will be my own original work.

I will be polite and cooperative with my teacher and classmates. I won't try to put anything over on them, or ask them to make exceptions for me.

I will try to always stay awake during class.

I will endeavor to keep my mind open to the ideas presented and really consider how they affect my life.

I will put forth effort in taking this class.

Signature: _____

A second way of setting up a positive classroom environment comes from the Communication faculty at Santa Barbara City College. They put the following "Standards for Student Success" in all course packets and review the expectations at the outset of each semester:

STANDARDS FOR STUDENT SUCCESS IN COMMUNICATION DEPARTMENT COURSES

To Our Students:

Welcome to the Communication Department! Your instructor may choose to share the ten expectations below with you. These standards or norms for success address attitudes and behaviors beyond the good practices you have already acquired in your years of experience in educational environments. Some of these are givens that fall under the heading of routine but sometimes unstated premises that operate in healthy classrooms. We believe that noting expectations early in the semester will help you to be a successful learner, provide benefits for other students in the class, save time, and assist your instructor in conducting effective class sessions that offer every student the opportunity to be heard and acknowledged as a productive course participant.

Box continued

Your instructor will discuss variances in the expectations with you. We are, after all, individuals whose standards may differ. We hope you will talk to your instructor about your expectations as well. The most constructive classroom environment will be one that encompasses the best that everyone—instructor and students alike—can offer to produce a positive learning experience . . . and that is what Santa Barbara City College is all about.

The Communication Faculty at Santa Barbara City College

1. **Attend classes regularly, be on time, and stay for the entire class period.** In most courses, students receive attendance credit/points but the points are less important on a day-to-day basis than what you will miss by unnecessary absences and what your classmates will lose in not having your discussion contributions. Late-comers are a distraction to everyone. Anticipate challenges and try to plan for them. For example, it is well known that finding a parking spot at 10:00 a.m. is difficult. Plan your schedule with enough flex time to accommodate circling the lots until you find a slot.

2. **Participate in class discussion.** Some courses have participation points and others do not. Your discussion contributions are important in either case. Be a positive force in your classroom interaction. Ask questions, express your opinions, and make yourself known as someone who is actively involved.

3. **Use the instructor's office hours.** This time is set aside explicitly for you to talk with your teachers. You don't have to come with a monumental issue or problem (although these are good times to drop by). Students often use office hours to:
   a. introduce themselves to the instructor.
   b. provide important information about unique challenges such as learning disabilities, child care issues, and potential conflicts with work responsibilities outside the college. Crucial factors known in advance are likely to be better accommodated than last-minute surprises.
   c. ask questions about course material and/or discuss individual problems. In many cases, the instructor will never know your concerns unless you speak up.
   d. pass the time of day sharing insights and observations. The office hour is yours. A casual and non task-oriented visit may produce positive results on both sides.

4. **Avoid speaking with your instructor about significant issues immediately before and after class** as s/he is trying to either get everything ready for one class or prepare for the one starting in 10 minutes. Use office hours, e-mail, or telephone messages to contact the instructor on important items. The SBCC voice mail allows you 24-hour access. We will return calls promptly if we are not in when you call. (Leave your name and phone number.)

5. **Understand that instructional memory is not flawless.** Many of us have 150 students and more. It is hard to recall all the details of your class performance without help. If you want to discuss, for example, your progress from one assignment to the next, bring along instructor critiques and any other helpful notes to the meeting with your instructor. Be prepared to explain your issue or complaint. If videotape is available, review it before discussion with your instructor. If you have questions about a grade, write out your reasons so your teacher can see the specifics.

6. **Take notes in class.** Informed discussion is far more likely to arise from documented notes than hazy recall. Notes will also aid study for exams.

7. **Read assignments in the text and comply with homework expectations on the dates assigned.** Bring materials required (Scantron answer sheets, pencils, etc.) when needed. Don't expect others to bail you out if you neglect your responsibilities.

8. **Review the syllabus periodically.** Ask questions if you have them. Know what is expected. If you don't know, ask.

9. **Participate in class activity appropriately.** This involves such disparate behaviors as listening to others and acknowledging opposing viewpoints, choosing language that avoids uselessly antagonizing others (obscenity, personal attacks, hostile or sarcastic comments, etc.), blatantly reading *The Channels* or some other non-course-related text while class matters are in progress, talking with other students while someone else (who has the floor) is trying to speak, and taking a nap during class. Some of these negative behaviors may seem barely worth mention but they do occur and they do influence classroom interaction. Most of the courses in the Communication Department are relatively small. One person's distracting behavior can have a larger impact than you might imagine. For the student or students trying to present a speech, a group project, a review of the literature, and so forth, audience members who appear to be dozing or paying no attention whatever, present an extremely bothersome problem. Your responsibility as a student of Communication theory and practice includes being an open, alert, courteous, and receptive listener, as well as a competent presenter.

10. **Take responsibility for your education.** Excuses and rationalizations should be eliminated from your academic repertoire. Know that your instructors are human and predisposed to trust rather than doubt you. If you get away with a faked illness or fabricated emergency, you may find that the inevitable result hurts you more than anyone else. In one recent course, the instructor distributed a take-home quiz with instructions to use the text as a resource but work alone in discovering the answers. A student inquired, "How will you know if we cheat?" The teacher responded, "I probably won't ever know . . . but you will."

Learning is not a game or a contest to discover who is most adept at bending/breaking the rules to suit individual needs. It is an opportunity to prepare for life, professional requirements, and individual success—both as a singular human being and a contributing member of an enduring social network. You are attending Santa Barbara City College in the interest of your own professional advancement and the enhancement of the society in which you live. We are here to help you give both of these aims your best shot. Help us, and we will do our best to help you.

METHODS OF EVALUATION

A good evaluation system should serve at least two purposes:

1. It should give the student feedback on his or her mastery of the skills under study to answer the question, "How well do I understand the subject?"

2. It should give the instructor feedback on how successful he or she has been in communicating the subject matter to the students to answer the question " Which areas have I taught successfully and which do I need to cover in greater depth or in a different way?

At the same time, a good system of evaluation should avoid the trap of inviting and rewarding unproductive behaviors—busy work, deceit, and "shooting the bull."

At first, we despaired of finding a useful system of grading that would help rather than hinder students and teachers. But experience has shown that there are several good alternatives. In addition, we have found that no matter which grading system we used, it was very important to delineate clearly the method of grading, the student assignments, and the assignment due dates at the outset of the course. We've also found it important to collect work on the assigned date. These practices seem to reinforce the seriousness of the work involved, increasing respect for the instructor and the course.

A number of grading alternatives follow, which can be used either singly or in combination. For each, we have listed both advantages and disadvantages.

Traditional Examinations

The biggest advantage of traditional examinations is the greater likelihood that students will read and study the text with care. We have found that giving a quiz before the discussion of each chapter works well. Test questions are for checking comprehension after the unit has been studied. We have included over 1100 questions in true/false, multiple choice, matching, and essay formats. The questions appear in print in this manual, and on computer disk (in either PC or MAC formats) for adopters of *Looking Out/Looking In*.

The principal disadvantage of a grading system based only on tests is that it may not actually measure the most important goals of the class, namely improving the student's everyday communication behavior. For example, it is entirely possible for a student to describe in writing a number of effective listening behaviors, but he or she may never practice any of them. Thus, tests may measure skill in taking tests about communication and little else.

Practice tests can be a good study aid for students. With the large number of test items available in this test bank, it is relatively easy to create short exams for practice. Whether you do it in class or a laboratory situation, students can grade themselves and review items to prepare for the graded exam.

Student-Planned Examinations

In this procedure, students split into small groups, each of which submits several possible examination questions. All questions are then displayed to the entire class, with the understanding that the instructor will select several of them for the actual test.

Although this method carries the same disadvantage as the traditional method just described, students do study the material more intensively as they select and draw up questions. Another challenge is students' unfamiliarity with writing exam questions; it can take some time before items of quality emerge.

Written/Oral Skill Assignments

In this approach, the emphasis is placed on performance of the skills introduced in *Looking Out/Looking In*. After the presentation of material in class, students use many of the exercises from the *Student Activities Manual* to practice the concepts in class. Then written and/or oral exercises are assigned as tests of the skills introduced.

A major advantage of this approach is that instructors can evaluate the student's ability to operationalize the skills introduced. Both written and oral abilities are assessed, and students who score poorly on objective tests can often demonstrate their knowledge in essay and oral formats. Another advantage is the amount of involvement students feel in the class when they see one another performing the skills they have studied; this also serves to help students to individualize the skills, to make them realistic by noting real-life situations in which they are used, and to move toward integrating the communication skills into their everyday lives.

A disadvantage of this approach is that it can take a lot of class time. Any videotaping facility on campus can help here by allowing students to practice oral skills and tape them for playback in class. A communication laboratory with videotape cameras and communication tutors can ease the burden on the instructor.

Student-Instructor Contracts

In this system, students and instructor develop a specific program of study that the students agree to undertake, in return for which they receive a predetermined grade. Contracts can cover work corresponding to units of study, or they can be written for term projects, which may take the place of a final examination. Projects can take many forms—research papers, interviews, dramatic productions, surveys, journals.

There are two advantages to such a plan. First, it demands student initiative in proposing a course of study—a pleasant contrast to more passive types of assignments in which students play less creative roles. Also, such a format allows students some latitude in choosing how to channel their energies. Research and experience show that the quality of work and motivation are higher when students work on subjects with a high degree of personal interest.

Two disadvantages often occur in the contract method. First, some tasks that students choose may not focus on concepts that the instructor deems most important. However, this difficulty can be remedied by defining acceptable areas of study—for example, "Develop a project demonstrating three factors influencing perception and communication." The second disadvantage lies in the inability of some students to be self-motivated scholars. After being trained for twelve or more years in the passive art of test taking, it is difficult to suddenly have to define and pursue one's own course of study.

Journal (Diary) Assignments

In place of examinations, some instructors substitute journal assignments in which students reflect on how topics under study apply to their personal lives. Journals may either be graded or returned to the student for revisions until they are satisfactory.

The advantage of such an approach to evaluation lies in extending the concepts discussed in the classroom into the student's everyday relationships. The value of such applications is obvious in a course designed to improve the participant's communication skills.

One potential disadvantage lies in the failure of journals to focus clearly on key concepts discussed in class. We think this problem can be remedied by assigning journals that concentrate on specific topics, for example, "Record the number and types of destructive styles of conflict you use during the next week." Many assignments in the *Student Activities Manual* follow this method; a collection of these from each chapter would make a substantial journal. Most of the exercises labeled "Invitation to Insight" in the *Student Activities Manual* are useful as journal entries.

Book Reports/Exercises

Book reports may be assigned to students to encourage more in-depth study of a particular subject.

The greatest disadvantage of book reports as a method of evaluation is that students often prepare reports that only regurgitate what was said in the book. To overcome this disadvantage, when assigning book reports, we have asked students to create an activity from the book they have read. The activity should be designed to teach others in the class one important thing (cognitive or affective) that the student gleaned from the book. We suggest that students look in the text for model exercises. Then we periodically set aside a class session for students to work out their activities with their classmates. Class members are asked to give feedback evaluating each student's exercise. The book report/exercise method seems to reinforce learning of the basic tenets of each book, and most students seem to enjoy sharing discoveries with their classmates.

Self-Evaluation

This method operates on the assumption that in many respects, the student is in the best position to judge his or her own progress in the course. Instructors who use self-evaluation systems ask each student to select a grade that reflects that person's effort and gain in understanding key ideas. Usually, the student is asked to write an explanation for the chosen grade.

The first advantage of this approach is its emphasis on self-judgment. It demonstrates that the student is responsible for his or her own growth and that whatever grade appears on the transcript is merely a symbol of that growth. Second, asking a student the question "What grade do you deserve?" often generates much more self-reflection about effort expended than any other system of evaluation.

The most obvious disadvantage is the potential for abuse. There is no guarantee that a lazy student will not take a high grade. A second shortcoming is the absence of any feedback from the instructor, who presumably has some valuable information about the student's progress. A remedy is to have the instructor reserve the right to give the final grade.

Peer Evaluation

In this system, the students assign each other individual grades based on the assumption that in a communication course, the perceptions of one's peers are a good indication of improvement and mastery of skills. The most efficient method of peer evaluation we've discovered involves reproducing the names of every class member, four to six names to a page. The names are equally spaced down the left side of the paper, and horizontal lines are drawn to separate the area on the paper that will be used to write comments to the student named there. (The back side of each student's space may also be used if the writer needs more room.)

Copies of this special evaluation roster are then distributed to everyone in the class. Each student records a grade and a statement of specifics that supports the assigned grade for each classmate. Ample time should be allowed for this assignment. In-class time seems to result in the best feedback.

The completed pages are collected. Like pages are stapled together and then cut with a paper cutter into individual packets. At the first opportunity, these packets are returned to the individual student. If all has gone well, the student will receive a sheaf of papers containing a grade and an evaluation from every member of the class.

The greatest advantage of peer evaluation is the feedback each student receives. If the class has been successful, students should know each other well enough to make many valuable comments. Assuming that class members are a representative sampling of the general population, the comments should be a fair reflection of the way a student is perceived outside of class.

The biggest disadvantage of this method is the desire of students to be nice to avoid any negative feedback—thus turning the exercise into an experience reminiscent of signing high school yearbooks. On the other hand, there is always the danger (although experience shows it to be extremely rare) that some unfavorable feedback can be psychologically damaging to the student.

GRADING SYSTEMS

Recognizing the strengths and weaknesses of each method of evaluation, you may want to combine several of them to suit your needs. Several possible grading systems follow as illustrations. We have successfully used each of these systems. You'll find that we have personalized each system by choosing to emphasize different areas. In addition, each grading system also posits a slightly different type of student-teacher relationship.

Grading System Option 1: *Student Activities Manual* Emphasis (Examinations, Quizzes, Attendance, Written and Oral Exercises)

Objective This grading system places added emphasis on the individual student's involvement with the various units covered in the course. It asks that students demonstrate their knowledge on traditional exams and quizzes and also in written exercises or oral skill checks from the *Student Activities Manual*. The philosophy underlying this approach is that communication skills should be studied and practiced and then performed orally to demonstrate knowledge of the material. It is believed that students will be more likely to use communication skills in their personal lives that they have practiced in a number of ways in class.

Examinations	35% of the final grade
Quizzes	10% of the final grade
Oral/Written Assignments	40% of the final grade
Attendance	10% of the final grade
Participation/Extra Assignment	5% of the final grade

Here are the points you will need to earn the grade of your choice:

A = 900–1000

B = 800–899

C = 700–799

D = 650–699

Here are the activities that will earn you points:

100 points. Attendance. Everyone will start with 100 points. You are entitled to a certain number of absences without penalty (3 for classes that meet 3 times a week, 2 for classes that meet 2 times, and 1 for a class that meets only once). Beyond these, each missed meeting will cost you points (correspondingly 6, 9, and 18), on the assumption that you need to be present to learn and practice the skills introduced in the course. Anyone who drops below 75 points in this area may be dropped.

50 points. Class Activities. Fifty points are available here for quality of class participation, extra assignments, or other activities assigned by the instructor.

100 points. Quizzes. There will be ten brief quizzes, designed to check your reading of the text. These quizzes are simple recall quizzes and are aimed only at being sure you've read the assigned pages. To take the quizzes, you'll need a packet of Scantron quiz-strips—the 15-question size. (10 quizzes x 10 points = 100 points)

350 points. Tests. There will be two 100-point midterms and a 150-point final exam. These exams will consist of objective questions (multiple choice, true/false and matching). For the exams you will need a packet of 100-item Scantron test strips. (100 + 100 + 150 = 350 points)

200 points. Written Exercises. Written exercises from the *Student Activities Manual* will help you apply course information to your own life. Entries will be assigned periodically, and selected assignments will be collected and graded. Exercises turned in late will be penalized for each class session they are overdue. (5 exercises x 40 points = 200 points)

200 points. Oral Skill Demonstrations. These dyadic exercises from the *Student Activities Manual* will help you orally practice the skills covered in class by applying them to your experience and receiving feedback from a partner. Anyone not in class when these exercises are conducted forfeits the points. (5 exercises x 40 points = 200 points)

NOTE: Some exercises may need to be videotaped in class or in the communication laboratory. You will be able to review videotaped oral skills after they are graded by the instructor.

Grading System Option 2: Attendance, Tests, Quizzes, Papers, Projects, Book Reports

The grade you earn in this class will depend on the amount of work you choose to do as well as its quality. Following is a list of activities, each of which will earn you a number of points. None of these activities is required. You choose the grade you want and pick the tasks that look most appealing that will earn you that grade.

Here are the points you will need to earn the grade of your choice:

    A = 420–500
    B = 340–419
    C = 220–339
    D = 180–219

Here are the activities that will earn the points:

100 points. Attendance. Everyone will start with 100 points. You are entitled to a certain number of absences without penalty (3 for MWF classes, 2 for TTh classes, 1 for evening classes). Beyond these, each meeting you miss will cost you points (10 for MWF classes, 15 for TTh classes, 30 for evening classes), on the assumption that you need to be present to learn and practice the skills introduced in this course. Anyone who drops below 50 points in this area will be dropped from the class.

150 points. Tests and Quizzes. There will be seven brief 10-point quizzes, designed to check your reading of the chapters of *Looking Out/Looking In*. These quizzes will be simple and are aimed only at being sure you've read the assigned pages.

In addition, there will be a 40-point midterm and a 40-point final examination, designed to test your understanding and your ability to apply the information discussed in this class.

150 points. Papers. You will be given a number of opportunities to write papers throughout the semester. You may write on up to six of the topics presented. Each paper will be worth 25 points.

These papers aren't tests. Their purpose is to help you see how the ideas we discuss apply to your everyday life. They will lead you to think about the way you presently communicate, offer you some alternatives, and invite you to try these alternatives to see if they help.

100 points. Projects and Book Reports. The project gives you an opportunity to focus on whatever area of interpersonal communication especially interests you. It might take the form of an experiment in which you try out different behaviors to see which work best, a research paper in which you explore an area of personal interest, or a questionnaire or survey to learn how other people see you or deal with a situation similar to yours. You may want to keep a journal to record certain kinds of communication, which you will then analyze.

In any case, if you are interested in doing a project, you will need to complete and turn in a contract form by _____. It will include a description of the area you want to explore, why that area interests you, how you plan to work on that area, and what you will hand in. In addition, it will indicate how many points you want to work for on your project. The instructor will look over your contract and either sign it or negotiate revisions with you. After signing it, the contract becomes the standard against which the quality of your work will be measured. All projects must be typewritten and are due no later than _____.

Book reports may be done on any book in the bibliography you will receive in class or on any title you clear with the instructor in advance. You may write up to two reports, each of which will be worth up to 50 points.

Your reports must be typewritten and should include a chapter-by-chapter discussion of the book in which you (1) describe the author's ideas in the chapter and (2) discuss how these ideas relate to your life.

Finally, you should write a conclusion in which you summarize your opinions of the book and how it relates to your own life.

Optional Paper Topics. The following paper topics are designed to help you see how the ideas discussed in class apply to your own life. These papers aren't tests. Their purpose is to help you think about the way you presently communicate, offer you some alternatives, and invite you to try out these alternatives to see if they help.

You can earn up to 25 points for each paper you write, and you may write as many as six papers. (In addition to the papers described on this sheet, you may propose in writing any other paper assignment that you believe will help you apply the concepts discussed. With the instructor's approval, such assignments will substitute for one or more of the papers.) In each case where there is more than one paper described for a chapter, you may do only one of the papers described. The last dates each paper will be accepted will be announced in class, and no work will be accepted after those dates.

The format for each paper involves:

1. Following the instructions in the text.

2. Writing a summary that describes

    a. What (if anything) you learned about yourself in following the instructions.

    b. How you feel about this learning (satisfied, indifferent, depressed, resolved, etc.).

    c. Anything you want to say about the exercise (suggest changes, describe difficulties, etc.).

Paper Topics
Chapter 1: A First Look at Interpersonal Relationships
1. Expanding your Communication Effectiveness (1.2 in *Student Activities Manual*)

Chapter 2: Communication and Identity: Creating and Presenting the Self
2. Who Do You Think You Are? (2.1 in *Student Activities Manual*)
3. Reevaluating Your "Can'ts" (2.4 in *Student Activities Manual*)

Chapter 3: Perception: What You See Is What You Get
4. Shifting Perspectives (Pillow Method) (3.3 in *Student Activities Manual*)
5. Your Call—Perception (3.8 in *Student Activities Manual*)

Chapter 4: Emotions: Thinking, Feeling, and Communicating

6. Recognize Your Feelings (text, p. 133)

7. Disputing Irrational Thoughts (4.5 in *Student Activities Manual*)

Chapter 5: Language: Barrier and Bridge

8. Effective Language (5.5 in *Student Activities Manual*)

9. Your Call—Language (5.7 in *Student Activities Manual*)

Chapter 6: Nonverbal Communication: Messages beyond Words

10. Ambiguity, Contradiction & Congruence (6.3 in *Student Activities Manual*)

Chapter 7: Listening: More than Meets the Ear

11. Listening Choices (7.4 in *Student Activities Manual*)

Chapter 8: Communication and Relational Dynamics

12. Discovering Dialectics (8.1 in *Student Activities Manual*)

13. Relational Stages (8.2 in *Student Activities Manual*)

Chapter 9: Intimacy and Distance in Relational Communication

14. Reasons for Nondisclosure (9.2 in *Student Activities Manual*)

Chapter 10: Improving Communication Climates

15. Understanding Defensive Responses (10.1 in *Student Activities Manual*)

16. Your Call—Climate (10.7 in *Student Activities Manual*)

Chapter 11: Managing Interpersonal Conflicts

17. Understanding Conflict Styles (11.1 in *Student Activities Manual*)

18. Win-Win Problem Solving (11.4 in *Student Activities Manual*)

Grading System Option 3: Instructor, Peer, and Self-Evaluations

Objective

To give each student as much control over his or her grade as possible while dealing with the responsibility this control demands.

Overview of Policy

To be successful and receive credit for this class, the following requirements must be met:

1. Attendance in class must be satisfactory.

2. All homework assignments must be completed and satisfactory.

3. Participation in class activities must be satisfactory to peers, self, and instructor.

If these requirements are met satisfactorily, you will receive a C grade.

The B-grade requirement may be met by reading two books, twelve articles, or a combination of one book and six articles.

If you wish to receive an A grade, you must complete satisfactorily the C and B requirements and, in addition, design and carry out a project concerning some aspect of interpersonal communication.

Details on Option 3 System

Attendance Requirement. The student's attendance will account for 30 percent of his or her grade. Each student will receive a notice of attendance requirements at the beginning of the course. To illustrate, here is a set of regulations for an MWF class:

0 to 1 class period missed	=	A for attendance part of grade
2 class periods missed	=	B for attendance part of grade
3 class periods missed	=	C for attendance part of grade
4 class periods missed	=	D for attendance part of grade
5 or more class periods missed	=	F for attendance part of grade

Adjustments would be made for classes meeting twice (TTh) a week or once a week. Students should be reminded that attendance governs only part of the grade and that missing four class periods doesn't necessarily mean that a semester grade of D will result. It would depend on the grades in the other areas and the amount of work the student completes.

Homework Requirements. There will be nine to twelve homework assignments. They will consist of journals, inventories, self-observation, and so on. There will be no letter grades on these assignments. Each assignment will be evaluated as satisfactory, unsatisfactory, or incomplete. To fulfill this requirement, the student must have all assignments handed in, completed, and satisfactory. Opportunity may be given to bring unsatisfactory homework up to a satisfactory level.

Quizzes. Quizzes will be given on the first class meeting after the class has been assigned to complete the reading of a chapter in the text. These quizzes will be graded but will be counted only to help the student achieve a higher grade. In other words, you will be rewarded if you have done the assigned reading and scored well on the quiz. You may take the quiz only when it is given to the entire class—no make-ups of quizzes.

Participation Requirements. You are already aware that attendance is extremely important in this class. There is a considerable amount of student participation during each class meeting. There is no available way to make up the activities and exercises that involve the class. However, just being present in the classroom will not satisfy the participation requirement. It is necessary for you to take an active part because you will be evaluated by fellow classmates, instructor, and yourself. Heading the listed criteria for these evaluations will be class participation.

Instructor's Evaluation. The instructor's evaluation will account for 30 percent of your grade. In arriving at that grade, your homework and classroom participation (with particular attention to improvement and attitude) will be reviewed. All class participants are expected to cooperate with the various activities and exercises in class and to be supportive of classmates. You should realize that some of the instructor's grade will come from impressions formed of your actions and reactions in the class. In other words, the instructor will form a subjective opinion of your effort in the class.

Peer Evaluation. This will account for 20 percent of the final grade. Each student is required to grade all the other students in the class. This evaluation will be done with criteria that have been published and in most cases developed by the class.

In this feedback process, students should place special emphasis on improvement that has been observed and improvement that needs to be made.

To make this process manageable, we will use the following method. Twice during the term, you will be asked to give feedback to your classmates—at about the halfway point and again at the end of the semester. The second evaluation will include a grade from each member of the class. You will arrive at your final peer-evaluation grade by finding the average of all the grades you receive.

Self-Evaluation. This will count for 20 percent of your final grade. At the end of the course, you will assign yourself a grade, which you must be able to justify in terms of criteria worked out before this assignment. Should there be any question about the self-grade assigned, the instructor will confer with the student so that they may reach an understanding.

B Grade. Attendance, instructor's and peer evaluation, and self-evaluation must be satisfactory before a student is eligible for a C grade. If a student wants to pursue a B grade, he or she must complete the previous requirements plus the following:

Select from the book list provided two books, read them, and write reports on the forms provided and/or give an oral report to a small group of classmates. In either case, the student must demonstrate that he or she has read the book, from the information given in the report.

or

Select twelve articles from a list of articles that have been collected and placed on reserve in the library by the instructor. These articles are to be read and reported on by completing an Article Report Form that will be provided for each article. The student may also be required to give oral reports to small groups in class.

or

Do a combination reading assignment of one book and six articles. Article and book reports that are not written in acceptable form—complete sentences, correct spelling, sensible paragraphs, and so on will be returned as unsatisfactory. They may be corrected and resubmitted, provided there is enough time for the instructor to review them a second time.

A Grade. If a student expects to receive an A grade, he or she must demonstrate the capacity to do superior work.

In this class, this will take the form of some kind of project concerned with interpersonal communication.

This project will earn an A grade only if it is of excellent quality and both the B and C grade requirements are met.

The A project must follow this schedule:

Within the first ten class hours, a plan must be submitted to the instructor. Remember, designing your own individual project is part of the assignment. Under no circumstances will the instructor give you a project to complete.

At the halfway mark, the instructor will meet with each student attempting an A project. It will be determined at that time if the project is of a kind that will be informative for all the class. If this is the case, it would be presented during a class period. If not, it would be submitted in written form. The specific written form will be agreed on at this time.

As soon as the projects are finished, they should be presented in class or submitted in writing. No project will be received for credit during the last two class meetings.

Some projects that have been attempted in the past follow.

Research Papers

How to Break Up and Remain Friends

Giving and Receiving Criticism Effectively

Interpersonal Communication in Personnel Management

A Study in How We Learn to Be Parents

An Investigation into the Language of Men and Women

Methods for Improving the Handling of Human Conflict.

Personal Projects

Improving my relationships with my coworkers

Becoming a better partner in my marriage

Improving the quality of communication with my fourteen-year-old daughter

Increasing my participation in class

Improving my relationship with my stepfather

Showing more positive independence around my parents

Other Projects

Do T-shirts communicate? (presented as a slide show to the class)

How conditioned are we to our sex roles? (class participation)

How do married couples want their mates to say, "I love you"?

How much does another's expectations of me influence my actions?

Establishing effective family meetings.

All of the projects were acceptable. Not all of them, however, earned their designer an A—not because of the subject matter but rather because of an insufficient amount of effort on the student's part.

SUGGESTED COURSE SYLLABUS

The following course syllabus is a sample outline that uses *Looking Out/Looking In* as the basic text. You may find a part or all of this syllabus useful in designing your own course outline. Since the lengths of semesters vary, we have arbitrarily assumed a 15-week duration for this course with classes meeting three times a week for 50-minute sessions. You can see and download customizable syllabi for 16-week (2 classes per week) and 10-week (3 classes per week) courses at the *Looking Out/Looking In* instructor's website.

Week 1

Class 1

Topic: Getting Started

The instructor explains the nature of the course and completes normal beginning-of-course housekeeping chores. Particular emphasis should be made on the classroom participation that will be expected from each student.

To reinforce the participation dimension of the course, begin at once with the exercise Name Chain, wherein each member of the group learns the names of all the others.

Exercise: Name Chain

(Find under Chapter One Notes following this section of *Instructor's Resource Manual*.)

Assignment: Obtain your own copy of *Looking Out/Looking In* and the *Student Activities Manual*. Begin Chapter One.

NOTE: Students should read all the material presented in each chapter, including the poetry, quotations found in the page margins, pictures and cartoons, exercises, and the regular text. All the material in each chapter is part of the message.

Class 2

Topic: Getting to Know One Another

Activity: Explain the importance of knowing one another in a communication skills class. It is important that students feel as comfortable as possible to experience less anxiety in trying out new communication behaviors.

Exercise: Introductions

(Find under Chapter One Notes following this section of *Instructor's Resource Manual*.)

Assignment:

Complete your communication skills inventory (1.1 in *Student Activities Manual*).

Read Chapter One (quiz to verify reading—next class session).

Complete the *Study Guide* section of the *Student Activities Manual* for Chapter 1.

Class 3

Quiz: Chapter 1

Topic: The Importance of Human Communication

Activity: Encourage discussion of basic human needs and how communication is necessary to obtain them. Use the student's Communication Skills Inventory to identify goals for the class.

Assignment: Expanding Your Communication Effectiveness (1.2 in *Student Activities Manual*)

Week 2

Class 1

Topic: Effective Communication

Exercise:

CMC—Computer-Mediated Communication (channels) (1.3 in *Student Activities Manual*)

Your Call—Communication Basics (1.4 in *Student Activities Manual*).

Assignment:

Read Chapter Two of text.

Complete the *Study Guide* section of the *Student Activities Manual* for Chapter 2.

Class 2

Quiz: Chapter Two

Topic: The Self-Concept

Activity: Instigate discussion of the different ways in which our self-concept may have developed.

Exercise: Who Do You Think You Are? (2.1 in *Student Activities Manual*)

Assignment: Self-Concept Inventory (2.2 in *Student Activities Manual*)

Class 3

Topic: Characteristics of Your Self-Concept

Exercise:

Discuss Self-Concept Inventory (2.2 in *Student Activities Manual*).

Ego Boosters and Busters (2.3 in *Student Activities Manual*)

Assignment: Reevaluating Your "Can'ts" (2.4 in *Student Activities Manual*)

Week 3

Class 1

Topic: Self-fulfilling Prophecies/Changing the Self-Concept

Exercises: Reevaluating Your "Can'ts" (2.4 in *Student Activities Manual*)

Assignment: Prepare Mediated Messages—Identity Management (2.6 in *Student Activities Manual*)

Class 2

Topic: Managing Impressions

Exercise:

Discussion groups compare their prepared responses to Mediated Messages—Identity Management (2.7 in *Student Activities Manual*)

Success in Managing Impressions (2.5 in *Student Activities Manual*)

Assignment:

Read Chapter Three for quiz.

Complete the *Study Guide* section of the *Student Activities Manual* for Chapter 3.

Class 3

Quiz: Chapter Three

Topic: The Process of Perception

Activity: Discuss the process of perception; students give examples and discuss in groups how perception influences communication. Relate to concept of self and how clear messages are or are not given. Use Your Perceptual Filters (text, p. 86).

Assignment: Guarding Against Perceptual Errors (3.1 in *Student Activities Manual*)

Week 4

Class 1

Topic: Accuracy and Inaccuracy of Perception

Exercise:

Discuss Guarding Against Perceptual Errors (3.1 in *Student Activities Manual*) in class. Compare and discuss in groups physiology and perception.

In the same groups, discuss New Body, New Perspective (text, p. 95) and compare group findings with class.

Assignment: Examining Your Interpretations (3.2 in *Student Activities Manual*)

Class 2

Topic: Role of Culture and Society in Perception

Activity: Discuss physiological influences, social roles, and cultural influences in the perceptual process. Use the Perception-Checking Stimulus games in this Instructor's Resource Manual (see Perception-Checking Stimuli the Notes on Class and Student Activities for Chapter 3) or Perception Checking (3.6 in *Student Activities Manual*.

Assignment: Prepare perception-checking statements to deliver in class based on today's activity (3.5 and 3.6 in *Student Activities Manual*)

Class 3

Topic: Empathy

Activity:

Deliver perception-checking statements (3.5 and 3.6 in *Student Activities Manual*).

Discuss differences between understanding someone and agreeing with that person.

Exercise: Punctuation Practice (text, p. 90)

Assignment:

> Read Chapter Four for quiz.
>
> Complete the *Study Guide* section of the *Student Activities Manual* for Chapter 4.

Week 5

Class 1

Quiz: Chapter Four

Topic: Emotions: Thinking and Feeling

Exercise: Recognizing Your Emotions (text, p. 125)

> Discuss difficulty we have in expressing our emotions. Explore benefits resulting from being able to express our emotions and the variations in expression due to culture and gender.

Assignment:

> The Components of Emotion (4.1 in *Student Activities Manual*)
>
> Your Call—Expressing Emotions (4.7 in *Student Activities Manual*)

Class 2

Topic: Emotions and Thought/Talking to Yourself

Exercise:

> Talking to Yourself (text, p. 144)
>
> Discuss overcoming irrational thinking, using How Irrational Are You? (text, p. 149)

Assignment:

> Express the Feelings (4.2 in *Student Activities Manual*)
>
> Self-Talk (4.4 in *Student Activities Manual*)

Class 3

Topic: Expressing Feelings

Exercise:

> Stating Emotions Effectively (4.3 in *Student Activities Manual*)
>
> Discuss minimizing debilitative emotions and when and how to share feelings.

Assignment:

> Read Chapter Five for quiz.
>
> Complete the *Study Guide* section of the *Student Activities Manual* for Chapter 5.

Week 6

Class 1

Quiz: Chapter Five

Topic: Words and Meanings

Exercise:

> In groups, students discuss Your Linguistic Rules (text, p. 168).
>
> Discuss meanings people have for words and their emotional reaction to words.

Assignment: Complete Misunderstood Language (5.1 in *Student Activities Manual*).

Class 2

Topic: Abstraction and Language

Activity: Discuss the nature of language (a symbol system) and abstraction. Introduce and have class members work with the abstraction ladder and the assignment exercises from the last class.

Assignment: Behavioral Language (5.2 in *Student Activities Manual*)

Class 3

Topic: Responsibility in Language

Activity: Discuss communication issues involved with the Language of Responsibility. Complete Responsible Language (5.3 in *Student Activities Manual*).

Assignment: Prepare "I" Language (Oral Skill) (5.4 in *Student Activities Manual*) for next class.

Week 7

Class 1

Topic: "I" Language

Activity: "I" Language (Oral Skill) (5.4 in *Student Activities Manual*)

Assignment: Down-to-Earth Language (text, p. 162)

Class 2

Topic: Language in Action

Activity: Effective Language (5.5 in *Student Activities Manual*)

Assignment: Record at least ten examples of language that is gender- or culture-related for the next class.

Class 3

Topic: Language, Gender, and Culture

Activity:

Discuss how gender and cultural variables affect language use.

Discuss in groups Mediated Messages—Language (5.6 in *Student Activities Manual*) and Your Call—Language (5.7 in *Student Activities Manual*).

Assignment:

Read Chapter Six for quiz.

Complete the *Study Guide* section of the *Student Activities Manual* for Chapter 6.

Week 8

Class 1

Quiz: Chapter Six

Topic: Nonverbal Communication

Exercise:

Reading "Body Language" (text, p. 207)

Discuss awareness of nonverbal communication.

Assignment: Describing Nonverbal States (6.1 in *Student Activities Manual*)

Class 2

Topic: Characteristics of Nonverbal Communication

Exercise: Describing Nonverbal Behaviors (6.2 in *Student Activities Manual*)

Assignment: Ambiguity, Contradiction & Congruence (6.3 in *Student Activities Manual*)

Class 3

Topic: Nonverbal Functions/Congruency

Activity: Discuss the six functions of nonverbal communication and relate them to the congruency and incongruency of verbal and nonverbal messages. Use Ambiguity, Contradiction & Congruence (6.3 in *Student Activities Manual*) to build upon the text.

Assignment: Your Call—Nonverbal (6.5 in *Student Activities Manual*)

Week 9

Class 1

Topic: Types of Nonverbal Communication

Exercise:

Distance Makes a Difference (text, p. 225)

Discuss proxemics, kinesics, paralanguage, clothing, territoriality, chronemics and environment.

Assignment:

Read Chapter Seven for quiz.

Complete the Study Guide section of the *Student Activities Manual* for Chapter 7.

Class 2

Quiz: Chapter Seven

Topic: Listening versus Hearing

Exercise:

Your Call—Listening (7.8 in *Student Activities Manual*)

Discuss types of ineffective listening and why we don't listen. Discuss benefits of talking less and listening more.

Assignment: Listening Diary (7.1 in *Student Activities Manual*)

Class 3

Topic: Becoming a More Effective Listener

Exercise:

One-Way and Two-Way Communication (Chapter Seven notes following this section in the Instructor's Resource Manual)

Effective Questioning (7.2 in *Student Activities Manual*)

Assignment: Paraphrasing (7.3 in *Student Activities Manual*)

Week 10

Class 1

Topic: Paraphrasing/Listening Responses

Activity:

Compare and contrast paraphrasing with other listening styles discussed in the text.

Discuss types of listening and when to use each.

Listening and Responding Styles (oral skill) (7.6 in *Student Activities Manual*)

Assignment:

Read Chapter Eight for quiz.

Complete the *Study Guide* section of the *Student Activities* Manual for Chapter 8.

Class 2

Quiz: Chapter Eight

Topic: Interpersonal Attraction/Building Positive Relationships.

Exercise: Discuss characteristics of relational communication, breadth and depth of relationships.

Class 3

Topic: Developmental Stages in Intimate Relationships

Exercise: Your Relational Stage (text, p. 278)

Assignment: Relational Stages (8.2 in *Student Activities Manual*)

Week 11

Class 1

Topic: Relational Dialectics

Exercise: Discuss characteristics of relational dialectics. Your Dialectical Tensions (text, p. 283)

Assignment: Discovering Dialectics (8.1 in *Student Activities Manual*)

Class 2

Topic: Communicating about Relationships

Exercise: Recognizing Relational Messages (8.4 in *Student Activities Manual*)

Assignment:

Read Chapter Nine for quiz.

Complete the *Study Guide* section of the *Student Activities Manual* for Chapter 9.

Class 3

Quiz: Chapter Nine

Topic: Intimacy in Relationships

Exercise: Breadth and Depth in Relationships (9.1 in *Student Activities Manual*)

Week 12

Class 1

Topic: Self-Disclosure in Relationships

Exercise:

Have class discuss Johari Window and self-disclosure.

Appropriate Self-Disclosure (text, p. 316)

Assignment: Degrees of Self-Disclosure (9.3 in *Student Activities Manual*)

Class 2

Topic: Benefits and Risks of Self-Disclosure

Exercise:

Mediated Messages (9.5 in *Student Activities Manual*)

Your Call—Relational Dynamics (9.6 in *Student Activities Manual*)

Assignment:

Reasons for Nondisclosure (9.2 in *Student Activities Manual*)

Class 3

Topic: Alternatives to Self-Disclosure

Exercise:

Discuss alternatives to self-disclosure.

Disclosure and Alternatives (9.4 in *Student Activities Manual*)

Assignment:

Read Chapter Ten for quiz.

Complete the *Study Guide* section of the *Student Activities Manual* for Chapter 10.

Week 13

Class 1

Quiz: Chapter Ten

Topic: Confirming and Disconfirming Communication

Exercise: Discuss Gibb Categories Evaluating Communication Climates (text, p. 336) and Defensive and Supportive Language (10.2 in *Student Activities Manual*)

Assignment: Understanding Defensive Responses (10.1 in *Student Activities Manual*).

Class 2

Topic: Handling Defensiveness

Exercise: Discuss defensiveness and defense mechanisms and ways to cope with defensiveness. Defense Mechanism Inventory (text, p. 340), and Nondefensive Responses to Criticism (10.4 in *Student Activities Manual*)

Assignment: Prepare Coping with Criticism (10.5 in *Student Activities Manual*) for next class.

Class 3

Topic: Building Clear Messages

Exercise: Writing Clear Messages (10.3 in *Student Activities Manual*)

Week 14

Class 1

Topic: Coping with Criticism

Activity: Coping with Criticism (10.5 in *Student Activities Manual*/ Study Guide)

Assignment:

> Read Chapter Eleven for quiz.
>
> Complete the *Study Guide* section of the *Student Activities Manual* for Chapter 11.

Class 2

Quiz: Chapter Eleven

Topic: Conflict Is Natural and Normal for All Persons

Activity: Discuss attitudes we're learning concerning conflict. Encourage personal testimony. Discuss how we behave in avoiding conflict and how these behaviors tend to drive us crazy.

Assignment: Understanding Conflict Styles (11.1 in *Student Activities Manual*)

Class 3

Topic: Conflict Styles

Activity: Your Conflict Rituals (text, p. 383)

Assignment: Your Conflict Styles (11.2 in *Student Activities Manual*)

Week 15

Class 1

Topic: Types of Conflict Resolution

Activity: Discuss win-lose, lose-lose, compromise, and win-win problem solving.

Assignment: The End vs. the Means (11.3 in *Student Activities Manual*)—prepare this to provide background for win-win problem solving next class.

Class 2

Topic: Effective Problem Solving

Exercise: Win-Win Problem Solving and Conflict Resolution Dyads (11.4 and 11.5 in *Student Activities Manual*). Use these to role-play the resolution of conflicts. Discuss effectiveness.

Assignment: Review for final exam.

Class 3

Topic: Conclusion of course

Activity: Give final examination and remarks.

USING INTERNET LINKS IN THE INTERPERSONAL COMMUNICATION COURSE

Making use of the Internet to enrich classroom instruction is easy. We provide a number of links below that we have found useful. They connect you to journals, publications, collections, bibliographies, teaching strategies, and other course-related materials such as audiotapes and videotapes. You will want to use some of the information yourself, but others can provide a valuable supplement to reading, lecture, discussion, and other activities in the classroom. Many thanks to **Heidi Murphy** from Central New Mexico Community College for the following.

Chapter 1: A First Look at Interpersonal Relationships

Making Friends in Cyberspace
Achieve a deeper understanding of cyber-friendships by reading this 1996 scholarly article entitled "Making Friends in Cyberspace."
http://jcmc.indiana.edu/vol1/issue4/parks.html

Fundamental Interpersonal Relations Orientation: Schutz's Theory of Interpersonal Needs
This article explains and give examples of interpersonal needs.
http://www.afirstlook.com/archive/firo.cfm?source=archauth

Interpersonal Competence Resources
This site provides a brief definition of interpersonal competence and links to many sites related to interpersonal competencies.
http://novaonline.nv.cc.va.us/eli/spd110td/interper/relations/relationsscomp.html

Focus on Feelings Rather Than Content
Read about the content and relational dimensions of interaction.
http://www.coping.org/dialogue/model.htm

Interpersonal Communication Workbook
Check out this comprehensive interpersonal communication course workbook, which includes articles, case studies, quizzes, and class exercises.
http://www3.shastacollege.edu/communication/rsaunders/workbooks/10workbook/S10WBF04.pdf

The Seven Challenges: Communicating More Cooperatively
Explore seven challenging interpersonal communication skills in this excellent, comprehensive online book.
http://www.coopcomm.org/workbook.htm

Models of Communication
Read a detailed analysis of how communication models developed over time.
http://www.shkaminski.com/Classes/Handouts/Communication%20Models.htm

Building Effective Interpersonal Communication Skills: A Self-Assessment
Evaluate your level of interpersonal effectiveness at work, and receive tips about how to be a good communicator.
http://spot.pcc.edu/~rjacobs/career/effective_communication_skills.htm

Communication Skills for School Leaders
This digest provides practical suggestions for school leaders who want to increase the effectiveness of their communication interactions. Suggestions focus on the following skills covered in your textbook: improving understanding, becoming a better listening, checking your perceptions, giving feedback, describing behavior, using "I" messages, expressing feelings, and improving nonverbal communication.
http://eric.uoregon.edu/publications/digests/digest102.html

Communication Skills Test

Use this self-test to evaluate your *general* level of communication skill ability. A comprehensive score interpretation requires a fee.

http://www.queendom.com/tests/relationships/communication_skills_r_access.html

Self-Assessment of Interpersonal Communication Competence

This self-test measures your abilities in the following interpersonal communication areas: adaptability, conversational involvement, conversation management, empathy, effectiveness, and appropriateness. This test requires an honest self-assessment. Even if you don't like what you learn about yourself, you can use the results of the test set goals for improving your communication.

http://www.austincc.edu/colangelo/1318/interpersonalcommunicationcompetence.htm

Interpersonal Communication Skills Enhance Employability

To get some insight into how important communication skills are in the workplace, read the article "Employers Cite Communication Skills as Key." In this annual survey, employers repeatedly identify communication skills as the most desirable of all entry-level job qualities.

http://www.naceweb.org/press/display.asp?year=&prid=235

Myths of Effective Communication

A communication scholar cautions readers that several widely professed interpersonal ideologies are false when taken to the extreme.

http://www.winstonbrill.com/bril001/html/article_index/articles/301-350/article349_body.html

Effectively Meeting Communication Goals

At this site, the theory of constructivism is explained and related to communication goals and cognitive complexity.

http://www.uky.edu/~drlane/capstone/interpersonal/construct.html

Toward Theorizing Japanese Interpersonal Communication Competence from a Non-Western Perspective

This scholarly article explores and challenges the traditional Western conceptualization of Japanese interpersonal competence.

http://www.acjournal.org/holdings/vol3/Iss3/spec1/Miyahara.html

Theory of Interpersonal Competence

Check out this brief explanation of and citations related to Spitzberg's & Cupach's theory of interpersonal competence.

http://www.uky.edu/~drlane/capstone/interpersonal/competence.htm

Technology and Immediacy

Read this scholarly article describing a series of studies that address mediated forms of immediacy.

http://www.communication.ilstu.edu/posull/homepage/mediated_immediacy.pdf

Strategic Interpersonal Communication

This extensive online book featuring research that examines how people meet their goals through communication.

http://www.questia.com/PM.qst;jsessionid=G2SNDjV3LVVxZMc2fp9Q2dPSZvhDRqJGV0yvHm8h2sp21r GTWLwn!-961595462!-1956466795?a=o&d=9656663

Exploring Relational Messages in Sales Interactions

This scholarly article examines the strategic use of relational messages in the sales profession.

http://www.allbusiness.com/periodicals/article/644393-1.html

Web Exercise 1.1: Why Communicate Cooperatively?

Visit the Cooperative Communication Skills Internet Resource Center. The author lists seven benefits/reasons for learning and adopting a more cooperative communication style. What are these seven

benefits? Which of these benefits would you like to apply in your own life? Explain why you chose the benefits you did, and give specific, concrete examples of how you might implement these benefits in your own life. For example, if one benefit you agree with is "more respect," state that you would like to have more respectful relationships with your children or co-workers, and explain what that "respect" might look like. What are the barriers to success? What steps can you take to overcome these barriers?
http://www.newconversations.net/communication_skills_workbook_introduction.htm

Web Exercise 1.2: What are Your Communication Strengths and Weaknesses?
Read the five steps for improving communication competence at "What's Wrong With You? Why Don't You Understand Me?" According to these suggestions, where do your strengths lie and where do you feel you need to improve?
http://www.selfgrowth.com/articles/Menechella12.html

Web Activity 1.3: Your Communication Style
Take the Communication Quiz at Cyberparent.com. Did you detect a pattern in your answers? What, if any, insight did you gain about yourself from this activity? Describe the communication style of a person you admire. Why do you admire this style? How is it different from your style? What relational goals can you achieve with this style?
http://www.cyberparent.com/talk/quiz.htm

Web Activity 1.4: A Personal Communication Inventory
Print and complete the worksheet at the webpage "Affirm Your Communication Strengths." Write a short essay describing any insights you gained from this activity.
http://sfhelp.org/02/evc-strengths.htm

Web Activity 1.5: Comparing and Contrasting Communication Models
Visit the Pragmatic Communication Model website. Read the explanation and then, in your own words, summarize the similarities and differences between the pragmatic model at this site and the transactional model in your textbook. What does each have in common? What does one model explain better than the other? Which one do you prefer and why?
http://www.aligningaction.com/prgmodel.htm

Web Activity 1.6: Interpersonal Communication Skills Enhance Employability
In an annual survey, employers repeatedly identify communication skills as the most desirable of all entry-level job qualities. Ironically, year after year, they also claim that communication skills are often what many candidates lack. Read the article "Employers Cite Communication Skills as Key" and then take a few moments to question your employer (or a potential employer), asking him or her about communication abilities the company desires in employees. Ask your employer to clarify specific skills that go beyond the broad terms provided in the article (e.g., interpersonal skills, teamwork skills) and to get more specific as to how and when an employee would need to apply these skills. Further, ask your employer to clarify the reasoning behind *why* specific interpersonal skills are desirable.
http://www.naceweb.org/press/display.asp?year=&prid=235

Chapter 2: Communication and Identity: Creating and Presenting the Self

Mediated Impression Management
This academic research study explores the uses of technology in impression management.
http://www.communication.ilstu.edu/posull/homepage/dont_know.pdf

Self Quiz: How Well Do You Know Yourself?
This simple quiz gives you a brief assessment of your self-awareness and reasons to get to know yourself better.
http://www.americanbaby.com/ab/quiz.jhtml?quizId=/templatedata/lhj/quiz/data/HowSelfAwareAreYouQ uiz_07152004.xml&catref=cat4620054&_requestid=258688

Self Quiz: What is your Myers-Briggs personality type?
Take an informal test that will approximate your personality type according to the dimensions of the Myers-Briggs Type Indicator.
http://www.personalitypathways.com/type_inventory.html

Little Ego Boosters
Check out these tips for parents on how to increase a child's confidence and self-esteem in the early years.
http://www.parenting.com/parenting/babytalk/article/0,19840,1197808,00.html

Ego-Busting Behaviors at Work
Take a look at seven types of ego-busting behaviors in the workplace and tips for helping ourselves and others improve the communication environment.
http://www.findarticles.com/p/articles/mi_qa4086/is_200410/ai_n9462175

Body Image
Learn how body image is shaped through the processes of reflected appraisal and social comparison.
http://www.myparentime.com/articles/03/article301b.shtml

Grow Your Self-Esteem
Play three games that help you increase your self-esteem and avoid negativity.
http://www.selfesteemgames.mcgill.ca/games/index.htm

Culture, Gender and Self-Concept
This scholarly article is about the various influences of culture and gender on self-concept and the effects of these differences on individuals' thoughts and perceptions.
http://sitemaker.umich.edu/culture.self/self-concept_and_possible_selves_publications

Incompetent People Are Blind to their Own Failings
Research findings conclude that people who do things badly are usually supremely confident of their abilities. The authors of this article explore one aspect of self-monitoring: that the skills needed for competence are often the same skills needed to recognize competence.
http://www.sfgate.com/cgi-bin/article.cgi?file=/chronicle/archive/2000/01/18/MN73840.DTL

Why Do Women Feel their Self-Worth is Tied to the State of their Body?
Read this detailed and informative look at the issues impacting the way we feel about our bodies.
http://www.jrn.columbia.edu/newmedia/projects/masters/bodyimage/toc.html

Self Quiz: How is Your Body Image
Take this brief quiz and reflect on the way you feel about your physical appearance.
http://www.queendom.com/tests/minitests/fx/body_image.html

The Personalized License Plate as a Form of Impression Management
This academic study explores the phenomenon of the personalized license plate and how it fosters and controls impressions.
http://www.engr.usask.ca/dept/techcomm/CSSR/rhetor/2004/seiler.pdf

Management Secrets: The Power of the Pygmalion and Galatea Effects
Learn how managers can increase employee performance by communicating positive expectations and helping people believe in themselves and their efficacy.
http://humanresources.about.com/od/managementtips/a/mgmtsecret.htm

When Teachers Have Low Expectations
Read this article exploring the relationship between teacher expectations and student achievement.
http://www.ncrel.org/sdrs/areas/issues/educatrs/leadrshp/le0bam.htm

Face
This site provides an explanation of "face," its relevance in different countries, and its role in intercultural communication.
http://www.beyondintractability.org/essay/face/

Diagram of a Self-Fulfilling Prophecy
Through description and diagram, business consultants feature a specific example of how initial beliefs can influence behavioral outcomes in an organization.
http://www.systems-thinking.org/theWay/sss/ssx01.htm

Changing Our Self-Concept and Building Self-Esteem
As part of a self-help online book, this material describes a step-by-step procedure to analyzing the self and taking steps to change the self-concept and improve self-esteem.
http://mentalhelp.net/psyhelp/chap14/chap14b.htm#a

Developing Self-Esteem Through Interactions With Others
Check out this list of annotated citations for academic and popular articles about the relationship between communicating with others and building self-esteem.
http://novaonline.nv.cc.va.us/eli/spd110td/interper/self/linksdevselfesteem.html

Good or Bad, What Teachers Expect From Students They Generally Get!
An education scholar explains the mechanisms of the self-fulfilling prophecy as it applies to teachers and students.
http://www.kidsource.com/education/good.bad.expect.html#credits

How Can We Strengthen Our Children's Self-Esteem?
An expert in early childhood education explains what adults can do to help strengthen children's self-esteem.
http://www.kidsource.com/kidsource/content2/strengthen_children_self.html

Identity Management in Cyberspace
Read about five interlocking factors that are useful in understanding how people manage identities in cyberspace.
http://www.rider.edu/~suler/psycyber/identitymanage.html

Increasing Self-Awareness
As part of a self-help online book, this material provides an excellent description of several chapter concepts including: self-monitoring, perceived self, and resisting self-concept change.
http://mentalhelp.net/psyhelp/chap14/chap14e.htm

Methods for Changing Our Thoughts, Attitudes, Self-Concept, Motivation, Values and Expectations
As part of a self-help online book, this skill-based chapter takes a comprehensive look at communication and self. Sub-topics include changing your self-concept and building self-esteem; increasing self-awareness; challenging irrational ideas; determinism; trying a new lifestyle; paradoxical intention; increasing motivation; straight thinking; common sense and good arguments; developing attitudes that help you cope; and self-hypnosis and mental imagery.
http://mentalhelp.net/psyhelp/chap14/

Self-Esteem Self-Evaluation Survey
Evaluate your self-esteem by responding to a brief survey.
http://www.self-esteem-nase.org/jssurvey.shtml

Self-Esteem Test
Take a comprehensive quiz to assess your general level of self-esteem. A detailed score interpretation requires a fee.
http://www.queendom.com/tests/personality/self_esteem_r_access.html

Self-Monitoring Test
Take this self-test to assess your general levels of interpersonal (public) and intrapersonal (private) self-monitoring. A detailed score interpretation requires a fee.
http://www.queendom.com/tests/personality/self_monit_access.html

Self-Monitoring: Do You Censor What You Say?
This self-test helps you assess whether you are a low or high self-monitor.
http://www.outofservice.com/self-monitor-censor-test/

Shaping Body Image
Read about how theories of social comparison and reflected appraisal play roles in shaping negative body image.
http://www.hc-sc.gc.ca/fn-an/nutrition/weights-poids/leaders_image-chefs_image_e.html

Strategies for Building Self-Esteem
Check out these twelve tips for building self-esteem.
http://www.vivaconsulting.com/counselling/selfesteem.html

Symptoms of Low Self-Esteem
This employment seeker's manual lists 19 symptoms of low self-esteem.
http://www.jobbankusa.com/lowse.html

US/Chinese Memories Show Impact of Culture on Self-Concept
Read this interesting short article that summarizes the differences between Chinese and Americans in how the self is recalled through memories.
http://www.news.cornell.edu/Chronicle/01/6.28.01/memory-culture.html

Web Activity 2.1: Self-Fulfilling Prophecy
Based on the example provided at the "Self-Fulfilling Prophecy" webpage, create your own labeled diagram and explanation of a self-fulfilling prophecy that has played out in your own life.
http://www.systems-thinking.org/theWay/sss/ssx01.htm

Web Activity 2.2: Self-Awareness and Self-Deception
Based on the descriptions provided in the article "Applying Learning Principles to Thoughts," speculate about your level of self-awareness (high, low, medium). Explain your answer using information from this article, your textbook, or both. Read the information on self-deception. Analyze your own level of self-deception. Give specific examples of times you have been guilty of these defensive deceptions.
http://www.mentalhelp.net/poc/view_doc.php?type=doc&id=9745&cn=353

Web Activity 2.3: Building Self-Esteem
Examine the list of suggestions for building self-esteem in the article "Strategies for Building Self-Esteem." Which of these might be relevant to your life situation? Select strategies that relate to you and elaborate on the specific steps you could take to proceed with building self-esteem. For example, are your life goals realistic and achievable? If you believe there are any irrational "shoulds" in your life, what are they? Can you dispute them? How? Do you have a "cruel inner critic?" If so, what does he/she say? Can you argue with this critic? What would you say?
http://www.vivaconsulting.com/counselling/selfesteem.html

Web Activity 2.4: Increasing Self-Awareness
Take the ten-question self-awareness quiz provided at AmericanBaby.com. (Don't worry, it's a quiz for adults.) What do you think about your score? In your opinion, is it accurate or not? Explain. In the score report, what reasons are given for increasing one's self-awareness? What are your reasons, if any? Make a short list of areas in which you'd like to increase your awareness (suggestions are given in score report). Then, next to each item, indicate a specific step you could take to accomplish increased awareness (e.g., take more quizzes, make lists, keep a journal).
http://www.americanbaby.com/ab/quiz.jhtml?quizId=/templatedata/lhj/quiz/data/HowSelfAwareAreYouQuiz_07152004.xml&catref=cat4620054

Chapter 3: Perception: What You See Is What You Get

Stereotyping of Native Americans
Read this brief discussion of the stereotypical portrayal of Native Americans in elementary education, which includes tips for avoiding stereotypes.
http://www.unr.edu/nnap/NT/i-8_9.htm

Do You Perpetuate Stereotypes?
This brief article asks you to consider your own role in perpetuating stereotypes.
http://www.intergrouprelations.uiuc.edu/dim2000/page2.html

The Self-Serving Bias in Relational Context
This research study examines the existence of self-serving bias in close and distant relationships.
http://www.soton.ac.uk/~crsi/Theselfserv.pdf

Does the Halo Effect Occur in the Elderly?
This interesting research study finds that the halo effect exists in the elderly despite the prediction that wisdom would eliminate this judgmental bias.
http://www.findarticles.com/p/articles/mi_qa3852/is_199801/ai_n8801895

The Accuracy and Power of Sex, Social Class and Ethnic Stereotypes
This lengthy research article examines the accuracy and power of sex, social class, and ethnic stereotypes in person perception. A comprehensive and useful list of related references follows the article.
http://www.psychology.iastate.edu/faculty/madon/accuracy.sex.socialclass.pdf

Basic Self-Controls to Interact Effectively With People
This article reviews skills of self-control, including perception checking, that can help us enhance our business and career success.
http://www.motivator-on-call.com/selfcontrol2.htm

Empathy and Listening Skills
Authored by a retired clinical psychologist, this site provides information about the power of using empathy and listening skills to promote productive relationships.
http://www.psychological-hug.com/listeningskills.htm

Different Drummers
Personality theorist David Keirsey provides an explanation of how and why people are different. Keirsey emphasizes that relational harmony comes from understanding and accepting differences, rather than trying to change another person to your ways of thinking.
http://keirsey.com/Drummers.html

Typical Stereotypes and Misconceptions
This site provides a description of some typical stereotypes and misconceptions Westerners hold about Islam and people living in the Middle East and vice-versa. In addition, find links to other sites with accurate information about the Middle East.
http://www.pbs.org/wgbh/globalconnections/mideast/questions/types/index.html

Test Your Hidden Racial Biases
Explore this unique site that allows you to test your hidden biases towards race, gender, age, and disability.
http://www.tolerance.org/hidden_bias/index.html

Self Quiz: Discover Your Emotional Empathy Profile
Assess your ability to empathize, and receive a detailed interpretation that gives suggestions for improving empathy in parenting, intimate relationships, and friendships.
http://www.eiskills.com/index.php?page=tests/empathy.php

Experiencing Empathy Online
This book chapter outlines a recent study that explored the presence of empathy in online communities.
http://www.ifsm.umbc.edu/~preece/paper/17%20ricekatz11.pdf

The Difference Between Jurors' Perception of Self and Others
This article explains the issues of self-serving bias and fundamental attribution error in the courtroom.
http://www.decisionquest.com/litigation_library.php?NewsID=218

Checking Out Our Interpersonal Hunches
As part of an online psychological self-help book, this article suggests specific strategies for clarifying our interpersonal assumptions.
http://mentalhelp.net/psyhelp/chap13/chap13k.htm

The Empathy Belly
Read about the "Empathy Belly," which is a product that helps men understand what it's like to be pregnant.
http://www.empathybelly.org/expectant_fathers.html

Self-Quiz: Empathy Quotient
Take this self-quiz to determine your empathy quotient. The empathy quotient is intended to measure how easily you pick up on other people's feelings and how strongly you are affected by other people's feelings.
http://www.guardian.co.uk/life/news/page/0,12983,937443,00.html

Empathy and Emotional Intelligence
Read about empathy and its connection to emotional intelligence.
http://www.eqi.org/empathy.htm

Influence of Stereotyping on Guilty Verdicts
Read this scholarly research article that describes the effects of stereotyping in a study where race seemed to influence guilty verdicts.
http://web.nwe.ufl.edu/~jdouglas/8.pdf

Understanding Cultural Relativism
This article clarifies the meanings of polar opposite concepts: ethnocentrism and cultural relativism.
http://rosado.net/pdf/Cultural_Relativism.pdf

Understanding Cultural Preferences
This site provides a brief explanation of four cultural dimensions: individualism, power distance, certainty, and achievement. Explanation and examples of each are given, and a self-quiz allows you to discover your preference for certainty.
http://www.itapintl.com/culturalpreferences.htm

Web Activity 3.1: Walking in My Shoes: Empathy Building
Read the information about the "empathy belly" at the Birthways Childbirth Resource Center website. This product helps men build empathy and understand a bit of what it's like to walk in someone else's shoes. Create a "suggestions for building empathy" guide that includes your own creative and helpful ideas about how one might understand more about what it's like to walk in the shoes of others. For example, if I want to understand what it's like to be homeless, what are some ways I could go about doing that? Could I dress like a homeless person and walk through the streets? Could I volunteer at a homeless shelter? Interview a homeless person? If I want to understand what it's like to be blind, what could I do? As a class, share your guides with each other and pick suggestions to act on. After participating in and carrying out one of your suggestions, write an essay about what it's like to "walk in the shoes of another."
http://www.empathybelly.org/expectant_fathers.html

Web Activity 3.2: Inaccurate Stereotypes and Cultural Misconceptions
Read the information about stereotypes, Islam, and the Middle East at pbs.org's Global Connections site. As you read, conisder how we often inaccurately prejudge other people, cultures, and places until we actually meet someone or experience something for ourselves. See if you can find four to five people who have traveled to other countries and realized that their prejudgments were inaccurate. Interview them and ask how their views have changed, how their communication has changed, and how their own lives have changed as a result of experience. Write an essay summarizing your interviews and draw your own conclusions using concepts from the chapter.
http://www.pbs.org/wgbh/globalconnections/mideast/questions/types/index.html

Web Activity 3.3: Stereotyping in Film
At this site, find a lengthy explanation of the causes and effects of the *librarian* stereotype. Based on this information and on your own thoughts consider the characteristics of the stereotypical librarian. Scroll down to the section called "Let's Go to the Movies" and read about how several films portray librarians in ways that are exceptionally different from the conventional stereotype. Choose your own stereotype category (see your textbook for examples) and make a list of films that both perpetuate and challenge the stereotype. What are your experiences with people who fit within this category? According to your textbook, what are some of the communication problems that can result from stereotyping?
http://home.earthlink.net/~cyberresearcher/stereotypes.htm

Web Activity 3.4: Reduce Ethnocentrism and Promote Cultural Relativism
Examine the four steps suggested by authors at the webpage "Reduction of Ethnocentrism and Promotion of Cultural Relativism," which provides information about confronting the culturally unfamiliar. Consider a time when you encountered behavior you considered strange from a person who is culturally different from you. For example, in international tourist spots within the United States, it is common to see foreigners who do not exhibit the customary behaviors of lining up single file (referred to as "queuing") for tickets. To Americans, this may be perceived as rude and could result in an uncomfortable or angry exchange. Recall your own situation or hypothesize about a new one, and use the four steps to explain how you could interact in that situation in a culturally relative way.
http://www.uwec.edu/minkushk/Anth161%20ETHNOCENTRISM%20.htm

Chapter 4: Emotions: Thinking, Feeling, and Communicating

Self Quiz: Emotional Intelligence Test
Take a comprehensive 70-question quiz to find out your general level of emotional intelligence. A detailed score interpretation requires a fee.
http://www.queendom.com/tests/iq/emotional_iq_r2_access.html

Self Quiz: Test Your Emotional Intelligence Quotient
Take this brief 12-question quiz to get your EQ score along with a brief interpretation and suggestions for improvement.
http://www.ihhp.com/quiz.htm

Self Quiz: Why Do I Feel the Way I Do?
This 10-question quiz that measures levels of shame, fear, anger and sadness "is designed to help you know how you came to feel as you do, and may help you identify how you can change your situation for the better."
http://www.allthetests.com/quiz15/quizpu.php?testid=1123475164&katname=EQ%20Tests%20emotional%20tests

Emotional Maturity
This site is rich with self-help articles that explain how and why to manage your emotions for the better.
http://www.hodu.com/ECS-Menu6.shtml

Experiencing and Expressing Emotions
Check out these self-help suggestions for identifying and expressing emotions.
http://www.couns.uiuc.edu/Brochures/Emotions.htm

The Ripple Effect: Emotional Contagion and its Influence on Group Behavior
This scholarly article explores the process of emotional contagion in groups.
http://www.findarticles.com/p/articles/mi_m4035/is_4_47/ai_107762239

Are You Infected by the Moods of Others?
Scroll down and take the "Mood Infection Quiz" to determine how easily you may be affected by someone else's mood. The surrounding article addresses a variety of methods to achieving emotional control.
http://www.buildfreedom.com/tl/tl12.shtml

Self Quiz: How Angry Are You?
Take this quiz to determine how frequently or easily you are angered.
http://www.kalimunro.com/self-quiz_anger.html

Self Quiz: Fuel For Success
This measure of emotional intelligence breaks down into five subcomponents and includes discussion of workplace applications and suggestions for improvements.
http://www.canadaone.com/magazine/eq080498.html

Culture and Emotion
This site provides a listing of scholarly publications (including many live links to PDF files) based on research at Stanford University's Culture and Emotion Lab.
http://www-psych.stanford.edu/~tsailab/

Seven Empowering Success Beliefs
Read this article explaining seven perspectives that support growth and well-being.
http://selfhelparticles.com/?Seven-Empowering-Success-Beliefs&id=939

Self Quiz: Mood Monitor
Take this short quiz to measure and monitor possible depression.
http://mood-monitor.perbang.dk/

EQ International Site
This useful and comprehensive site provides a list of over 2,000 feeling words in addition to detailed explanations of primary and secondary emotions, causes behind emotions, tips for managing negative emotions, history and explanation of "emotional intelligence," and links to other resources on emotions.
http://eqi.org/index.htm

Advice for Couples: How to Control Anger
This article makes suggestions for couples on how to control anger and problem-solve.
http://www.sensiblepsychology.com/improving_anger.htm

How Do You Feel Today?
See if you can describe how you are feeling today by looking at 65 faces representing a variety of emotions.
http://www.oaktreecounseling.com/feelings.htm

Thinking Quiz
Take this true/false quiz to explore what you know about how our emotional responses are controlled by our thought processes.
http://www.helpself.com/thinker.htm

Who is the Only Person in the World Who Can Make You Angry?
This site provides a diagram and explanation of how our thoughts cause our emotions. The author also gives suggestions for anger control.
http://members.aol.com/AngriesOut/grown1.htm

Using Rational-Emotive Therapy to Control Anger
Learn how to use rational emotive therapy to control anger. The examples given are illustrative and accessible.
http://www.palace.net/~llama/psych/ret.html

Rational-Emotive Behavior Therapy
At this site, a clinical psychologist gives the reader tools for identifying and overcoming the source of emotional difficulties.
http://www.threeminutetherapy.com/rebt.html

Who Controls You?
This site provides explanation and examples of how rational emotive and cognitive behavior therapy can help you change unwanted emotions and behaviors.
http://www.rational.org.nz/public/intro.htm

Understanding Yourself
This page describes four purposes emotions can serve in your life, and gets you ready to begin expanding your emotion-vocabulary.
http://www.region.peel.on.ca/health/commhlth/selfest/emotions.htm

Expressing Emotions by Expanding Your "Feelings" Vocabulary
Use the "feelings vocabulary" and practice being expressive with your emotions by responding to hypothetical situations.
http://www.region.peel.on.ca/health/commhlth/selfest/vocab.htm

Managing Emotions
Read about six ways to help you begin to understand, interpret, and manage your feelings.
http://www.region.peel.on.ca/health/commhlth/selfest/2emotion.htm

"Cool-Down" Strategies
Expand your list of "cool-down" strategies.
http://www.region.peel.on.ca/health/commhlth/selfest/cooldwn.htm

Managing Emotions as a Part of Conflict Resolution
Read a series of questions you might ask yourself when learning to manage and express emotions.
http://crnhq.org/freeskill6.html

Albert Ellis Institute
Read more about Albert Ellis and rational emotive therapy at the Albert Ellis Institute homepage.
http://www.rebt.org

Methods for Coping with Depression
As part of a self-help online book, this material reviews several methods for coping with depression. The methods relate to: behavior, emotions, skills, cognition and unconscious factors.
http://mentalhelp.net/psyhelp/chap6/chap6s.htm

Challenging Irrational Ideas
As part of a self-help online book, this material provides helpful exercises on how to challenge irrational ideas.
http://www.mentalhelp.net/psyhelp/chap14/chap14i.htm

Producing Desired Emotions: How to Be Happy
As part of a self-help online book, this material provides lengthy advice on producing desired emotions and includes a section on "how to be happy."
http://www.mentalhelp.net/psyhelp/chap12/chap12e.htm

Methods for Handling Our Own Aggressions/Anger
Part of an online self-help book, this material provides advice on how to handle our own anger and aggression.
http://www.mentalhelp.net/psyhelp/chap7/chap7n.htm

Directory of Emotional Intelligence Internet Sites
This site provides a comprehensive clearinghouse of sites, resources and organizations dedicated to the study and practice of EQ (emotional intelligence quotient).
www.eq.org

Web Exercise 4.1: Practicing the ABCs of Rational Emotive Therapy
The author of "Using Rational Emotive Therapy to Control Anger" expands on the textbook description of rational emotive therapy. Using the ABC approach described in this article, create an example problem of your own and practice applying rational emotive therapy to the problem. Be sure to include all the steps, A through G. After you finish, describe the consequences that could result in this relationship from choosing to apply this approach.
http://www.palace.net/~llama/psych/ret.html

Web Exercise 4.2: Express Your Emotions
Using the exercise Expressing Emotions by Expanding Your Feelings Vocabulary provided at the Peel Public Health website, practice expressing your emotions with a wide range of word choices For suggestions, see the table of feelings in Chapter 4 of your textbook, or click on "feeling word possibilities" at the bottom of the website. Review the guidelines for expressing emotions in your textbook, and practice describing your feelings by writing statements for each of the hypothetical situations listed at the website.
http://www.region.peel.on.ca/health/commhlth/selfest/vocab.htm

Web Exercise 4.3: Challenging Irrational Thoughts
This site, part of an online self-help book, *Methods for Coping With Depression,* reviews several methods for coping with depression. The methods relate to behavior, emotions, skills, cognition, and unconscious factors. After reading the material, list some negative thoughts you hold about yourself. Next to each thought, make a list of the external forces you blame for these negative qualities. Now, as the author says, challenge any faulty perceptions, irrational ideas, automatic ideas, faulty conclusions, and excessive guilt. Review the fallacies in your textbook and change any irrational self-talk. Did you change any of your original thoughts? If so, why? If not, why not? How might changes influence communication and relationships?
http://www.mentalhelp.net/poc/view_doc.php?type=doc&id=9857&cn=353

Web Activity 4.4: Are Your Thoughts Causing You Distress?
Explore your own irrational beliefs in this thinking quiz. For each statement given, describe the underlying belief using one or more of the seven fallacies explained in your textbook. For example, note that statement 7 on the website reflects the fallacy of causation because it indicates that calling someone nasty names *causes* hurt feelings. The site also provides helpful suggestions for improving your thinking and, consequently, the resulting emotions. After reading the chapters and the excerpts at this site, rewrite each statement in a way that more accurately reflects healthy thinking.
http://www.helpself.com/thinker.htm

Web Activity 4.5: Develop Your Emotional Intelligence
Take this self-test and read the explanations and suggested answers. Based on this self-analysis, where are your emotional strengths and weaknesses? Be specific and give examples. Using suggestions from your textbook and from this site, describe steps you can take to improve your emotional intelligence.
http://www.helpself.com/iq-test.htm

Chapter 5: Language: Barrier and Bridge

Gender Differences in E-mail Communication
This academic research article examines the implications of gender differences on language use in electronic mail discussion groups.
http://iteslj.org/Articles/Rossetti-GenderDif.html

Basic Differences Between Men and Women
The author of this site describes many types of gender differences and makes skill recommendations for improving relationships. Scroll down to "Basic Differences between Men and Women."
http://www.familycare4u.com/male_female.htm

Gender Differences in Communication
Read more about gender differences in communication and access a lengthy list of online links related to the topic.
http://www.geocities.com/Wellesley/2052/genddiff.html

Styles of Communication: Direct and Indirect
Read more about high- and low-context communication styles, and test your knowledge with a quiz.
http://www.peacecorps.gov/wws/educators/enrichment/culturematters/Ch3/stylescommunication.html

Why Men and Women Don't Always Understand Each Other
Get more information about how gender differences can prevent men and women from understanding each other.
http://www.mediatraco.com/interper.html

Language: Say What You Mean
Click any link under "Language: Say What You Mean" to read humorous examples of equivocal language.
http://www.coping.org/write/percept/language1.htm

How Much Do You Know About How Men and Women Communicate?
Test your knowledge of gender communication differences. Detailed answers follow the quiz.
http://www.glc.k12.ga.us/pandp/guidance/schoices/sc-f20.htm

Gender Styles in Computer-Mediated Communication
This article briefly reviews the current state of research on gender communication styles in computer-mediated communication.
http://www.georgetown.edu/faculty/bassr/githens/cmc.htm

Gender Differences in Communication
Check out this informative article describing gender differences in communication.
http://pages.towson.edu/itrow/wmcomm.htm

Avoiding Emotive Language in Writing
See examples of how to avoid emotive language in academic writing.
http://unilearning.uow.edu.au/academic/2diq2_feedback.html

Direct and Indirect Communication Styles
Read a description of and examples of low and high context communication styles.
http://www.pierce.ctc.edu/tlink/general/context.html

Getting Along With Americans
For an outsider's perspective on U.S. behaviors and styles of communication, read the information at this site for international students.
http://www.ufic.ufl.edu/handbook10.htm

Expressing Yourself More Clearly and Completely

This excellent, comprehensive online book explores seven challenging interpersonal communication skills. This chapter expands on "I" statements and offers a step-by-step methodology for assertively expressing yourself clearly and completely (also a variation on the clear message format explained in your textbook).
http://www.coopcomm.org/w7chal3.htm

Rethinking "I" Statements

The author of this page suggests revisions to the traditional format of "I" messages, in order to adapt to students' unique cultures and further reduce defensiveness.
http://www.state.oh.us/cdr/schools/contentpages/Istate21.htm

Gender Communication Differences in Business

Read what business educator and speaker Candy Tymson says about gender communication differences and about how to deal effectively with the opposite gender in business.
http://www.tymson.com.au/articles.html

Gender Differences in Communication: An Intercultural Experience

A scholarly article that argues the appropriateness of viewing gender communication as a form of intercultural communication. The author includes a primer on gender differences in communication, and provides suggestions for applying effective intercultural communication skills to the situation of gender communication.
http://www.cpsr.org/cpsr/gender/mulvaney.txt

The Linguistic Relativity Hypothesis

This site provides an academic explanation and review of linguistic relativity and the Sapir-Whorf hypothesis.
http://plato.stanford.edu/entries/relativism/supplement2.html

Linguistic Relativity: Does Language Shape Thought?

This research article includes good examples of how having different ways of describing the world leads speakers of different languages to also have different ways of thinking about the world.
http://www-psych.stanford.edu/~lera/papers/mandarin.pdf

Linguistic Relativity and Linguistic Determinism

This essay explains and compares linguistic relativity and linguistic determinism using a few interesting and specific examples from the Turkish and American Indian languages.
http://www.lsadc.org/info/ling-fields-thought.cfm

What Happens When People from Japan and the United States Meet

Read an account of what often happens when people from Japan and the United States meet. Japanese translator Etsuko Ueda writes about the differences between Japanese and U.S. culture and communication styles, and emphasizes intercultural understanding for sake of the global economy.
http://fly.hiwaay.net/~eueda/japguest.htm

The Power of Language

This essay looks at the power of using words as weapons or as tools in problem-solving.
http://www.mtoomey.com/book_language.html

Levels of Abstractions

This essay reviews and provides examples of the concept of abstraction.
http://thisisnotthat.com/gs/gs_litaa.html

Abstraction and Assumptions

Check out these tips for improving communication by being aware of abstract language and the assumptions that result from its use, and by listening deeply to discover authentic meanings.
http://www.authenticbusiness.co.uk/archive/authenticcomms/

When in Rome Should We Do As the Romans?
This essay discusses the pros and cons of adapting to the conversational style of others.
http://www.hodu.com/romans.shtml

Identity in Language
This article discusses the ways in which we use subtleties in language to express relational messages.
http://www.tamu.edu/chr/agora/winter00/sterling.pdf

Web Exercise 5.1: Identifying Direct and Indirect Communication Styles
The article at this site about direct and indirect communication styles provides several examples of the differences between direct (low-context) and indirect (high-context) communication styles. Which style is being illustrated in the last example about the late teacher? How do you know? Create 2 to 3 additional communication situations in which you illustrate both direct and indirect styles by writing and labeling thoughts, dialogue, or actions.
http://www.pierce.ctc.edu/tlink/general/context.html

Web Exercise 5.2: Personalizing "I" Statements
The author of the article "Rethinking 'I' Statements" makes a point about how the traditional structure of "I" statements do not always work in students' cultural climates. In addition, the author mentions that the traditional "I" statements include several "you"s that could potentially be interpreted defensively. The author makes suggestions for how to revise "I" statements to fit personal communication styles and to further reduce defensiveness. Follow the example on this webpage and create several traditional "I" statements for your own real-life situations. Then revise them according to the author's suggestions. Give your opinion about which structure might work best for you and explain why.
http://disputeresolution.ohio.gov/schools/contentpages/Istate21.htm

Web Exercise 5.3: Practicing "I" Messages
Read the information and examples about I-Messages at MentalHelp.net. Think of a situation from your own life for which the use of an "I" message might be useful. State at least two reasons for why an "I" message might be effective in this situation. Write 5 to 7 "you" statements that apply to your situation, and label them according to the names given on the webpage. Now turn these "you" statements into effective "I" statements.
http://www.mentalhelp.net/poc/view_doc.php?type=doc&id=9765&cn=353

Web Exercise 5.4: Linguistic Relativity & Linguistic Determinism
Read the essay "Language and Thought." According to its author, what is the hypothesis of linguistic determinism? What evidence is given in support of and against the argument for determinism? What questions might you ask a bilingual in order to test this hypothesis? Carry out an experiment by interviewing one or more bilingual persons to determine how language and thought are related.
http://www.lsadc.org/info/ling-fields-thought.cfm

Web Exercise 5.5: High Context & Low Context Cultures
The webpage "Your Japanese Guests" provides an account of what often happens when people from Japan and from the United States meet. Japanese translator Etsuko Ueda writes about the differences between Japanese and U.S. culture and communication styles, and emphasizes intercultural understanding for sake of the global economy. Read the portion of the article titled "The art of communication." Are the Japanese high-context or low-context communicators? Using 2 to 3 examples from the article, explain the differences between high-context and low-context communication styles.
http://fly.hiwaay.net/~eueda/japguest.htm

Web Exercise 5.6: Intercultural Misunderstandings
Based on your understanding of high- and low-context communication from your textbook and the webpage "Styles of Communication: Direct and Indirect," create two short role plays that illustrate a potential misunderstanding that could occur as a result of these style differences. For example, in the quiz at the bottom of the page, statement 8 is "'Yes' means I hear you." If "yes" can mean "I hear you" to high-

context communicators, but it means simply "yes" to low-context communicators, what might happen if a low-context communicator asks a high-context communicator if he accepts her price offer in a business deal? Your dialogues should illustrate 1) a U.S.-apanese business negotiation gone bad and 2) an embarrassing incident with your high-context in-laws. Label the speech parts with "high-context" or "low–context" and act out your role plays in class.

http://www.peacecorps.gov/wws/educators/enrichment/culturematters/Ch3/stylescommunication.html

Web Exercise 5.7: Gender Communication Differences

Read the research on gender communication differences summarized in the quiz answers on the webpage "Gender Communications Quiz." Think of some common difficulties between men and women in both personal and work relationships. Do you think any of these difficulties can be explained by the gender communication differences explained in either your textbook or the quiz answers? Explain your answer and give examples.

http://www.glc.k12.ga.us/pandp/guidance/schoices/sc-f20.htm

Web Exercise 5.8: Moving Down the Abstraction Ladder

Read over the lesson in the article "Communication Skills: Using the Five 'Why's' to Create Specific, Descriptive Verbal Messages" and practice applying the five "whys" to create your own specific, descriptive verbal messages. How effective were the "why" questions in helping you determine specifics? Explain.

http://www.ag.iastate.edu/centers/ftcsc/media/fivewhys6.pdf

Web Exercise 5.9: Using Emotive Language

Read the article on denotation, connotation, and emotive language at VirtualSalt.com. Note that most of the emotive language examples illustrate how perceptions and attitudes of *issues* can be influenced by words. Your task is to illustrate and explain how perceptions and attitudes of *people* can be influenced by words. Imagine you are asked to write a peer evaluation of a fellow employee that you've never really liked. She works hard and gets her job done, but her personality annoys you. Write a one-paragraph evaluation of her performance, using highly emotive language designed to influence your supervisor's perception of her in a negative direction. Next, rewrite the evaluation with specific, descriptive, emotive-free language. Discuss the differences between the two evaluations in terms of (1) which one might be taken more seriously by your supervisor, (2) which one is fairer to the employee being evaluated, and (3) which one provides more useful, accurate information. Explain your answers.

http://www.virtualsalt.com/think/semant2.htm

Chapter 6: Nonverbal Communication: Messages Beyond Words

Nonverbal Communication in Japan

Prepare for travel to Japan with this article that describes some of the nonverbal norms and customs in the following areas: silence, facial gestures, touching, showing respect to objects, gestures, dress, Tatami rooms, seating and standing protocol, being on time, rank, elevators, table seating, cars, table manners, slurping, dishes, toasting, and smoking. Click on the drop-down menu under "Japanese Culture" at the left side of the screen for access to different articles.

http://www.traveltst.ca/index.php?pageId=60

South-African Gestures

Check out this photo-illustrated dictionary of South-African gestures.

http://www.aaanet.org/sla/jla/jla14_2_brookes.htm

Nonverbal Communication in Text-Based Virtual Realities

This academic master's thesis investigates the forms and functions of nonverbal communication in MUDs (multi-user dimensions), similar to chat rooms on the Internet.

http://www.johnmasterson.com/thesis/

Business Card Etiquette
This article explains the importance of the business card exchange in international business relations.
http://www.hodu.com/card.shtml

Dress for Success
Tips on the specifics of appropriate business dress in five countries.
http://getcustoms.com/2004GTC/Articles/new003.html

Nonverbal Communication in Asian Cultures
Read a lengthy and comprehensive explanation of the differing meanings behind American and Asian gestures.
http://www.csupomona.edu/~tassi/gestures.htm

Nonverbal Communication Abstracts
This site provides a useful listing of nonverbal communication-related abstracts for scholarly articles published in academic journals. You may find this list useful when searching for research paper resources.
http://www.faculty.ucr.edu/%7Efriedman/nvcabstract.html

Nonverbal Communication Helps Us Live
Read a variety of brief anecdotes and news items about nonverbal communication.
http://www.csun.edu/~vcecn006/nonverb.html

Chinese Emotion and Gesture
Check out this excellent photo-illustrated article that explains Chinese gestures.
http://www.ling.gu.se/~biljana/gestures2.html#neg

Gender Differences in Nonverbal Communication
This site provides a brief bulleted listing of the major differences in nonverbal communication behaviors between males and females.
http://www.colostate.edu/Depts/Speech/rccs/theory20.htm

The Nonverbal Dictionary of Gestures, Signs and Body Language Cues
This site provides a comprehensive resource for understanding human nonverbal behaviors. It offers an extensively researched dictionary of nonverbal communication terms and illustrations.
http://members.aol.com/nonverbal2/diction1.htm#The%20NONVERBAL%20DICTIONARY

How's Your Personal Distance—Watch This Space
This excellent article is aimed at exploring perceptions of nonverbal behavioral norms between U.S. and Russian cultures.
http://www.friends-partners.org/oldfriends/spbweb/lifestyl/122/how.html

The Body Language of Proxemics
This concise essay is about how spatial relationships and territorial boundaries directly influence our daily encounters.
http://members.aol.com/katydidit/bodylang.htm

Lack of Nonverbals: How Can Email Communication Affect Your Business?
Read about problems that can occur in email communication because of the lack of body language, voice tones, and shared environments.
http://www.pertinent.com/articles/communication/chrisCom1.asp

Nonverbal Negotiation Skills
Read a sales consultant's advice about using nonverbal skills in the negotiation of sales.
http://www.everyonenegotiates.com/negotiation/nonverbalnegotiation.htm

I'm Running Late: The Silent Signals of Time
What does being late communicate to others? Find out in this article.
http://www.expertmagazine.com/articles/late.htm

Links, Links, and More Links to Information on Nonverbal Communication
This site provides a virtual clearinghouse of nonverbal communication links!
http://www3.usal.es/~nonverbal/introduction.htm

Emoticons
Check out these links to sites of emoticon galleries.
http://novaonline.nv.cc.va.us/eli/spd110td/interper/message/Linkscmcemoticons.html

Body Language Quiz
Test your understanding of body language.
http://www.janhargrave.com/quizes.htm

More Nonverbal Communication Links
More links to a variety of websites related to nonverbal communication websites.
http://novaonline.nv.cc.va.us/eli/spd110td/interper/message/linksnonverbal.html

The Detection of Deception via Nonverbal Deception Cues
Read about nonverbal behavioral cues common in deception.
*http://www.personal.psu.edu/krm10/PSY083%20student%20readings/10-
27%20%20with%20questions.pdf*

Nonverbal Communication Articles
This site provides a variety of useful articles related to nonverbal behaviors in everyday life.
http://www.hodu.com/effective-communication-skills-menu.html#bod

Use Nonverbal Communication to Improve Relationships
Check out these ten brief pieces of advice on using nonverbal behavior to improve relationships.
http://www.selfgrowth.com/articles/Albright2.html

Quiz: Hidden Aspects of Communication
Take a college practice quiz on "hidden aspects of communication."
http://anthro.palomar.edu/language/quizzes/langqui6.htm

Paralanguage
Hear sound-byte examples of vocalizations and test your knowledge of their meanings.
http://www.esl-lab.com/para.htm

Nonverbal Library
This site provides a virtual library of information about nonverbal behavior and related topics. Subject headings include proxemics, kinesics, gestures, touch, paralanguage, smell, attractiveness, light and colors, and applications of nonverbal studies.
http://digilander.libero.it/linguaggiodelcorpo/biblio/

How Do Attractiveness and Stereotypes Affect Development?
A research lab studies how facial attractiveness and associated stereotypes affect development.
http://homepage.psy.utexas.edu/homepage/group/langloislab/NewFormat/OurResearch.html

Turkish Body Language
Read about the meaning behind Turkish gestures and other body language.
http://www.business-with-turkey.com/tourist-guide/turkish_body_language.htm

Quiz: Gestures Around the World
Test your knowledge of gestures around the world.
http://www.isabellemori.homestead.com/questionsgestus.html

Brazilian Gestures
Go to this site for photos and explanations of Brazilian gestures.
http://www.maria-brazil.org/brazilian_body_language.htm

Nonverbal Communication in the Vietnamese Culture
Read this summary of nonverbal behaviors and their meanings in the Vietnamese culture.
http://www.adoptvietnam.org/travel/non-verbal.htm

French Gestures
Go to this site for photos and explanations of French gestures.
http://french.about.com/library/weekly/aa020901a.htm

Nonverbal Communication in International Business
This article explains the importance of nonverbal communication to intercultural effectiveness.
http://www.sideroad.com/Business_Communication/business-communication-nonverbal.html

Your Distinct Hand Gestures
This article is by the president of the International Society for Gesture Studies, who studies the way people use and respond to hand gestures in conversation, particularly in the workplace.
http://www.utexas.edu/features/archive/2003/gestures.html

Quiz: Spot the Fake Smile
Test your ability to spot the subtle differences between a fake smile and a real one.
http://www.bbc.co.uk/science/humanbody/mind/surveys/smiles/index.shtml

Quiz: General Knowledge of Nonverbal Communication Concepts
Test your knowledge of nonverbal communication.
http://www.quia.com/pop/1704.html

Emotion and Facial Expression
Access various photos of facial expressions and read analysis of the expressive elements of emotions illustrated by the face.
http://face-and-emotion.com/dataface/emotion/expression.jsp

Web Exercise 6.1: Gender Differences in Nonverbal Communication
Read the information in the article "Gender Differences in Nonverbal Communication." Develop a research strategy to observe nonverbal behaviors in males and females. Using the information at this site, develop a research question or a hypothesis and an instrument that you can use to keep track of your observations. Observe nonverbal behaviors in a public place, such as a shopping mall, restaurant, or bus station. Analyze and write up your results in a report describing observed differences and similarities between males and females. Do your results match those in stated in this webpage? Do they match what your textbook says?
http://www.colostate.edu/Depts/Speech/rccs/theory20.htm

Web Exercise 6.2: Asian and American Nonverbal Differences Can Lead to Misunderstandings
First, read the article "Gestures: Body Language and Nonverbal Communication," and then complete the exercise. Using Table 6-2 on p. 228 of your textbook as a model, create a table with the following columns: In column A, describe 5 to 6 gestures; in column B, list the U.S. interpretation of the gesture: in column C, explain how the gesture might be interpreted by an Asian culture (be specific about which culture: Korea, China, Japan, all Asian cultures, etc.); in column D, explain any misunderstandings that could occur as a result of the different interpretations. Discuss the following questions with your classmates: How different is Asian nonverbal communication from U.S. nonverbal communication? Why is it different at all? How can we prevent misunderstandings when traveling or doing business with other cultures?
http://www.csupomona.edu/~tassi/gestures.htm

Web Exercise 6.3: Nonverbal Communication Quiz: Types and Functions
Click on the "Quiz" link at JanHargrave.com and make guesses about nonverbal behaviors and meaning. Submit and check your answers. How well did you do? Refer to *true* answers 4, 6, 7, 9, and 10, and describe the *type* of nonverbal communication that is being described in each question (according to your textbook). For each question, also describe the *function* of the nonverbal behavior being described.
http://www.janhargrave.com/

Web Exercise 6.4: Exploring Cultural Differences in Nonverbal Communication: An Interview
After reading the article "How's Your Personal Distance--Watch This Space," interview several people who have recently spent some time living in another country. Find out what each person observed and learned about differences in the 12 areas of nonverbal communication discussed in your textbook. Also ask each person to give examples of nonverbal misunderstandings she or he has experienced. Write a report on your findings.
http://www.odu.edu/ao/oip/elc/s_imai.pdf

Web Exercise 6.5: Guide to Effective Nonverbal Communication
Synthesizing information from your text and any of the web links for Chapter 6, create a "Nonverbal Communication Advice Guide" in one of the following areas: Improving Male-Female Relationships, Successful Intercultural Travel, Nonverbal Essentials for the Workplace, Nonverbal Communication Online.

Chapter 7: Listening: More Than Meets the Ear

Be All Ears
Check out this article about how listening is more important than talking.
http://nie.redding.com/newsarchive/20020526cu055.shtml

Active Listening Skills
This site provides specific examples of paraphrasing and other listening strategies.
http://www.taft.cc.ca.us/lrc/class/assignments/actlisten.html

Quiz: What is the Speaker Feeling?
Test your ability to listen for feelings.
http://www.gov.mb.ca/agriculture/homeec/cba20s04.html

Improving Listening Skills
Read more about effective listening and practice improving your own skills with the suggested activities.
http://www.coping.org/dialogue/listen.htm

Improving Responding Communication Skills
Read more about effective responding and practice improving your "listening to give help" skills with the suggested activities.
http://www.coping.org/dialogue/response.htm

Quiz: Are You a Really Good Listener?
Take this self-test to assess whether you are really a good listener.
http://www.stand-deliver.com/star_ledger/030505.asp

Quiz: How Well Do You Really Listen?
Take this self-test to assess how well you listen.
http://www.powercommunicator.com/test1a.asp

Quiz: How Well Do You Listen to Your Children?
Take this self-test to assess how well you listen to your children.
http://www.powercommunicator.com/test2a.asp

Quiz: Measure Your Listening Abilities
Take this self-test to measure your listening abilities.
http://www.careerjournal.com/myc/climbing/20021224-raudsepp.html

Empathy and Listening Skills
At this site, a retired clinical psychologist provides information about the power of using empathy and listening skills to promote productive and positive relationships.
http://www.psychological-hug.com/

Listening Skills: A Key Element to Learning to Communicate Well
Read about the importance of and strategies for listening with "understanding," which allows us to see an idea and attitude from another person's point of view or frame of reference.
http://www.itstime.com/aug97.htm#skills

Listening—With Your Heart As Well As Your Ears
Read about the following topics: 1) why being a good listener is important, 2) how listening affects family and work life, 3) some styles of poor listening, and 4) ways to improve listening skills.
http://www.utahmarriage.org/index.cfm?id=6S73xz0lgb

International Listening Association
This home page belongs to the International Listening Association, a professional organization that promotes the study, development, and teaching of listening and the practice of effective listening skills and techniques. Links provide the following information about: membership; organization calendar; members, board and staff; conferences, seminars and workshops; discussion group; exercises; resources; quotes and factoids about listening.
http://www.listen.org/index.html

Quiz: Check Your Own Listening Skills
Check your own listening competency in the areas of: attention, empathy, respect, response, memory, and open-mindedness.
http://www.highgain.com/SELF/index.php3

Listening: Recommended Reading
A training organization that specializes in listening offers an annotated bibliography of resources related to listening and communication.
http://www.highgain.com/html/recommended_reading.html

Sssh! Listen Up! How to Bring the Critical Skill of Listening Into Your Business
A free monthly online newsletter provided by a professional training organization specializing in listening and other communication skills. Articles feature advice and tips about the importance of listening skills for success in business.
http://www.highgain.com/newsletter/hg-enews-current.html

Back issues of Sssh! Listen Up!

http://www.highgain.com/newsletter/back-issues/back-issues-main.html

Listening More Carefully and Responsively
Read this chapter from a comprehensive online book that explores seven challenging interpersonal communication skills. The chapter addresses the practice of responsive listening, and focuses on the practice of separating the acknowledgement of the thoughts and feelings that a person expresses from approving, agreeing, advising, or persuading.
http://www.coopcomm.org/w7chal1.htm

How Do You Rate Your Listening?
A self-test.
http://www.facetofacematters.com/assessments/Listening101.doc

Listening and Empathy Responding
As part of an online psychological self-help book, this page provides a detailed, step-by-step methodology for developing listening and empathic response skills.
http://www.psychologicalselfhelp.org/Chapter13/chap13_8.html

Habits to Differentiate Good from Poor Listening
This site provides a brief comparison of poor and effective listening habits.
http://www.managementhelp.org/commskls/listen/gd_vs_pr.htm

Tests for Listening
This site suggests questions to ask ourselves while listening in order to test (a) whether we're prepared to listen, (b) how well we're understanding, (c) how thoroughly we have listened, and (d) our level of empathy.
http://www.dhemery.com/cwd/2004/01/tests_for_listening.html

Emphatic Listening
This site provides an explanation and example of how to use deep listening to gain a stronger understanding of what is being conveyed both intellectually and emotionally.
http://www.mindtools.com/CommSkll/EmphaticListening.htm

Active Listening
This site features a script of a virtual student discussion about active listening techniques. It includes explanations, examples, and practice activities.
http://istudy.psu.edu/FirstYearModules/Listening/ListeningInformation.html

Listening to Ourselves
Check out these tips for mindful listening.
http://www.innerself.com/Relationships/listening.htm

Web Exercise 7.1: Assessing and Improving Communication Between You and Your Partner
Take the Listening Skills self-evaluation quizzes at The Positive Way website and then click on "ratings discussion and listening advice." If you find there is room for improvement in your relationship, develop a dialogue between you and your partner that resembles a recent conflict in which neither partner practiced good listening skills. However, revise the dialogue to include the suggested advice on this page. Label your responses with the following terms: paraphrasing, clarification, effective feedback, awareness of body language. Did the outcome of the conflict change? If so, why? Practice using these listening skills during your next conflict.
http://www.positive-way.com/listenin.htm

Web Exercise 7.2: Identifying Barriers to Listening
Choose a story topic from the dozens of listening quizzes in Russell's ESL Cyber Listening Lab. Listen to the whole story and then take the comprehension quiz. If you did not score 100 percent, try to identify which listening barriers might have interfered. Repeat this exercise with other stories. Which barriers might be more prevalent in your life and why? Explain. What could you do to reduce ineffective listening? Apply some of the tips for informational listening from your chapter and see if your retention and recall improves. Practice these listening techniques in your next lecture class.
http://www.esl-lab.com/

Web Exercise 7.3: Practicing Empathic Responding
Read the information and examples on listening and empathy responding at the Psychological Self-Help website. Get together with two classmates and practice listening to each other relate a problem from your past or present. One of you should rate your empathy responses on the scale provided by the author. How did you do? Take turns speaking, listening/responding, and rating. Discuss your ratings. What were common problem areas? Did any low-rated responses relate to the barriers discussed in the beginning of the chapter? If so, which ones? What concrete steps can each of you take to improve your empathy responses?
http://www.psychologicalselfhelp.org/Chapter13/chap13_8.html

Web Exercise 7.4: Learning to Acknowledge What you Hear
Read "Challenge One: Listen First & Acknowledge" in this online workbook about cooperative communication skills. With another classmate, discuss a topic that is fairly controversial. (A current news event usually works best). Be sure that the topic is one in which you take opposing sides. Decide which one of you will speak first (person 1) and which one of you will listen (person 2). Give person 1 two minutes to present his/her take on the issue. After two minutes, person 2 must accurately summarize and state what the other person said without approving, disapproving, agreeing, disagreeing, advising, or persuading. Start this statement by saying "I hear you saying that . . . ." Use the skills suggested in Chapter 7 to listen more responsively. Person 1 must agree that this statement is an accurate reflection of what was said before person 2 can take a turn. Now repeat the process, with person 2 taking a turn to give his/her side of the issue. How did you do? How difficult was the task of summarizing and acknowledging? How is this type of conversation different from what you are used to? Can you think of a personal example of a situation where someone could have benefited from using this technique?
http://www.newconversations.net/communication_skills_workbook_challenge_one.htm

Web Exercise 7.5: Ineffective Listening Styles
Compare and contrast the ten ineffective listening styles described at Coachville.com and the seven styles described in your textbook. Which ones are similar? Write five scenarios that illustrate a situation in which one person demonstrates an ineffective listening style. Trade scenarios with your classmates and try to guess which styles are being illustrated.
http://topten.org/public/BN/BN153.html

Web Exercise 7.6: Payoffs for Effective Listening
Scroll down and read over the nine payoffs for effective listening in the online article "Listening--With Your Heart As Well As Your Ears." Which ones can you relate to specifically? Give *specific* examples of positive payoffs that might result in *your life* if you improved your listening skills.
http://www.utahmarriage.org/index.cfm?id=6S73xz0lgb

Web Exercise 7.7: Empathy & Listening Skills in a Conversation
Read the conversation between two friends at the webpage "Empathy and Listening Skills: Second Conversation." Find and describe 2 to 3 examples of Anita's ability to empathize with Tanya. Summarize the end result. Create your own situation and dialogue: Respond to a friend in need using similar empathic responses. Speculate about the possible consequences of empathizing in a variety of contexts.
http://www.psychological-hug.com/listeningskills.htm

Web Exercise 7.8: Taking Action to Improve Your Listening Skills
At WorkingMatters.com, scroll down to the two-column table of "actions to improve your listening skills." For each action, note the reasoning given. Then, develop a role play script for a scenario that illustrates the importance of the stated reasoning. For example, the reasoning given behind the listening improvement of "At intervals, try to paraphrase what people have been saying" is "this gives you the opportunity to learn what you think they've been saying." A role play could illustrate the problems that may be caused by not trying to learn what you think another person has been saying (e.g., an employee makes an embarrassing move because he/she didn't fully understand the information given by the manager). Demonstrate the scenarios in class and discuss the purpose and goals of improving our listening skills.
http://www.workingmatters.com/archives/YaffeMay06ListeningV2.html

Chapter 8: Communication and Relational Dynamics

Interpersonal Theories and Examples
Scroll down to find the following links to useful analyses, in-depth explanations, and concrete examples of the following chapter-related theories: interpersonal deception, relational dialectics, social exchange, and Knapp's stages of relationship development.
http://www.uky.edu/~drlane/capstone/interpersonal/

Can Marital Success Be Predicted and Improved?
As part of an online self-help book, this chapter comprehensively reviews the topic of marital relationships and focuses on: the nature of attraction and love, prediction and improvement of marital success, stages and types of marriages, and handling marital problems.
http://www.psychologicalselfhelp.org/Chapter10/

Relational Dialectics
An introduction and brief explanation of Baxter & Montgomery's theory of relational dialectics. Also provided are several links to student-created pages relating to research, application, and critique of the theory.
http://oak.cats.ohiou.edu/~pc406097/rd.htm

Social Exchange Theory
This student-created site introduces and briefly explains Thibaut & Kelley's social exchange theory. Also provided are links to student-created pages relating to research, application, and critique of the theory.
http://oak.cats.ohiou.edu/~al891396/exchange.htm

Quiz: Compatibility and Interest Guide
Take this quiz with your partner to determine and communicate about how compatible you are.
http://www.positive-way.com/compatibility.htm

Quiz: What's Your New Couple Quotient?
Take this self-test to find out what your new couple quotient is.
http://www.newcouple.com/couplequiz.html

Social Exchange Theory
This site provides a comprehensive explanation of social exchange theory.
http://www.afirstlook.com/archive/socialexchange.cfm?source=archther

Do Opposites Attract? Not Really.
This study suggests that when finding a mate, "likes" may attract better than opposites.
http://my.webmd.com/content/article/70/80965.htm

Put On a Happy Face
This study suggests that men find positive personality traits more attractive in women than physical traits.
http://www.psychologytoday.com/articles/pto-20010101-000015.html

Marriages Do Better When Personalities Are Similar
A 2005 study finds that married couples whose partners are more alike in personality report happier marriages.
http://www.jyi.org/news/nb.php?id=178

Quiz: Match the Couples
Test your ability to spot the couples in a group of photos.
http://www.bbc.co.uk/science/hottopics/love/matchmaking_quiz.shtml

Quiz: Are You On the Same Wavelength?
Determine whether you and your mate are a "great minds think alike" couple or an "opposites attract" couple.
http://www.lhj.com/lhj/quiz.jhtml?quizId=/templatedata/lhj/quiz/data/AreYouOntheSameWavelengthQuiz_12132002.xml&catref=cat1950004

Quiz: What State Are Your Relationships In?
Reflect on the levels of compatibility, passion, and effective communication in your love relationship.
http://www.therelationshipgym.com/couples_quiz.htm

Relationship Quiz: Copasetic, Caution, or Conundrum?
Assess the likelihood of your relationship being a success in the long term.
http://www.selfgrowth.com/articles/Hartwell1.html

Rubber Bands and Sectioned Oranges: Dialectical Tensions and Metaphors Used to Describe Interpersonal Relationships
This scholarly article takes a unique look at dialectical tensions and metaphors that emerge from individuals' perceptions of romantic relationships.
http://www2.edutech.nodak.edu/ndsta/pawlowski.htm

How Much Time Do You Invest In Relationship Maintenance?
This article stresses the importance of reflecting on the time you spend in relational maintenance.
http://valueprep.com/relationship-maintenance.html

Personality and Love Style Test
Discover your personality and love style types, and get suggestions for possible romantic matches in your area.
http://www.weattract.com/TestsPersonality.html

Metatalk
This site provides many great examples of metacommunication for all types of relational situations.
http://sfhelp.org/02/meta-wks.htm#xampls

Quiz: Is Your Relationship Fun Enough?
Consider the levels of predictability and novelty in your relationship.
http://www.lifetimetv.com/reallife/relation/quiz/fun.html

So What Is Love, Really?
This article defines love as an attitude, a lifestyle, a belief system, and more.
http://www.hodu.com/love2.shtml

How to Forgive Another for Past Hurts
Read this article to explore why it is a good idea to forgive people who have wronged us and how best to do it.
http://www.hodu.com/forgive.shtml

Quiz: Are You a Giver or a Taker?
Determine your ratio of give and take.
http://www.oaktreecounseling.com/giver%20or%20taker.htm

Cyber-Attraction: The Emergence of Computer-Mediated Communication in the Development of Interpersonal Relationships
In this article, a scholar examines the effects of computer-mediated communication on interpersonal communication and on the development and process of attraction in cyberspace.
http://www.vepsy.com/communication/book3/3CHAPT_10.PDF

Quiz: How Effective Is Your Relational Communication?
Examine the effectiveness of your communication with a loved one.
http://www.austincc.edu/colangelo/1311/relationalcommtest.htm

Quiz: Are Some of Your Beliefs and Attitudes Hurting Your Relationship?
Examine the flexibility and inflexibility of your beliefs, and use the quiz as a catalyst for discussion in your relationship.
http://www.kalimunro.com/self-quiz_relationship.html

Personal Relationships **Article Archive**
A huge variety of topics from Chapter 8 in your textbook are explored in more than 100 scholarly articles published in *Personal Relationships*, an academic journal.
http://lilt.ilstu.edu/personalrelationships/contentsofissues/since1994/default.htm

Web Exercise 8.1: Factors of Attraction in Your Own Relationships
Read the online lecture "Interpersonal Attraction." Make a list of people you are attracted to (people you like). Review the factors of attraction and make a list of which factors apply to the people on your list. In other words, why are you attracted to the people you listed? Because they are physically attractive? Similiar to you? Competent? Which factors appear most on your list? Which factors appear least?
http://www.nd.edu/~rwilliam/xsoc530/attraction.html

Web Exercise 8.2: Evaluating Relational Outcome in a Movie Relationship
Read a student's application of social exchange theory to the movie *Jerry Maguire*. Think of another movie relationship and write a similar short essay in which you apply the theory to determine the rewards and costs. Evaluate the decision that was made to stay together or break apart using the following concepts: rewards, costs, outcome, comparison level (CL), and comparison level of alternatives (CLalt).
http://oak.cats.ohiou.edu/~cc383997/exchange.htm

Web Exercise 8.3: A Relationship Diagram
Read the section in your textbook on relational development, and then read the example dialogue in the relational stages at this site. Think of a romantic or platonic relationship you are no longer involved in. Diagram your relationship using your perceptions of what occurred at each stage and include sample dialogue. Did your relationship proceed through all ten stages? If not, which ones were missing? How much time did you spend at each stage? What insight, if any, did you gain about your relationship through this exercise?
http://www.uky.edu/~drlane/capstone/interpersonal/reldev.html

Web Exercise 8.4: Examine and Discuss Your Relational Communication
Print and take the quiz "How Effective Is Your Relational Communication?" Ask your partner, family member, or friend to take the quiz also. Hold a discussion with the other person and metacommunicate about your answers and scores. Then, write a brief essay addressing the questions at the bottom of the quiz page. What did you notice about content and relational dimensions of your discussion? Was the metacommunication productive in any way? If so, how—and why?
http://www.austincc.edu/colangelo/1311/relationalcommtest.htm

Chapter 9: Intimacy and Distance in Relational Communication

Honesty and Intimacy
This scholarly article (also published in the *Journal of Social and Personal Relationships*) analyzes and argues the importance of honesty in developing and sustaining intimate relationships.
http://www.stpt.usf.edu/hhl/papers/honesty.htm

Battle of the Genders
Read about the intimacy differences in males and females.
http://www.cyberparent.com/gender/battle3.htm

Intimacy: Recommended Reading for Men
This site provides a comprehensive listing of books for men on the topic of intimacy.
http://www.menstuff.org/books/byissue/intimacy.html

Equivocal Communication
This book review includes a brief summary, explanation of, and examples of equivocal communication.
http://oak.cats.ohiou.edu/~sa102596/ITResearch.htm

Quiz: Self-Disclosure
Take a self-test (small fee required) to determine your willingness to self-disclose to family members, friends, acquaintances, and strangers. Submit your answers and obtain a detailed analysis of your results in addition to tips on "how to get closer."
http://www.queendom.com/tests/relationships/self_disclosure_general_access.html

The Johari Window Model: Brief Explanation
This site provides a sample diagram and brief explanation of the Johari Window model of self-disclosure.
http://www.knowmegame.com/johari_window.html

The Johari Window Model: Lengthy Explanation
This site features a sample diagram and lengthy explanation and interpretation of the Johari Window model of self-disclosure.
http://www.noogenesis.com/game_theory/johari/johari_window.html

Johari Window and Self-Disclosure Discussion
This site features a diagram, explanation, and brief discussion of the benefits and risks of self-disclosing.
http://www.cultsock.ndirect.co.uk/MUHome/cshtml/psy/johari.html

Excuses, Emotions, and In-Between
This scholarly essay about excuse-making addresses the question, What makes us view a message as an excuse, and what are the emotional consequences of doing so?
http://research.haifa.ac.il/~benzeev/excuses.htm

Self-Disclosure and Openness
As part of an online self-help book, this material gives comprehensive skill advice for self-disclosure and openness.
http://www.psychologicalselfhelp.org/Chapter13/chap13_39.html

Social Penetration Theory
This student-created site introduces and briefly explains Altman & Taylor's social penetration theory. Also provided are links to student-created pages relating to research, application, and critique of the theory.
http://oak.cats.ohiou.edu/~bz372497/socpenbz.htm

Common Interpersonal Problems and Needed Skills
As part of an online self-help book, this material discusses many of the problems associated with making and keeping friends, including fear (risk) of approaching someone, fear (risk) of rejection, hints for becoming a good conversationalist, and the importance (benefits) of self-disclosure.
http://www.psychologicalselfhelp.org/Chapter9/chap9_76.html

Quiz: A Self-Disclosure Test for Couples
Take this self-test to assess your level of self-disclosure with your partner.
http://www.queendom.com/tests/minitests/self_disclosure_couples_abridged_access.html#h

Quiz: Are You an Open Person?
Take this self-test to determine whether you are an open person.
http://members.fortunecity.co.uk/siukaice/openness.htm

Friendships Through Instant Messaging
This scholarly article examines the relationship between instant messaging and intimacy.
http://jcmc.indiana.edu/vol10/issue1/hu.html

Interactive Johari Window
This unique site allows you to configure your own online Johari window. You choose adjectives to describe yourself and ask friends and family to visit your "window" site and do the same.
http://kevan.org/johari

Interactive Nohari Window
This inversion of the interactive Johari window allows you to explore perceived and unrecognized weaknesses.
http://kevan.org/nohari

Building Trust in Relationships
Check out these ten suggestions for building trust in a relationship.
http://marriagepartner.com/relationships/943.php

Quiz: What's Your Intimacy IQ?
Take this test to explore your knowledge of the concept of intimacy.
http://www.consum-mate.com/quiz01.htm

Quiz: What's His Intimacy IQ?
This short quiz asks women to reflect on the level of intimacy between themselves and their mates.
http://quiz.ivillage.com/cosmopolitan/tests/intimacyiq.htm

Quiz: Do You Keep Too Many Secrets?
Take this self-test to determine whether you keep too many secrets.
http://www.lifetimetv.com/reallife/relation/quiz/rel_quiz_honesty.html

Quiz: How Honest Are You?
Take this self-test to assess how honest you are in relationships.
http://lhj.com/lhj/quiz.jhtml?quizId=/templatedata/lhj/quiz/data/HowHonestAreYouQuiz.xml&catref=lcat103

Quiz: Do You Reveal Too Much Personal Information?
Take this self-test to assess whether you reveal too much personal information.
http://lhj.com/lhj/quiz.jhtml?quizId=/templatedata/lhj/quiz/data/1145557392363.xml&catref=lcat103

Ten Ways to Create More Intimacy
Check out these ten suggestions for how to have fun, spend more time together, and surprise each other.
http://marriage.about.com/od/intimacy/tp/createintimacy.htm

Relationship Rules
This site outlines the basic ingredients for healthy, intimate relationships.
http://www.psychologytoday.com/articles/pto-20031224-000002.html

Web Exercise 9.1: Configure Your Johari Window
Visit kevan.org/johari and follow the directions to describe yourself from the list of adjectives provided. Send an email to several friends and family asking them to also rate you with the same list of adjectives. If you are brave, visit kevan.org/nohari, and repeat the activity using antonyms of the adjectives provided at kevan.org/johari. After receiving feedback from others, visit the windows you created at the site. What is your reaction? What do you think about the accuracy of the model(s) drawn for you? What do you think about the words others used to describe you? How receptive are you to feedback from others? How willing are you to know and learn things about yourself from others? How willing are you to self-disclose to others? What did this activity reveal about your level of self-awareness? Do you feel that there is anything about your communication style that you want to change? If so, why? If not, why not?
http://kevan.org/johari
http://kevan.org/nohari

Web Exercise 9.2: Blocks to Trust and Effective Communication
As a small group, read the list of blocks to developing trust and effective communication at a site produced by the New England Regional Leadership Program. Add your own ideas and then try to reach consensus about the 5 most serious blocks. Share reasons for making your choices and discuss ways to overcome these blocks. Include a discussion of self-disclosure and how it is connected to trust and effective communication.
http://crs.uvm.edu/gopher/nerl/group/b/j/Exercise18.html

Web Exercise 9.3: Building Intimacy
After reading the short online article "Top 10 Ways to Create More Intimacy Today," make your own list of suggestions for building intimacy in your relationships. Justify the choice for the items on your list with explanations and reasoning from Chapter 9 in your textbook.
http://marriage.about.com/od/intimacy/tp/createintimacy.htm

Chapter 10: Improving Communication Climates

Life Skills: Being Nice
Read about the power of being nice.
http://www.pamf.org/teen/parents/emotions/lifeskills/lifesks3.html

Quiz: Evaluate Your Relationship
Take a self-test to assess the level of effective and positive communication in your relationship with a partner. Then read the explanations that follow for suggestions on how to more effectively communicate in your relationship.
http://www.positive-way.com/communic.htm

Handling Criticism With Honesty and Grace
Read useful and practical suggestions for responding to another's criticism with honesty and grace. The focus is on how to actually gain new insights about yourself and the other person in the process.
http://www.pertinent.com/articles/communication/kareCom8.asp

Know Yourself and the Communication Climate
Scroll down to the section titled "Predicting the weather, or setting the stage for a positive communication climate." This section offers brief explanations and concrete examples of indicators and strategies for positive communication climates.
http://www.allenshea.com/knowyourself.html

Open Communication Climate
Read about supportiveness, defensiveness, and communication barriers as they as they relate to open and closed communication climates in organizations.
http://atc.bentley.edu/faculty/wb/printables/opencomm.pdf

Assertiveness Training: Responding to Criticism
As part of an online self-help book, this material reviews strategies for responding to criticism with assertive responses.
http://www.psychologicalselfhelp.org/Chapter13/chap13_18.html

Expressing More Appreciation, Gratitude, Encouragement and Delight
A chapter in an excellent, comprehensive online book that explores seven interpersonal communication skills. The chapter addresses research on the relational power of expressing appreciation and gratitude. The author also gives a step-by-step methodology for fully expressing appreciation (similar to the steps involved in the clear message format).
http://www.coopcomm.org/w7chal6.htm

Translating Complaints and Criticisms Into Transformative Requests
A chapter in an excellent, comprehensive online book that explores seven interpersonal communication skills. In order to gain more cooperation from others, learn how to ask for what you want by using specific, action-oriented requests rather than generalizations.
http://www.coopcomm.org/w7chal4.htm

Keeping Cool While Under Fire
Here are some "tools" to add to your "toolbox" for the next time someone is upset and is taking it out on you.
http://www.pertinent.com/articles/communication/kareCom.asp

Invalidation—The Opposite of Empathy
This article about empathy and communication provides some excellent examples of disconfirming responses.
http://www.selfgrowth.com/articles/winnett2.html

Acknowledgement While Talking and Communicating
Read examples of confirming communication in this article.
http://www.cyberparent.com/talk/acknowledge.htm

The One Eyed Turtle: Invalidation
This site provides a compilation of commentaries and examples of invalidation.
http://www.newciv.org/nl/newslog.php/_v175/__show_article/_a000175-000246.htm

Quiz: Defensive?
Take this self-test to determine which defense mechanisms you rely on most.
http://www1.excite.com/home/health/diet_center_article/0,20766,420,00.html

Quiz: Are You Too Critical?
Take this self-test to determine how critical you are of others.
http://www.lovingyou.com/content/advice/communication/content.shtml?ART=critical

Non-Defensive Exercises
This series of exercises can help you understand your nondefensive strengths and the areas that need improvement.
http://www.pndc.com/exercises/NonDefensiveExercises.htm

Defensive Exercises
This series of exercises can help you understand your own defensive patterns, a vital step in the process of change.
http://www.pndc.com/exercises/DefensiveExercises.htm

The Power of Non-Defensive Communication
A collection of stories about the power of using non-defensive communication in real-life situations.
http://www.pndc.com/stories/index.php

How Does One Handle Negative Criticism? It's Your Choice!
An educator offers his perspective about how to handle negative criticism:
http://home.earthlink.net/~bmgei/educate/docs/aperson/thinking/negative.htm

Transforming a Defensive Climate
Read more information about responding nondefensively and transforming a defensive climate.
http://www.aligningaction.com/climate.htm

Non-Defensive Communication Tools
Read a summary of nondefensive communication tools suggested by the author of a book entitled "Taking the War Out of Our Words."
http://www.mediate.com/articles/ford7.cfm

Accepting Criticism
An organizational psychologist describes three common emotional reactions we experience in the face of criticism. He also explains how these emotional reactions can prevent us from learning from feedback and using constructive problem-solving methods.
http://www.innerself.com/Behavior_Modification/warren03203.htm

Communication Climate
Read more about Gibb's pairs of defensive and supportive behaviors, and about creating positive communication climates.
http://www.bsu.edu/classes/flint/climate.html

Dealing With People You Can't Stand
In these online sample chapters and in fun, interactive exercises, learn methods that help us deal more effectively with difficult people.
http://www.thericks.com/dpcs/dpcs-library.htm

Self Quiz: Communication Climate Inventory
Reflect on your supervisor's communication style and measure the extent to which your organizational environment seems supportive or defensive. The scoring provides ratings for each of the 12 climate characteristics defined by Gibb in your textbook.
http://www.cps.usfca.edu/ob/studenthandbooks/321handbook/climate.htm

Self Quiz: How's Your Team Spirit?
Assess your perception of the atmosphere that exists within your team.
http://www.coachingandmentoring.com/Quiz/teamspirit.html

Responding to Criticism Without Being Defensive
Read practical advice about how and why to respond nondefensively at home and at work.
http://fatherhood.about.com/cs/discipline/a/criticism.htm

Assertive Communication
Read practical advice about assertiveness: what it is, why it's important, and how to apply it in your life.
http://www.uiowa.edu/~ucs/asertcom.html

The 411 on Constructive Criticism
This site provides hints about the art of constructive criticism.
http://www.inc.com/articles/2001/08/23257.html

The Politeness of Requests Made Via Email and Voicemail
This study explores the differences in the degree of politeness between voicemail messages and email messages.
http://jcmc.indiana.edu/vol11/issue2/duthler.html

The Unconscious Art of Verbal Defense
This site provides specific examples and characteristics of defense mechanisms.
http://inst.santafe.cc.fl.us/~mwehr/Personality/02DefenseMechanisms.doc

Web Exercise 10.1: Translating Your Criticisms and Complaints into Clear Requests
After reading the online article "Challenge Four: Translating Criticisms and Complaints into Requests," make a list of five common criticisms and complaints you might make in your own life (such as "clean up this house;," "do this correctly next time," "you'll never amount to anything"). Using the suggestions from Chapter 10 of your textbook, revise these complaint statements into specific action requests or clear explanatory clauses. According to the chapter, what are the benefits of communicating in this manner?
http://www.newconversations.net/w7chal4.htm

Web Exercise 10.2: Expressing Appreciation in Your Own Life
Read the online article "Challenge Six: Expressing More Appreciation," then list five things you are grateful to other people for. Using the three-part method for expressing appreciation mentioned in Chapter 10 of your textbook, develop clear statements for each thing on your list. Be sure to describe behavior, feelings, and consequences. What are the benefits of expressing appreciation to others? How does expressing appreciation relate to communication climates?
http://www.newconversations.net/w7chal6.htm

Web Exercise 10.3: Analyzing the Communication Climate in Your Own Relationship
After obtaining the results from your self-assessment quiz, write a short essay describing a relationship you have or have had with someone. Use terms from Chapter 10 of your textbook such as communication climate, defensiveness, supportiveness, spirals, responding to criticism, Gibb's behavior pairs, and confirming and disconfirming communication. Describe problems as well as specific skills or behaviors that could be used to improve the relationship.
http://www.positive-way.com/communic.htm

Web Activity 10.4: Non-defensiveness: A Growth Opportunity
Read the online article "How Does One Handle Negative Criticism" and reflect on your own defensiveness. Think of a time recently in which you were actually at fault but chose to respond defensively. Which of the nine defensive reactions mentioned in your textbook best describes your reaction? Why do you suppose you chose to react defensively instead of nondefensively? Replay the incident in your head and change your reaction to a nondefensive one. What would you say? Which of the nondefensive strategies mentioned in your textbook would allow you to best understand and acknowledge your error? What personal and relational outcomes do you envision in this replay?
http://home.earthlink.net/~bmgei/educate/docs/aperson/thinking/negative.htm

Web Exercise 10.5: Communication Climate Assessment
In order to better understand the characteristics of defensive and supportive climates, complete and score a communication climate inventory provided by the University of San Francisco's College of Professional Studies. Base your answers on a job you now hold or one you held in the past. How did your organization score on measures of supportiveness and defensiveness? Imagine you are a consultant hired to submit a diagnostic and prescriptive report to your organization's supervisor regarding the communication climate. Write a short summary of where the supervisor's strengths and weaknesses lie according to Gibb's climate characteristics. Explain and give specific examples. Then, write up a short paragraph of specific recommendations that will help the supervisor maintain or better build a supportive climate.
http://www.cps.usfca.edu/ob/studenthandbooks/321handbook/climate.htm

Web Exercise 10.6: Why Not Be Assertive?
Read the section entitled "Why Is Assertiveness Important" at the University of Iowa's online counseling service. Reflect on the list of eight negative consequences one might experience from lack of assertiveness. Which ones, if any, can you relate to? Explain and give specific examples.
http://www.uiowa.edu/~ucs/asertcom.html

Web Exercise 10.7: Delivering Your Own Clear and Complete Messages
Carefully follow the steps and suggestions provided in the online article "Challenge Three: Expressing Yourself More Clearly and Completely" to develop three of your own clear and complete messages. Use all five steps and label your messages. What communicative results can a person achieve by using this method?
http://www.newconversations.net/w7chal3.htm

Chapter 11: Managing Interpersonal Conflicts

Family Life Skills
This site for teens contains three links to useful and practical information related to conflict resolution. The links (on the left in the orange box) are titled Beyond the Blame Barrier, Being a Skilled Negotiator, and Family Problem Solving.
http://www.pamf.org/teen/parents/emotions/lifeskills/

There Is No One-Size-Fits-All Approach to Conflict Resolution
This detailed essay explains the importance of cultural competency in conflict management. A useful list of additional online sources follows.
http://www.beyondintractability.org/essay/culture_conflict/

Interpersonal Conflict Transformation: A Checklist for Disputing Parties
This useful checklist offers many items to consider when involved in interpersonal conflict. Each item includes links to more information.
http://www.beyondintractability.org/checklists/interpersonal_adversaries.jsp

Culture-Based Negotiation Styles
The author of this article outlines some generalizations about cultural and national approaches to negotiation.
http://www.beyondintractability.org/essay/culture_negotiation/?nid=1187

Conflict Resolution
This site provides links to numerous articles about conflict resolution in the workplace.
http://www.hodu.com/BC-Menu5.shtml

Conflict: An Essential Ingredient for Growth
A trainer and educator makes a point about how growth in an organization is limited without conflict. The article also briefly explains five conflict styles.
http://www.pertinent.com/articles/communication/spilgrim4.asp

Managing Conflict Successfully
This comprehensive article describes the differences between conflict and disagreement, and provides procedures for resolving both successfully.
http://utahmarriage.org/index.cfm?id=T157P9tfyt

Resolving Everyday Conflicts Sooner
Get practical tips for resolving conflict.
http://www.pertinent.com/articles/communication/kareCom91.asp

Interpersonal Relationships and Conflict Resolution
This comprehensive article contains many useful suggestions for how to resolve conflicts and manage personality differences in groups.
http://www.ic.org/nica/Process/Relation.html

Gender, Conflict and Conflict Resolution
A conflict resolution practitioner discusses the role of gender in conflict.
http://www.mediate.com/articles/birkhoff.cfm

There Is No Such Thing As a Relationship Without Conflict
A marriage and family therapist discusses conflict styles, conflict resolution styles, attitudes needed for conflict resolution, and stages of conflict resolution.
http://www.drnadig.com/conflict.htm

Getting to Yes: Negotiating Agreement Without Giving In
This page contains a summary of a popular book, written by two negotiation experts, on the subject of negotiating.
http://www.colorado.edu/conflict/peace/example/fish7513.htm

The Conflict Resolution Information Source
This site provides an extremely comprehensive database of links related to conflict resolution and conflict research.
http://conflict.colorado.edu/

The Win-Win Method of Settling Disagreements
Read a step-by-step discussion of the win-win conflict resolution method.
http://www.psychologicalselfhelp.org/Chapter13/chap13_61.html

Win-Win Approach to Conflict Resolution
Check out this brief explanation of the win/win approach to conflict resolution.
http://crnhq.org/freeskill1.html

Conflict Prevention and Conflict Resolution in the Workplace
Read articles about conflict prevention in the workplace. Scroll down to access free articles.
http://www.work911.com/conflict/index.htm

Conflict Styles: What Are You Like?
Read a brief explanation of five different conflict styles. Also included is a brief self-test to determine your own conflict style.
http://jeffcoweb.jeffco.k12.co.us/high/wotc/confli1.htm

Quiz: How Self-Assertive Are You?
Take this self-test to see how assertive you are.
http://www.oaktreecounseling.com/assrtquz.htm

Quiz: Assertiveness Inventory
Determine your scores on passiveness, aggressiveness, and assertiveness.
http://www.humanlinks.com/manskill/assertiveness_inventory.htm

Quiz: How Do You Deal With Problems in Your Relationships?
Take this self-test to assess how you deal with problems in your relationships.
http://www.positive-way.com/communic.htm

Quiz: Adult Personal Conflict Style Inventory
Calculate your preferred method for dealing with conflict.
http://peace.mennolink.org/cgi-bin/conflictstyle/inventory.cgi

Quiz: Do you confront? Deny? Or run away screaming?
Take this self-test to assess how you deal with challenging situations .
http://www.pallotticenter.org/SharedVisions/Vol9%20No1/confront.htm

Quiz: How Assertive Are You?
Here's another self-test to help you determine how assertive you are.
http://www.queendom.com/tests/minitests/assertiveness_abridged_access.html

Quiz: Are You a Creative Problem-Solver?
This self-test generates brief results—more explanation requires a fee.
http://www.queendom.com/tests/career/create_ps_access.html

Intercultural Conflict Management: A Mindful Approach
This comprehensive scholarly article addresses cultural factors underlying conflict and suggests a mindful, competence-based approach to conflict management.
http://personal.anderson.ucla.edu/richard.goodman/c4web/Mindful.htm

Passive Aggressiveness Resources
This site provides a comprehensive collection of links to information on passive aggressiveness.
http://www.passiveaggressive.homestead.com/Links.html

Life Would Be Easy . . . If It Weren't For Passive-Aggressive People
The author of this article suggests that the first step to dealing with a passive aggressive-person is to take a close look at yourself and your own communication style.
http://www.conniepodesta.com/articles_life9.htm

Quiz: Fighting Fair Evaluation Guide
Gain insight into how fair your disagreements might be and what the implications might be for your relationship.
http://www.positive-way.com/wqfightingfarepage.htm

12 Skills for Conflict Resolution
The Conflict Resolution Network details twelve skills necessary for solving any conflict, including the "win-win approach" and "appropriate assertiveness."
http://www.crnhq.org/twelveskills.html

How Do You Handle Conflict In Your Marriage?
Read this list of "dirty fighting techniques" for a humorous look at ineffective methods for dealing with conflict in a marriage. Which methods have been used in your relationships?
http://www.geocities.com/lmft_99/conflict.html

A Communication Model of Problem-Solving
This site provides helpful hints for relational problem-solving.
http://www.coping.org/dialogue/probsolv.htm

Conflict in Cyberspace: How to Resolve Conflict Online
Read explanations for how heightened conflict and misunderstandings occur in online communication, and suggestions for how to effectively resolve conflict online.
http://www.rider.edu/~suler/psycyber/conflict.html

Communication and Conflict-Related Articles
Scroll down to the "Communication and Conflict-Related" sections to access articles that relate to managing conflict and building effective relationships in the workplace.
http://work911.com/articles.htm

Avoiding Conflict Online
This site provides a description of five key attributes to online communication and hints for avoiding conflict online.
http://www.fullcirc.com/community/avoidingconflict.htm

What Does Win-Win Problem-Solving Sound Like?
This detailed dialogue illustrates a win-win outcome in a family problem-solving situation.
http://www.stepfamilyinfo.org/02/win-win.htm

Ineffective Couple's Communication
This detailed dialogue illustrates a lose-lose outcome in a marriage conflict.
http://www.stepfamilyinfo.org/02/lose-lose.htm

Quiz: Do You Fight Fair?
Find out whether you fight dirty, are willing to walk in another's shoes, or are somewhere in between.
http://lhj.com/lhj/quiz.jhtml?quizId=/templatedata/lhj/quiz/data/DoYouFightFairQuiz_03312003.xml&cat ref=cat1950002

Don't Avoid Conflict and Confrontation With Your Spouse
This article explains the importance of facing and not avoiding conflict in your marriage.
http://marriagepartner.com/relationships/844.php

Quiz: Can You Identify the Abuse?
Practice identifying and analyzing different types of passive aggressive communication. The site includes transcripts and audio files of actual dialogue between a woman and her partner.
www.youarenotcrazy.com

Web Exercise 11.1: What is Your Conflict Style?

Take the online self-test "Conflict Styles: What Are You Like?" and determine which conflict style best represents you. Do you agree with the outcome of this test? Why or why not? Give specific examples of conflict situations in which you demonstrated characteristics of a particular style.
http://www1.orange.co.uk/about/community/downloads/customercare/CONFLICTSTYLESQUESTIONNAIREcc1.doc

Web Exercise 11.2: Handling Conflicts in a Cooperative, Win-Win Manner

Read about constructive problem solving in your textbook and about cooperative and integrative conflict approach at the Psychological Self-Help website. Consider the following conflict scenarios:

1. Sarah and Desidra have lived together harmoniously for a year. One day, Desidra brings home a new puppy, and Sarah is upset because she does not want to deal with the mess or care of this new animal. Sarah decides to approach Desidra about the problem.

2. Pedro and Roxanne are married and have just had a new baby. Pedro is a smoker, and Roxanne is worried about Pedro smoking around the baby. She decides to approach Pedro about the problem. Pedro states that he is not willing to quit smoking.

3. Malik and Mario have been good friends and employees of equal status, until recently when Malik was promoted to a supervisor position. Malik is now in charge of supervising Mario's work. Malik has been frustrated with Mario recently because Mario brings his input and revisions to Malik a few hours before a deadline. Malik is feeling pressure from his boss to turn in good work on time, and he wants to confront Mario. However, he is also worried about ruining their friendship.

For each situation, work through the steps of collaborative, cooperative negotiation until you reach a win-win solution. Show your work for each step. Consider what each character might think, say, or do in each situation, assuming each character is convinced and willing to apply the win-win approach. Give examples of specific dialogue that might occur in the process. If necessary, make up details about each person or about the situation. How is the win-win approach and outcome different from other conflict management methods? Which parts of the process were easy? Difficult? Did you experience any blocks? Were you satisfied with the win-win approach to these conflicts? If not, how could it be improved? Would you be likely to use this method of problem-solving in your own life? Why or why not?
http://www.psychologicalselfhelp.org/Chapter13/chap13_62.html

Web Exercise 11.3: One Story, Five Endings

Read the descriptions of the five conflict management styles at the website for the Ohio Commission on Dispute Resolution and Conflict Management. Scroll down to "Activity 1" and read the story and its five endings. Write your own story, illustrating a conflict in an interpersonal relationship with a relative, friend, coworker, or classmate. Make up a story or write one that is based on a real-life conflict. Similar to the example at the website, write (and label) five different endings based on the five styles described. Finish the story, illustrating the relational outcomes you think might occur in each scenario as a result of using different conflict styles. Relate the styles at the website to the methods of conflict resolution described in your textbook. What are the similarities and differences?
http://www.state.oh.us/cdr/schools/contentpages/styles.htm

Web Exercise 11.4: Problem Solving Mix and Match

Read the section on constructive conflict skills in your textbook and the "Steps for two people in solving a common problem" at Coping.org (scroll down about a bit from the top of the page). After doing so, choose a partner and select one of the "ten role play situations" listed near the bottom of the page. Write the following words on separate slips of paper: avoiding, accommodating, competing, compromising, collaborating. Each partner should randomly choose a conflict style and then develop a 2- to 3-minute role play in which each of you illustrates your chosen style. Role-play your script for the class and see if your classmates can guess which conflict styles you're illustrating. Discuss the pros and cons of each style.
http://www.coping.org/dialogue/probsolv.htm#two

Web Exercise 11.5: Examining Your Own Conflict Style

After taking the quiz "Fighting Fair Evaluation Guide" at The Positive Way website, reflect on your score. How can you specifically improve your approach to conflict in significant relationships, according to the suggestions at this site? Explain and give examples.

http://www.positive-way.com/wqfightingfarepage.htm

USING FEATURE FILMS IN THE INTERPERSONAL COMMUNICATION COURSE

"Are we going to see a movie today?" In most cases the sight of a video cassette or DVD player in the classroom results in this kind of question. Conditioned by the sophisticated production techniques and high entertainment value of many films and television programs, students often welcome the break of routine provided by video programming. When they learn that the "show" will be a feature film, their interest level goes up even more. Beyond entertainment, however, feature films provide a valuable supplement to the reading, lecture, discussion, and other activities more common in the classroom.

Uses of Film and Television

To Model Desirable Behaviors By providing positive models of skillful communication, instructors can capitalize on the power of the media to further their instructional goals. The empathic listening of Judd Hirsch in *Ordinary People*, the positive communication climate created by Robin Williams in *Dead Poets Society*, or the family values illustrated in *Running on Empty* help students understand how they can behave more effectively in their own lives.

To Illustrate Ineffective Communication In addition to providing positive models, film and television can provide illustrations of ineffective or counterproductive types of communication. The controlling behavior of Nurse Ratched in *One Flew Over the Cuckoo's Nest* provides a vivid portrait of the abuse of power. Valmont's manipulative strategies in *Dangerous Liaisons* offers a cautionary tale of the evils of deceit. Bull Meecham's autocratic domination of his family in *The Great Santini* can help future parents avoid the same sort of alienation he suffered from his children and wife.

To Provide Material for Description and Analysis Films are not only useful in skills-oriented parts of the interpersonal communication course; they can also provide outstanding examples when the goal is to illustrate or analyze communication behavior. Consider, for example, the subject of stages in relational development and deterioration. A good text and lecture can introduce various models of relational trajectories, but dramatic illustrations can make them real. Students who watch the rise and fall of the romance between Woody Allen and Diane Keaton in *Annie Hall* gain an understanding of relational stages that goes far beyond what they gain in a lecture that is not supported with illustrations. Likewise, the way a single incident can appear different from the perspectives of various observers and participants is illustrated dramatically in Akira Kurosawa's classic film *Rashomon*.

Advantages of Film and Television The value of film becomes clear when the medium is compared to the alternatives. Lecturing about how to communicate more effectively is important, but it is clearly a different matter from illustrating the actual behavior. Describing appropriate self-disclosure or use of "I" language, for instance, is no substitute for providing examples of how this behavior looks and sounds in common situations.

Films also can have advantages over students sharing their own personal experiences. While this sort of involvement can demonstrate the relevance of ideas introduced in a course, some topics do not lend themselves to personal examples. For example, it is unlikely that students or instructors will feel comfortable discussing their own experiences with deceptive communication, remediating embarrassment, or sexual involvement. With topics like these, films and television provide an ideal way to illustrate people realistically handling the issues without invading the privacy of students.

Role-playing appropriate behaviors has its advantages, but this sort of impromptu acting is often simplistic, artificial, and only remotely linked to how interactions occur in the "real" world beyond the classroom. Every instructor who has tried to demonstrate principles like self-disclosure or conflict management skills by staging a scene in the classroom knows that this approach can fall flat as often as it can succeed. Student actors are self-conscious, situations are often contrived, and the whole activity often lacks the spontaneity and dynamism that occurs in real life.

Nothing in this argument should be taken to suggest that all films or television programming can be legitimately or productively used to support instruction. Works with unrealistic plots or dialogue, poor acting, and shabby production values are likely to be unusable. Furthermore, some programming may be too upsetting or otherwise inappropriate for classroom use. But well-chosen examples, supported with commentary by an instructor, can be a legitimate and uniquely effective means of enhancing principles introduced by more traditional means.

Film is never likely to replace more traditional methods of instruction. The clarity of a good textbook, the lectures and commentary of a talented instructor, and the contributions of motivated students are all essential ingredients in successful instruction. But the addition of dramatizations from television and film provide a complement to these elements.

Advantages of Videotaped Films

Availability Not too many years ago, screening films for students was a time-consuming and expensive task. With the VCR, DVD, and film rental sources, literally thousands of titles are available quickly, easily, and inexpensively.

Flexibility In addition to their availability, another benefit of videotaped examples from film and television is their flexibility. They can be edited in advance, played repeatedly for examination and analysis, and they are highly portable. As the following section illustrates, they can be used in a number of ways.

What Film or Television Program to Use? How to Use It?

Films and TV programs should be selected and used carefully in the interpersonal communication course to avoid trivializing the subject matter or confusing students. The text has suggestions for films and TV programs at the end of each chapter. Look for thorough descriptions of the following films and TV programs in the text (TV programs are marked with an asterisk):

Chapter 1

About Schmidt (the importance of interpersonal communication)

* *Friends* (transactional communication)

* *The Office* (communication competence

World's Fastest Indian (communication competence)

Chapter 2

Akeelah and the Bee (influence on self-concept)

Bridget Jones's Diary (influence on self-concept)

Brokeback Mountain (identity management)

Catch Me if You Can (identity management)

Stand and Deliver (self-fulfilling prophecy)

Chapter 3

Crash (stereotyping)

The Doctor (building empathy)

Don Juan de Marco (narratives)

* *Lost* (stereotyping)

* *30 Days* (building empathy)

Chapter 4

Garden State (the significance of expressing emotions)

Riding in Cars with Boys (expressing emotions (ir)responsibly)

The Upside of Anger (debilitative and facilitative emotions)

Chapter 5

Mean Girls (linguistic convergence)

The Miracle Worker (the importance of language)

Nell (the importance of language)

The N-Word (cultural rules for language)

When Harry Met Sally (gender and language)

Chapter 6

The Birdcage (masculine and feminine nonverbal behavior)

Boys Don't Cry (masculine and feminine nonverbal behavior)

Freaky Friday (personality expression via nonverbal communication)

Life as a House (the power of touch)

Mrs. Doubtfire (masculine and feminine nonverbal behavior)

 * *Seinfeld* (nonverbal communication in everyday life)

Tootsie (masculine and feminine nonverbal behavior)

Chapter 7

Dead Man Walking (supportive listening)

Jerry McGuire (ineffective listening and its alternatives)

Chapter 8

Bend It Like Beckham (dialectical tensions)

*50 First Date*s (developmental models)

 * TV reality shows (relational attraction)

Chapter 9

About a Boy (the need for intimacy)

Before Sunset (the process of self-disclosure)

In Her Shoes (intimacy and self-disclosure in family and relationships)

Transamerica (intimacy and self-disclosure in family and relationships)

Liar Liar (alternatives to self-disclosure)

Chapter 10

 * *American Idol* (giving and receiving criticism)

Antwone Fisher (confirming communication)

Changing Lanes (communication spirals)

Office Space (defensive communication climate)

Stolen Summer (defensiveness)

Chapter 11

American Beauty (dysfunctional conflict)

The Joy Luck Club (culture and conflict)

The Secret Lives of Dentists (conflict styles)

Widely available films and topics illustrated

In addition to those films highlighted in the text, many more film summaries and applications are available at the **Film in Communication Database** on the Premium Book Companion Website, accessible through

ThomsonNOW for *Looking Out/Looking In*. Following is a list of available films, the chapter most closely associated with the film, and the general context of the film (e.g., friendships, work relationships, family, couple, etc.). Please see the website for more thorough descriptions.

Chapter 1: A First Look at Interpersonal Relationships

The Accidental Tourist (couple)

The Anniversary Party (friendship/acquaintances)

A Beautiful Mind (strangers)

The Breakfast Club (friendship/acquaintances)

Cast Away

Children of a Lesser God (work/organizations)

Dad (medical)

Dangerous Liaisons (couple)

Denise Calls Up (friendship/acquaintances)

Dominick and Eugene (family)

Erin Brockovich (communication competence)

Gung Ho (work/organizations)

Intimacy (family)

Italian for Beginners (couple)

Joy Luck Club (family)

Kramer vs. Kramer (friendship/acquaintances)

*Life Lessons (*in *New York Stories)* (couple)

My Family (Mi Familia) (family)

Nothing in Common (friendship/acquaintances, family, work/organizations)

An Officer and a Gentleman (work/organizations)

One Flew Over the Cuckoo's Nest

On Golden Pond (friendship/acquaintances)

Rain Man (family)

Ordinary People (family)

Parenthood (work/organizations)

Shrek (friendship/acquaintances)

Swept Away (couple)

Terms of Endearment (work/organizations)

The Unbearable Lightness of Being (couple)

Waking Life (friendship/acquaintances)

When a Man Loves a Woman (couple)

When Harry Met Sally (couple)

You've Got Mail (couple)

Chapter 2: Communication and Identity: Creating and Presenting the Self

Antz (work/organizations)

All About Eve (couple)

Boyz in the Hood (influences on the self-concept)

The Breakfast Club (friendship/acquaintances)

Bridget Jones's Diary (couple, work/organizations)

The Closet (work/organizations)

Clueless (school)

Children of a Lesser God (work/organizations, friendship/acquaintances)

The Color Purple (couple)

Dad (medical)

Finding Forester (strangers)

First Wives Club (friendship)

Grease (couple)

The Great Santini (family, work/organizations)

Gung Ho (work/organizations)

Kramer vs. Kramer (friendship/acquaintances)

Mr. Holland's Opus (family, school)

Parenthood (family, friendship/acquaintances, work/organizations)

Pay It Forward (family)

Pretty Woman (couple)

Riding in Cars with Boys (family)

The Right Stuff (work/organizations)

Shallow Hal (couple)

Shirley Valentine (school)

Stand and Deliver (school)

Stand By Me (friendship/acquaintances)

The Story of Us (couple)

The Truth about Cats and Dogs (couple)

Chapter 3: Perception: What You See Is What You Get

Annie Hall (family)

At First Sight

Being There (strangers)

Children of a Lesser God (couple)

The Doctor (work/organizational)

The First Wives Club (shared narratives)

The Outrage (strangers)

Rashomon (strangers)

Trading Places (friendship/acquaintances)

Waiting to Exhale (friendship/acquaintances, shared narratives)

White Man's Burden (friendship/acquaintances, multiple perspectives)

Chapter 4: Emotions: Thinking, Feeling, and Communicating

About Last Night (couple)

The Accidental Tourist (couple)

Annie Hall (couple)

The Big Chill

Broadcast News (couple; friendship/acquaintances)

Bull Durham (work/organizations)

Casablanca (couple)

Children of a Lesser God (couple)

High Fidelity (couple)

Intimacy (couple)

Monster's Ball (the significance of expressing emotions)

Remains of the Day (couple)

Shall We Dance? (couple)

Smoke (friendship/acquaintances)

Tootsie (couple; work/organizational; friendship/acquaintances)

Chapter 5: Language: Barrier and Bridge

Being There (couple)

Big (couple)

Gone with the Wind (couple)

Shirley Valentine (couple)

Meet the Parents (family)

The Miracle Worker (school)

My Fair Lady (strangers)

Nell (strangers)

Pushing Tin (couple)

Quest for Fire

Stand By Me (friendship/acquaintances)

A Thousand Clowns (friendship/acquaintances)

Chapter 6: Nonverbal Communication: Messages beyond Words

About Last Night (couple)

Alice (family)

Baby Boom (couple)

Beaches (friendship/acquaintances)

The Big Chill (friendship/acquaintances)

The Birdcage (couple)

Broadcast News (couple)

Life as a House (family)

Meet the Parents (friendship/acquaintances)

An Officer and a Gentleman (work/organizations)

The Paper Chase (school)

Philadelphia (work/organizational)

Sea of Love (friendship/acquaintances)

Tootsie (work/organizational)

Two Guys and a Girl (friendship/acquaintances)

Chapter 7: Listening: More than Meets the Ear

Children of a Lesser God (friendship/acquaintances)

Dead Man Walking (friendship/acquaintances)

Good Will Hunting (friendship/acquaintances)

Grosse Pointe Blank (friendship/acquaintances)

Kramer vs. Kramer (couple; work/organizations)

Office Space (work/organizational)

Rain Man (medical; couple)

Shirley Valentine (couple; family)

Chapter 8: Communication and Relational Dynamics

About Last Night (couple)

Annie Hall (couple)

Beaches (friendship/acquaintances; couple)

Broadcast News (couple)

The Brothers McMullen (family)

Dad (family)

Diner (couple)

Dominick and Eugene (family)

Down and Out in Beverly Hills (family)

The Fabulous Baker Boys (family)

Gone with the Wind (couple)

He Said, She Said (friendship/acquaintances)

Jerry McGuire (couple)

My Fair Lady (couple)

My Life (couple)

Parenthood (family)

Reality Bites (couple)

Romeo and Juliet (couple)

Chapter 9: Intimacy and Distance in Relational Communication

About a Boy (the need for intimacy)

Almost Famous (the need for intimacy; masculine and feminine intimacy styles)

Before Sunrise (the process of self-disclosure)

Before Sunset (the process of self-disclosure)

Liar Liar (alternatives to self-disclosure)

Magnolia (the need for intimacy; alternatives to self-disclosure)

Meet the Parents (alternatives to self-disclosure)

Secrets & Lies (benefits and risks of self-disclosure; alternatives to self-disclosure)

sex, lies, and videotape (intimacy and distance in romantic and family relationships)

Chapter 10: Improving Communication Climates

Annie Hall (couple)

Beaches (friendship/acquaintances)

Broadcast News (work/organizational)

Children of a Lesser God (school)

Dead Poets Society (friendship/acquaintances; school)

The Fabulous Baker Boys (couple)

Ghost World (friendship/acquaintances)

Gone with the Wind (couple)

My Fair Lady (couple)

One Flew Over the Cuckoo's Nest (medical)

One True Thing (family)

Parenthood (family)

Patch Adams (medical)

Tin Men (strangers)

Welcome to the Dollhouse (school)

When Harry Met Sally (couple)

Chapter 11: Managing Interpersonal Conflicts

American Beauty (friendship/acquaintances)

The Anniversary Party (couple)

Dangerous Minds (work/organizational)

Good Morning Vietnam (work/organizational)

Joy Luck Club (family)

Lost in America (couple)

Mississippi Masala (couple)

On Golden Pond (friendship/acquaintances; school)

Shirley Valentine (couple)

War of the Roses (couple)

Who's Afraid of Virginia Woolf (couple)

In every case, it is important for the instructor to view a film in advance of a class screening to become familiar with the material and determine how it can best be used to further instructional goals. Once a film has been identified as having instructional value, it can be used in one of several ways: **In class** Segments or complete films may be shown in class to illustrate points about a single topic (e.g., defense-arousing communication, self-disclosure) or to preview and/or review the entire course or major units. **In the college media center** Most campuses have a media center where students can view segments or entire films, and if desired complete workbook assignments. **As homework** Class members can all view the same film on their own time, or they may choose a variety of titles from a pre-approved list in order to complete an analytical assignment.

Available to Adopters of *Looking Out/Looking In,* Twelfth Edition

A film guide, *Communication in Film III: Teaching Communication Courses Using Feature Films*, prepared by Russ Proctor, describes how a wide array of movies can be used to illustrate how concepts from *Looking Out/Looking In* appear in realistic situations. This guide takes advantage of students' inherent interest in the medium of film, showing them how movies can be both entertaining and educational.

Part 2

Notes on Class and Student Activities

CHAPTER 1
A FIRST LOOK AT INTERPERSONAL RELATIONSHIPS

Objectives

After studying the material in Chapter One of *Looking Out/Looking In,* you should understand:

1. The types of needs that communication can satisfy.
2. The elements and characteristics of the transactional communication model.
3. The principles and misconceptions of communication
4. The differences between impersonal and interpersonal communication.
5. The characteristics of effective communicators.

Specifically, you should be able to:

1. Identify the needs you attempt to satisfy by your interpersonal communication and the degree to which you satisfy those needs.
2. Use the transactional model to:
   a) Diagnose barriers to effective communication in your life.
   b) Suggest remedies to overcome those barriers.
3. Identify the degree to which your communication is impersonal and interpersonal.
4. Improve your effectiveness as a communicator by broadening your repertoire of behaviors and your skill at performing them.
5. Identify the most appropriate communication behaviors in a variety of important situations.
6. Discover how satisfied you are with the way you communicate in various situations.

Notes on Class and Student Activities

A. Name Chain

Objectives

To learn the names of all the group members, thus forming a foundation for future interaction.

To achieve immediate participation from every class member.

To demonstrate that making mistakes is an acceptable, normal part of learning.

To provide an activity that calls for a minimal contribution with relatively little threat.

Note	WE STRONGLY RECOMMEND THAT THIS BE THE FIRST CLASS ACTIVITY! Over many semesters, it has proved to be one of the activities most often reported by the students as being of extreme value.

Instructions

1. Assemble your group, including instructor, so that everyone can see each other; a circle works well.

2. The first person (ask for a volunteer) begins by giving his or her name to the whole group, speaking loudly enough to be heard clearly by everyone. ("My name is Sheila.") Instructors may want to repeat what they've heard to check whether the speaker has been heard correctly. If you're not sure of a name, ask to have it repeated.

3. The group member seated on the first speaker's left will then give his or her own name followed by the first speakers. ("My name is Gordon, and this is Sheila.")

4. Now the person to the left of the second speaker gives his or her name, followed by the second and first speaker's names. ("My name is Wayne, this is Gordon, and that's Sheila.") This procedure is followed around the whole group so that the last person names everyone in the class. It sounds as if it will be impossible for the last few people, but when you try it, you'll be surprised at how many names are remembered.

5. Things to watch for:

    a) If you forget a name, don't worry; that person will help you after you've had a little time to think.

    b) If you don't catch the speaker's name, ask to have it repeated.

    c) You may want the person who begins the activity to end it also. After that, anyone who wants to should try to "name them all."

    d) Above all, keep the atmosphere informal. As you know, personal comments and humor have a way of lessening pressure.

Variations

Use first names only, or work with both first and last. Both approaches have their advantages. Try both methods to see which works best for you.

Have each person attach a descriptive word to his or her name, for example: Gardening (or Digger) Dan, Patient Cindy, and so on. The variety of names is good for several laughs, thus making the exercise an even better icebreaker.

Discussion Questions

1. Was remembering all the names as difficult as you expected? The answer is usually no, and you can make the point that what was true here will likely hold true for other activities, both in and out of class. Taking risks isn't always as dangerous as it seems.

2. What will you do if you can't remember someone's name the next time you see him or her? This is a good time to talk about a common problem. Is it better to pretend you remember a person's name, or come right out and tell the person you forgot? Just how valuable is "tact" in social situations?

3. How did you feel as your turn approached? How did you feel after you were done? This question invites the students to reveal the feelings of anxiety they had and to discover that their fears in social situations are not unique but are rather like their classmates.

4. Which name(s) do you think you'll remember easily? Why? This question invites discussion on what factors make names or people stand out in our memories. It is the differences that make individuals unique. This question leads into the next activity very naturally.

B. Introductions

Objective

To assist the students further in becoming acquainted by having them learn some personal characteristics of their classmates.

Instructions

1. Ask students to form dyads (groups of two), and to, if possible, pair up with someone they've not known previously. Use yourself to even out the dyads if necessary. In any event, someone should introduce the instructor to the class.

2. Each member of a dyad will interview the other. Try to allow about 20 minutes for this activity. Give students the following instructions.

   a) You should find three unique things to tell the group about the person you're introducing. These may be actions, characteristics, or experiences that set your partner apart from other people. (For example, the fact that your partner graduated from Lincoln High School probably isn't as important as the fact that he or she is thinking about getting married or planning an interesting career.) Remember that most people feel uncomfortable talking about themselves, so you'll have to probe to get those unique aspects from your partner.

   b) Use the name of the person you're introducing instead of the pronoun he or she. This will help everyone learn names.

   c) Back in the large group, students introduce their partners to the class until everyone has been introduced.

Discussion Questions

1. Did you feel scared or threatened during any of the steps in this exercise? If so, when? This question may encourage group members to discover something about beginning acquaintances.

2. How successful were you in finding out unique things about your partner? Why? Students may shed some light on the difficulty we seem to have in getting most persons to talk about themselves. The group may also discover the prevalence of clichés in our conversation.

3. This experience was different from the usual way you get to know someone. What parts of it did you like? Were there parts that you didn't like? Why?

4. Now that you know more about each other, have your feelings changed about any of the individuals? How? Have your feelings changed in regard to the group? How?

C. Autograph Party

Objective

To break the ice in the classroom and to help students get acquainted with others in the group.

Instructions

Give students the following instructions:

Your task is to find someone who fits each of the descriptions below, and get his or her signature on this sheet. Try to find a different person for each description.

Find someone who

is an only child _____

skipped breakfast today _____

drives an imported car _____

was born east (west) of the Mississippi _____

isn't getting enough sleep _____

plays a musical instrument _____

is a parent _____

is left-handed _____

is taller than you _____

has an unusual hobby _____

is married _____

goes to church regularly _____

knows someone you know _____

has schedule problems _____

writes poetry _____

has traveled overseas _____

has read a book you've read _____

is in love _____

speaks a language besides English _____

knows some information helpful to you _____

is self-employed _____

D. Comparing and Contrasting Communication Models
(*Invitation to Insight* activity in text, p. 14)

Objectives

To explain the role of models in learning.

To identify and clarify unique elements involved in interpersonal communication transactions.

Instructions

Assign the activity as homework and then conduct in-class discussion.

Discussion Questions

1. What similarities and differences occur between the two models?
2. In your opinion, what does one model explain better than the other, and vice-versa?
3. Which model do you prefer, and why?
4. What is the purpose of models in learning? Do they confuse or clarify? Explain.

E. How Personal Are Your Relationships (*Invitation to Insight* activity in text, p. 25)

Objectives

To enable the student to classify communication relationships along the impersonal-interpersonal spectrum.

To evaluate the relationship according to the characteristics of interpersonal communication.

Instructions

Use the activity as homework or as an in-class assignment, and then conduct a follow-up discussion.

Discussion Questions

1. What are the unique qualities of your relationships?
2. How irreplaceable are your relationships?
3. How much interdependence characterizes your different relationships?
4. Compare the amounts of self-disclosure present in your relationships along the p. 25 impersonal-interpersonal spectrum.
5. Distinguish the rewards (extrinsic and intrinsic) in your different relationships.

F. Communication Skills Inventory (1.1 in *Student Activities Manual*)

Objectives

To help students identify how satisfied they are with the way they communicate in various situations.

To help students identify goals and objectives for learning throughout the semester.

Instructions

Use the activity as homework or as an in-class assignment, and then conduct a follow-up discussion.

Discussion Questions

1. What patterns did you detect in your answers?
2. How satisfied are you with your ability to communicate? Are you more satisfied with your abilities in some contexts (e.g., work, family, friendships) than in others?
3. In what areas do you need improvement?
4. What concrete benefits do you envision gaining from improving your interpersonal communication behavior?

Variations

Combine this activity with the in-text *Skill Builder*, "Check Your Competence" (p. 33) and/or the in-text *Invitation to Insight* activity, "Assessing Your Communication Skills" (p. 28). Assign these activities as homework and ask students to turn answers into a brief report on their own strengths and weaknesses. Then, have them set specific goals for achievement in the course. They should consider ways to measure improvement, barriers to success, and possibilities for overcoming barriers. Have them repeat the activities for an end-of-semester evaluation and evaluate the process and progress of their goal achievements.

G. Expanding Your Communication Effectiveness
(1.2 in *Student Activities Manual*)

Objectives

To help students develop an awareness of a personal range of communication behaviors with people important to them.

To foster evaluation of the effectiveness of their current range of behaviors.

To increase awareness of effective communication behaviors that might widen the range of abilities to accomplish interpersonal goals.

Instructions

Use the activity as homework or as an in-class assignment, and then conduct a follow-up discussion.

Discussion Questions

1. Relate the range of behaviors observed to your own evaluation of your skill. Comment specifically on how a communicator can choose appropriate behaviors.

2. How accurate do you think you are in identifying effective models? Is there any reason why you might be inaccurate?

3. What behaviors that you don't engage in currently would you like to develop? Why?

4. How difficult was it to come up with specific examples of effective behaviors? (i.e., it's easy to suggest you want to become a better listener, but it's more difficult to describe exactly what that behavior looks like).

CHAPTER 2

COMMUNICATION AND IDENTITY: CREATING AND PRESENTING THE SELF

Objectives

After studying the material in Chapter Two of *Looking Out/Looking In,* you should understand:

1. How the self-concept is defined.
2. How biological and social factors influence the self-concept.
3. How the self-concept is developed and shaped.
4. Four reasons why the self-concept is subjective.
5. Problems involved with resisting change to the self-concept.
6. Influences on identity.
7. The role of self-fulfilling prophecies in shaping the self-concept and in influencing communication.
8. Four requirements for changing the self-concept.
9. Differences between public and private selves.
10. The characteristics of and reasons for identity management.
11. The ways in which identities are managed.
12. The ethics of impression management.

Specifically, you should be able to:

1. Develop a self-concept that enhances your communication by
   A) identifying the key elements of your self-concept.
   B) identifying the people who have had the greatest influence on your self-concept.
   C) describing the ways in which your self-concept may be inaccurate and suggesting ways of improving its accuracy.
   D) identifying the ways in which your self-concept influences your communication.
   E) recognizing and giving proper credit to your personal strengths.
2. Describe the ways in which you influence the self-concept of others.
3. Avoid destructive self-fulfilling prophecies that affect your communication and create positive self-fulfilling prophecies that can improve your communication.
4. Identify the differences between your public and private selves.
5. Manage impressions of yourself to meet your relational goals.

Notes on Class and Student Activities

A. Take Away (*Invitation to Insight,* text, p. 42)

Objectives

To demonstrate that the concept of self is perhaps our most fundamental possession.

Discussion Questions

1. What types of descriptors seem most fundamental to your self-concept?
2. What descriptors do you see as the most vulnerable to change?
3. Do you think others would describe you as you have yourself? Why or why not?

B. Ego Boosters and Busters
(*Invitation to Insight,* text, p. 47 and 2.3 in *Student Activities Manual*)
Objectives

To enable the student to see how messages from others affect his or her self-concept.

To enable the student to understand how his or her communication affects the self-concept of others.

Discussion Questions

1. What sorts of things were "busters"? Why did they affect your self-concept negatively? What sorts of things were "boosters"?
2. Are there any differences of opinions among class members about what indicates a booster or buster? Why might that occur? Are there any universal boosters and busters?
3. Is it possible to always send booster messages and avoid sending intentional and unintentional busters? If not, how can one deal with this state of affairs?

C. Recognizing Your Strengths (*Invitation to Insight,* text, p. 55)
Objectives

To illustrate the disproportionate emphasis we place on negative parts of the self-concept.

To demonstrate the value of feeling positive about oneself.

To build class cohesiveness and morale.

To further develop the acquaintance of group members.

Discussion Questions (see text, p. 55)

D. Reevaluating Your "Cant's"
(*Skill Builder,* text, p. 63 and 2.4 in *Student Activities Manual*)
Objectives

To demonstrate how an obsolete self-concept becomes a self-fulfilling prophecy that keeps the student from growing.

To help students understand the many ways they can change and develop their communication habits.

Discussion Questions

1. What did you discover about the differences between being *unable* and *unwilling* to do something?
2. What are some of the negative consequences that result from believing you "can't" do something?
3. How do "can't" and "won't" affect our abilities to accomplish goals?
4. What do you learn about yourselves, if anything, from doing this activity?

E. Your Personal Coat of Arms

Objectives

To help the group members search out some of the important and positive aspects of their identities.

To further acquaint the class members with each other.

Options

You may assign this as an out-of-class activity. Students may use pictures from magazines, snapshots, or their artistic talents to complete their own "coats of arms."

Display the completed assignments in the classroom for a few days so that students can see them and try to guess the owners.

Discussion Questions

1. When you have seen the coats of arms of your whole group, do you find any similarities?

2. In what ways are the coats of arms most alike? What could be an explanation?

3. In what ways are the coats of arms most different? Explain. There are no set answers to these questions, but they usually promote good discussion, and the search for explanations leads students to the areas of their lives that they share with most others and also those in which they differ.

Student Instructions

1. Create a personal coat of arms that represents important information about you, such as

   A) people who are important to you.

   B) locations that are significant to you.

   C) activities with which you are associated.

   D) personal traits that characterize you.

   E) your ambitions.

   F) physical features that identify you.

   G) talents and skills you have.

   H) anything else you think is an important part of you.

2. Remember that you needn't be a professional artist to complete this activity. This is a getting-acquainted activity, not a contest.

3. In addition to pencil or pen, you might use other materials to construct your coat of arms: photos, crayons, felt-tip pens, rub-on letters, paint, and newspaper or magazine clippings.

4. After completing your coat of arms, explain it to other class members.

F. Interpersonal Interviews

If you haven't done Introductions in Chapter One (Activity B in Instructor's Manual), a good, nonthreatening way to help all class members begin to talk to one another and in front of the class is to conduct interpersonal interviews.

Pair class members and ask them to exchange information about themselves (biographical, interests, values, family, school, work, etc.). Allow them about 15-20 minutes to interview one another, and ask them to take brief notes about the other person.

Stop the interviews and allow about 2-3 minutes for all persons to organize the information they have about their partners so that they can introduce their partners to the class.

Sitting in a circle so that everyone can see everyone else, ask class members to introduce their partners. After the introduction, other class members may ask questions of their partners or the partners may clarify or correct any information given about them to the class.

Variations

Do shorter interviews on a number of days, using one topic at time (e.g., only biographical information one day, only interests another, and only future goals another). Or, after the interviews have occurred, ask students to analyze how they have presented their self-concept to the partner (different from the way they present to others?) and how they would change the way they interacted if they could. Another idea is to have class members go around the circle after the interviews, using one positive adjective to describe each of the persons introduced.

G. Your Many Identities and Success in Managing Impressions
(*Invitation to Insight,* text, p. 67 and 2.5 in *Student Activities Manual*)
Objectives

To help students recognize how manner, appearance, and setting affect identity management.

To provide an opportunity for students to reflect on how, when, and why they might improve their levels of self-monitoring.

Discussion Questions

1. What role does self-monitoring play in presenting more or less successful "selves?"

2. What factors influence the ability to consciously manage better impressions (e.g., lack of knowledge, lack of skill, lack of confidence, etc.)?

H. Self-Monitoring Inventory (*Invitation to Insight,* text, p. 71)
Objectives

To recognize your level of self-monitoring.

To consider the appropriate level of self-monitoring in different situations.

Discussion Questions

1. What are the advantages of high self-monitoring? The disadvantages?
2. How can we balance paying attention to our own behavior with focusing on that of others?

I. Self-Concept Collage

Objectives

To provide students with opportunity to reflect on the social development of their own self-concepts.

To illustrate reflected appraisal and social comparison.

Instructions

Give students the following assignment. In class, put students in small groups and have them share their collages with each other. Provide questions (on board or on handout) that can guide their group discussion, such as:

Discussion Questions

1. Who are the people in our lives who have had the greatest influence on our self-concept? Identify ego-busters and ego-boosters. Share specific examples of ego-busting or ego-boosting comments or actions and explain how they have influenced your self-concept.
2. Relate the discussion in #1 to the textbook concept of reflected appraisal. What does it mean and how do the people mentioned above play a part in the process? How do these people contribute to the development of your self-concept?
3. Relate the discussion in #1 to the textbook concept of social comparison. What does it mean and how do the people mentioned above play a part in the process? Share some specific examples of comparisons you make between you and significant others. Between you and strangers? How do other people contribute to the development of your self-concept?
4. Share ways in which you think your current self-concept affects the way you interact in your interpersonal relationships.

Student Instructions

Purpose

The purpose of this activity is to reflect on and become aware of the people and communication events that have played and do play a role in the development of your self-concept.

Format

Because this is a creative assignment, no instructions are provided about how to specifically format the collage. Use words, phrases, quotes, images, drawings, photos, word balloons, etc. Use poster board, notebooks, photo albums, shoeboxes, fabric, or other materials. Make them 2D or 3D. However be sure that items are big enough for other class members to see when you share your collage during class time (in small groups). In your collage, include representations of:

people who are important to you

people who confirm your positive self-concept (ego-boosters) and *examples* of ego-boosting comments or behaviors

people who confirm your negative self-concept (ego-busters) and *examples* of ego-busting comments or behaviors

people to whom you compare yourself

CHAPTER 3
PERCEPTION: WHAT YOU SEE IS WHAT YOU GET

Objectives

After studying the material in Chapter Three of *Looking Out/Looking In,* you should understand:

1. How the processes of selection, organization, interpretation and negotiation operate in the perception process.
2. How physiological influences, cultural differences, social roles (including gender and occupational roles), and self-concept influence the perceptual process.
3. Five common tendencies that influence the accuracy and inaccuracy of our perceptions.
4. The purpose, components, and considerations of perception checking.
5. The dimensions of and requirements for developing empathy to improve the accuracy of perceptions.

Specifically, you should be able to:

1. Identify
   A) the physiological factors that influence your and others' perceptions.
   B) the cultural and social factors that influence your and others' perceptions.
   C) common perceptual errors that contribute to opinions of others.
2. Engage in perception-checking by
   D) using appropriate nonverbal behaviors (eyes, voice).
   E) describing clearly and accurately the behavior you observed.
   F) posing at least two possible interpretations of the behavior you described.
   G) requesting feedback from your partner about the accuracy or inaccuracy of your observation and interpretations.
3. Communicate empathy by
   H) using appropriate nonverbal behaviors (eyes, proximity, touch, voice).
   I) describing the correct or understandable elements of your position and/or the position of your partner.
   J) describing the incorrect or difficult elements of your position and/or the position of your partner.
   K) describing at least two different ways these elements might affect your relationship.

Notes on Class and Student Activities

A. Your Perceptual Filters (*Invitation to Insight,* text, p. 86)

Objectives

To help students recognize the perceptual, physical, role, interaction, psychological, and membership constructs that help them categorize others.

To encourage students to consider the validity of their constructs.

Discussion Questions

1. How do constructs limit our perceptions of others?

2. How do constructs help us relationally?

B. Punctuation Practice (*Skill Builder,* text, p. 90)
Objective

To help students discover the importance of punctuation in our perceptual organization.

Discussion Questions

1. In the examples, how might the different punctuating schemes affect the way each might respond to the other?

2. How can you use the concept of punctuation to appreciate the perception of others?

C. New Body, New Perspective (*Invitation to Insight,* text, p. 95)
Objective

To enable students to understand how perception can be changed by different physiological conditions.

Discussion Questions

1. How did the situation you chose differ when you changed the physiological "symptoms"?

2. Is it difficult to understand how someone else would "see" in each of those conditions? If so, why?

3. Did any of the people of your group foresee problems that may occur when under any of the different conditions?

D. Role Reversal (*Invitation to Insight,* text, p. 101)
Objective

To give students the opportunity for firsthand experience with an orientation or perspective different from his or her own.

Options

An effective warm-up is to have the class members name people, groups, or philosophical positions they do not understand at all—which should provide each student with several targets for the assignment. An alternate approach is to stage debates in which students are required to defend positions opposed to their own. You might even want students actually to assume the role they're playing, that is, have conservatives pretend they're radicals, children play parents, and so on. In many cases, you'll need to become the director to help students get into their roles. You may need to goad them into acting out contrasting positions, play alter ego, or just plain put words into their mouths until they get the idea.

Discussion Questions

1. What were your expectations prior to the experience?

2. How did the experience meet your expectations? Were there any surprises?

3. Did the experience change your own perspective, orientation, or the way you feel toward others? If so, in what ways?

4. How might this experience affect future relations with people who hold

different perspectives from you?

5. Are there people whom you wish would take a walk in your shoes for a day? If so, who are they?

E. Perception-Checking Stimuli

Objectives

To enable students to understand the perceptions of others.

To provide situations where perceptions can be aired, discussed and "perception checked."

Instructions

Here are two activities designed for group interaction.

The Gender Game. Divide the class into men and women. Each group is to come up with 5–10 questions they have always wanted to ask the opposite gender but, for some reason or another, never have. They are to rank their questions in importance because the class may not get to all the questions. Two simple rules govern the limits here: (1) you may not ask a question of the opposite gender that you are unwilling to answer yourself, and (2) you should avoid questions that are insulting (i.e., specific sexual behaviors that might embarrass some class members) or that tend to generalize about all members of a gender (e.g., "Why do women always go to the bathroom in pairs?").

Groups meet face to face after about 20 minutes allotted to question-generation, and the instructor acts as moderator as one "side" and then another asks one question at a time; each time the opposite side can put the question back to them. The instructor should encourage all members of the class to answer the question put to the group, but no one should be pressured if he or she feels uncomfortable.

The Intercultural Game. Using the same format as The Gender Game, this activity makes good use of any diverse population your institution may have. If your class has members of many cultures, you can divide them that way. Or, make use of foreign language classes or English as a Second Language (ESL) classes, and coordinate your activity with another instructor. In addition to providing a forum for perception checking, you can further interdisciplinary relationships at the same time.

Note: Both of these activities can be used as the stimulus for activity 3.5 in the *Student Activities Manual*. Ask students to keep track of perceptions they have during the course of the activity and prepare 2-5 perception-checking statements to be delivered to specific individuals during the next class. (Examples: "Shelley, when you said that men didn't take enough responsibility for birth control in relationships, I didn't know if you meant that men should bring up the subject of birth control first or if you thought that men should just take it upon themselves to be the ones that actually use protection. Did you mean either of those two things or something else?" Or "Jose, when you said most white people in the U.S. made no effort to understand you, I wondered if you were referring to just your language, or if you meant more than that—like trying to understand what you think and feel. What did you mean?")

Discussion Questions

1. What did you find out about the other gender (or about another culture) that you didn't know before?

2. Are your perspectives similar to or different from the others you interviewed?

3. What purpose did perception checking serve in this activity?

4. How do our perceptions influence communication with others? Give specific examples.

5. What effect might this activity have on future communication and relationships with people of the opposite gender (or of another culture)? Suggest specific ways we can improve communication.

F. Perception-Checking Practice
(*Skill Builder,* text, p. 109 and 3.5 and 3.6 in *Student Activities Manual*)
Objective

To assist students in the application and analysis of perception checking in a variety of situations.

Discussion Questions

1. What aspects of perception checking are most/least useful?
2. How can you use perception checking most effectively in your life?

G. Pillow Talk
(*Skill Builder,* text, p. 116–17
and Shifting Perspectives, 3.3 in *Student Activities Manual*)
Objective

To provide students with a systematic tool for exploring the perceptions of those who differ from them on important issues.

Note		
	1.	The pillow method is a culmination of the entire chapter. The measure of a student's success in understanding perceptual variability is the ability to move through the steps on a personal problem.
	2.	Working through the pillow becomes more difficult with the immediacy of the issue. You will most likely want to work through several cases in class. You may need to suggest to students some possible reasons for position 2, in which the "opponent" is right.
	3.	We urge you not to become discouraged when students say they "can't" understand a position different from their own. Although this kind of understanding is difficult, the reward of increased empathy is well worth the effort.

Discussion Questions

1. What insights can we gain about the perspectives of others when we apply the pillow method?
2. How has empathy (or lack thereof) affected communication in your past and current relationships?
3. How might these insights affect future communication in your relationships?

H. Empathy Skills
Objective

To give students practice in demonstrating their abilities to build common ground and express empathy.

Purpose

This assignment will allow you to demonstrate your ability to build common ground and empathy.

Student Instructions

1. Choose an interpersonal issue with a person who is important to you. This person may be a friend, family member, fellow student or worker, instructor, or any other person who matters to you. This person must be available to you for feedback during the time you are completing this assignment.

2. Compose a draft paper, describing the issue from the other's point of view. Write your description in the first person as if you were the other person. (You may choose to meet with the other person before writing your description to understand his or her perspective better.)

3. Show your completed draft to the other person to verify its accuracy. Based on the comments you receive, revise your description.

4. Show your revised description to your partner. If you have represented his or her thoughts and feelings accurately, have this person verify its correctness by signing the paper. If your description is still not accurate, keep revising it until the other person is willing to sign it.

Note   As you write your description, remember that you are not required to agree with the other person's position—only to understand it.

---

5. Add a written summary to your paper describing the following dimensions of the issue:

6. There are understandable reasons for the behavior of both parties in the issue.

7. Both parties have engaged in at least some erroneous thinking and behavior with regard to this issue.

8. In at least one way the issue may be seen as less important than the parties have perceived it to be.

I. Explore Your Perceptions

Objective

To illustrate the process and characteristics of students' perceptions.

Instructions

1. Have students pair up with classmates they have not yet interacted with or met.

2. Ask them to greet each other, get each others names and then sit down across from each other and number a blank piece of paper.

3. Write the following (or similar) items on the board, and tell them that, without talking to each other, they are going to guess these things about their partners (on paper):

   • major in school

   • job? If so, where?

   • hometown

   • mode of transportation

   • favorite place to travel

   • own pets? if so, which ones?

   • favorite music

   • favorite TV program

   • several adjectives that describe his/her personality and style of interaction

4. After their guesses are complete, have them talk with their partners about unrelated subjects (what's the last movie they've seen, what they did last weekend or plan to do the next weekend) for about 3-4 minutes. Tell them to avoid the guessed subjects if possible.

5. After their conversations, have them change any of their guesses if they see a need.

6. Then, give them time to share and compare answers and keep track of how many they got right or wrong (or partly right).

Discussion Questions

1. How many of you guessed more than half correctly? Less than half? Half?

2. What information did you use to base your guesses on (hairstyle, clothing, initial greeting, previous behavior in classroom, people you know who look like your partner, your own preferences, assumptions and generalizations about people)?

3. Did you change your answers after speaking? If so, why?

4. Which items were easiest to guess? Hardest? Why? What does someone look like that drives a truck? Owns a cat?

5. Were there any surprises? Did you get any ideas about how others view you?

6. How did it feel to make these guesses about someone?

7. Do you make these assumptions in real life? These are fairly trivial pieces of information that we attach meaning to. What are some other types of interpretations we make about people and their behaviors?

8. How do the stages of perception (selection, organization, interpretation, negotiation) to this exercise?

9. What lessons can we draw from this exercise?

CHAPTER 4
EMOTIONS: THINKING, FEELING, AND COMMUNICATING

Objectives

After studying the material in Chapter Four of *Looking Out/Looking In,* you should understand:

1. The four components of emotions.
2. The six influences on emotional expression.
3. Options for expressing emotions effectively.
4. The characteristics of facilitative and debilitative emotions.
5. The relationship between activating events, thoughts, and emotions.
6. Seven fallacies that result in unnecessary, debilitative emotions.
7. How the rational-emotive approach can assist in coping with debilitative feelings.

Specifically, you should be able to:

1. Identify the components of the emotions you experience.
2. Recognize the emotions you experience and the circumstances and consequences surrounding them.
3. Identify reasons that you and others may be more or less comfortable sharing emotions.
4. Distinguish true feeling statements from counterfeit expressions of emotions.
5. Distinguish between debilitative and facilitative emotions and label the emotions.
6. Express facilitative emotions you experience clearly and appropriately by using the guidelines for sharing feelings.
7. Minimize your difficult/debilitative emotions.

Notes on Class and Student Activities

A. How Would You Feel?

Objective

To provide situations involving emotions that will prompt an examination of students' feelings.

Instructions

1. In groups, have students generate situations in which they or their friends or family get emotional (e.g., weddings, funerals, birthdays, promotions, failures). They should write down specific situations.
2. Once the list is made, groups should discuss what emotions are felt in each situation. They should note how different people are likely to feel differently in each situation.
3. Next, the group should report back to the class about their discussion.
4. Discussion of each group's situations and responses will allow them to compare their individual reactions and group reactions.

Discussion Questions

1. How do these emotions manifest themselves in the body (both physically and nonverbally)?
2. How do labels influence emotions?
3. What intensity differences exist between different emotions?
4. Is it easy and/or common for us to verbally express our emotions in these situations? Explain.

B. Recognizing Your Emotions (*Invitation to Insight,* text, p. 125)

Objective

To further the student's awareness of his or her feelings and how these feelings register themselves physically in the body.

Options

- We find that when we provide a duplicated form for the diary/journal, the students tend to take the assignment a bit more seriously. Design a form to fit your situation.

- Another way of adding importance to the assignment is to collect the diaries and take a number of the better entries and publish them for the whole group. It goes without saying that this is done without disclosing the individual's name.

- You'll find that this diary technique is used on many occasions in the text. Our experience is that this is one of the best ways to promote out-of-class effort.

C. Feelings and Phrases (*Skill Builder,* text, p. 138 and Stating Emotions Effectively, 4.3 in *Student Activities Manual*)

Objective

To help students develop ways of expressing feelings clearly.

Instructions

In a group activity, have members evaluate the effectiveness of different forms of expressing emotions (or of not expressing the emotion at all). Encourage group members to comment on the clarity of each expression and emotion.

Discussion Questions

1. How does the expression of feelings vary from situation to situation . . . from receiver to receiver?
2. What are some reasons *for* and *for not* expressing true feelings in each situation with each receiver?

D. Talking to Yourself (*Invitation to Insight,* text, p. 144)

Objective

To help students better understand how their thoughts can shape their feelings.

Option

Conduct as group activity and have students compare answers.

Discussion Questions

1. How easy or difficult was it to identify the voice behind your self-talk?
2. Were there few or many differences between your and your classmates' reactions? Are there few or many ways to interpret an activating event?
3. How are feelings shaped by thoughts?

E. How Irrational Are You? (*Invitation to Insight,* text, p. 149)
Objectives

To help students to identify whether their self-talk contains any irrational thoughts.

To provide students with the opportunity to reflect on how their thoughts may cause debilitating emotions.

Option

Conduct as group activity and have students compare answers.

Discussion Questions

1. Which fallacies appeared most often in your groups? Why do you suppose there are some more popular than others?

2. Which subjects seemed to most commonly stimulate irrational thinking? Speculate about why.

3. How did your awareness of self-talk change, if at all, prior to and after this activity? Explain.

F. Rational Thinking (*Skill Builder,* text, p. 151)
Objective

To assist students in replacing irrational thinking with rational thinking.

To afford students a chance to practice the procedure before observers and make necessary adjustments.

To give students a chance to observe and analyze the effectiveness of the steps to minimizing debilitating emotions mentioned in the text.

Note	The instructor should probably demonstrate the exercise with two others, playing (perhaps the most difficult) role of the "little voice."

Discussion Questions

1. How did it feel to play the different roles? Which role was hardest and easiest to play? Why?

2. What were the easiest and hardest parts of the process? The most and least useful? Explain.

3. How easy or difficult could this be to apply in real-life situations? Explain.

G. Would You Share? Your Call—Emotions (4.7 in *Student Activities Manual*)
Objective

To assist students in deciding what emotions to share with others.

Option

Conduct as group activity and have students compare answers.

Discussion Questions

1. What conclusions can your group members draw about the appropriate sharing of emotions?

2. Describe a few other situations that involve expressing emotions, and make recommendations about expressing emotion for each.

CHAPTER 5
LANGUAGE: BARRIER AND BRIDGE

Objectives

After studying the material in Chapter Five of *Looking Out/Looking In,* you should understand:

1. The symbolic nature of language.
2. That language is rule-governed.
3. That language can shape our perceptions and reflect the attitudes we hold toward one another.
4. That language use contributes to understanding and misunderstanding.
5. Language that can provoke unnecessary disagreements.
6. That language describes events at various levels of abstraction.
7. The problems that occur when overly abstract language is used.
8. How behavioral descriptions clarify thinking and communicating.
9. The manner in which a speaker's language can reflect responsibility.
10. The similarities and differences between male and female language use.
11. Differences in the way language is used across cultures.
12. How language and the worldview of a culture are related.

Specifically, you should be able to:

1. Develop a greater awareness of your language goals, and make effective verbal choices that help to meet those goals.
2. Identify ways in which linguistic rules may affect your understandings of others' messages.
3. Identify language choices that can lead to unnecessary misunderstandings, and compose alternatives.
4. Avoid using language that can lead to unnecessary disagreements by identifying the problematic terms you use, and compose alternatives.
5. Label inferences contained in your statements and separate them from the facts in your language.
6. Identify overly abstract statements you and others make and propose less abstract alternatives.
7. Identify ways in which your language and the language of others reflects degrees of responsibility.
8. Increase the clarity of your language by using:
   - behavioral descriptions
   - lower-level abstractions
   - "I" statements

Notes on Class and Student Activities

A. Down-to-Earth Language (*Skill Builder,* text, p. 162)

Objective

To give students practice using lower abstractions.

To help students describe behavior effectively.

Note	In order to help them construct useful behavioral descriptions, it may be helpful to ask students "what does that behavior look or sound like?" or "what did that person do or say, specifically?".

Option

This exercise can be a good precursor to coping with criticism in Chapter 9, as it may enable students to criticize specifically and constructively themselves before having to cope with the criticism of others later.

Discussion Questions

1. How might communication outcomes change in each situation with the use of less abstract language? Why? Explain.

B. Your Linguistic Rules (*Invitation to Insight,* text, p. 168)

Objective

To give students awareness of their own and others' linguistic rules.

Option

Conduct as group activity and follow up with discussion questions.

Discussion Questions

1. Are there familiar syntactic rules that are commonly broken? Give examples.

2. What types of semantic misunderstandings occur frequently, and why?

3. Give examples of pragmatic rules that are shared by most of you.

4. Give examples of pragmatic rules that operate differently today than they may have in the past.

5. Give examples of individualized sets of pragmatic rules that operate in some of your relationships.

C. Conjugating Irregular Verbs (*Invitation to Insight,* text, p. 175)

Objectives

To give students some practice using emotive words.

To help students become sensitive to the frequent practice of using words that we think describe something or somebody but really announce to the receiver our attitude about it.

Note	This particular exercise seems to be one that the students like. It is, therefore, quite easy to get them to come up with their own "I am _____" and then pass it on to the next person in line for the "You are _____" and to a third person for the "He is _____" responses.

Options

Conduct as group activity and have students share answers.

Discussion Questions

1. To what degree did word choices change meanings? Explain.

2. Think of a few situations in which you have unconsciously used emotive language. How did words affect the interaction?

3. What are some problematic outcomes of using emotive language?

D. Responsible Language, (5.3 in the *Student Activities Manual*), and Practicing "I" Language (*Skill Builder,* text, p. 178, and 5.4 in the *Student Activities Manual*)

Objectives

To give students practice using "I" statements.

To give students practice speaking descriptively rather than evaluatively.

Note	This exercise can be very difficult for students who are not used to describing behavior. It is best to give them many examples before they actually do this exercise (e.g., change "You're not telling me the truth!" to "I heard from Jane that you went out with the boys last night and you just told me you stayed home and watched a movie").

Discussion Questions

1. Which parts were easy? Difficult? Why were some parts easier than others?

2. In which types of situations do you think "I" language could be effective? Not effective? Why?

3. What does "I" language do for us? What's the purpose of using "I" instead of "you?"

E. The World of Abstraction

Objective

To give students practice in identifying high level abstractions.

Instructions

1. Bring in newspaper and magazine articles. Get a good variety so that you will have stories from writers, quotes from politicians and comments from movie stars.

2. Have students identify the high level abstractions in each and discuss the effectiveness or ineffectiveness of each.

Discussion Questions

1. What were some common abstract phrases or words?

2. How did the words and phrases contribute to or take away from your understanding?

3. Suggest some alternative words and phrases that may make the original statements more effective.

F. Words That Hurt and Heal

Objective

To help students identify words that have powerful effects on themselves and others.

Instructions

1. Make two columns on the board: Words that Hurt, and Words that Heal.
2. For each column, have students brainstorm words that they or others respond to strongly. If the Hurt column seems longer than the Heal column (this is usually the case), challenge students to turn the Hurt column words into kinder terms.

Discussion Questions

1. Which list was easier to come up with? Why?
2. What impact do these words and phrases have on us and others?
3. Make suggestions about how to talk about things and behaviors that concern and bother you without using hurtful words.

G. Sample Dialogues

Objective

To give students practice at identifying, analyzing, and evaluating gender and/or culture differences in actual dialogue.

Note	This activity requires some prep time on the instructor's part.

Instructions

1. Create a few short sample dialogues illustrating problems that can occur as a result of gender and/or cultural differences. Copy to transparency for display in class.

   Ideas for illustration:

   - Frustration between a husband and wife that occurs because she wants to talk about the details of the day, and he doesn't see the point.
   - Frustration between a girlfriend and boyfriend that occurs because he offers advice to her about a problem she's discussing, and she only wants him to listen and acknowledge her.
   - A misunderstanding between a mother and son based on her misinterpretation of his competitive communication style.
   - A misunderstanding between a male and female coworker based on her misinterpretation of his direct conversational style.
   - A business deal gone wrong due to high and low context style differences.
   - Frustrations between class project group members due to culturally different verbal communication styles.

2. Have students identify the specific communication style differences that appear in the dialogue and describe how these differences led to problems.
3. Be sure students understand that language styles can be easily misinterpreted, especially if someone is not familiar with or doesn't take these differences into account during the interaction.
4. Have students make suggestions about skills from earlier chapters that can be used to "bridge" these differences and communicate effectively (e.g., perception checking, empathy, avoiding thought fallacies, metacommunication, etc.).

CHAPTER 6

NONVERBAL COMMUNICATION: MESSAGES BEYOND WORDS

Objectives

After studying the material in Chapter Six of *Looking Out/Looking In,* you should understand:

1. The definition of nonverbal communication.
2. The importance of nonverbal communication.
3. The five characteristics of nonverbal communication.
4. The seven functions of nonverbal communication.
5. The seven categories of nonverbal communication described in this chapter.
6. How gender and culture influences nonverbal communication.

Specifically, you should be able to

1. describe your and others' nonverbal behavior in a variety of situations.
2. exhibit nonverbal sensitivity in encoding and decoding
3. identify ways in which nonverbal communication contributes to identity management, relational messages, and emotional expression.
4. consider a variety of meanings for nonverbal behaviors.
5. identify examples of nonverbal behavior that repeat, substitute for, complement, accent, regulate, or contradict verbal messages.
6. identify cues of deception
7. explain why deception cues are not easy to detect.
8. describe another's nonverbal behavior and use perception-checking statements to verify its meaning.

Notes on Class and Student Activities
A. Greetings and Goodbyes
Objective

To help students develop awareness of several dimensions of nonverbal communication.

Instructions

1. Assign students to visit airports, bus terminals, or anywhere that they are likely to be able to observe people greeting and leaving one another (they can even do this in groups to increase the fun).
2. Have them write down every nonverbal behavior they see (students usually record touching behaviors and facial expressions, but review the other types of nonverbal communication so that they will remember to record things like any paralanguage they overhear, the clothing people are wearing, and the actual spacing of people).
3. Then, they should speculate on the meanings of the behaviors and on the relationship between the people.
4. Finally, they should write up a brief summary and bring their reports back to the class for discussion.

5. Make a list on the board of nonverbal behavior categories (e.g., proxemics, touch, eye behavior, facial expressions, gestures). Ask students to cite unique examples of observed nonverbal behaviors under the appropriate categories.

Options

Have students propose research hypotheses (e.g., females are more likely than males to use touch in greetings and goodbyes) and then use the data they collect to draw conclusions and support/reject their hypotheses.

Discussion Questions

1. What categories of nonverbal communication were most prevalent in the observed greetings and goodbyes?
2. Did you see any evidence of gender or cultural influences?
3. Is it easy or difficult to separate our observations of behavior from our interpretations of it? Explain. Why is this ability important?
4. How much confidence do you have that the meanings you assigned to the behaviors and relationships are accurate? Consider some alternative meanings.
5. If you tested a hypothesis, what were your results, and how do your results compare to the research stated in the text?

B. Reading "Body Language" (*Invitation to Insight,* text, p. 207)

Objectives

1. To increase the students' skills of observing nonverbal behavior.
2. To help students become more aware of some of the dangers inherent in interpreting nonverbal behavior.
3. To give students practice separating the observation of behavior from their interpretation of it.

Options

It is suggested that this exercise be done in pairs, but it also can be done in larger groups.

Discussion Questions

1. How easy or difficult was the observation portion? Explain.
2. How easy or difficult was the interpretation portion? Explain.
3. How easy or difficult was it to keep the observation of behavior and the interpretation of it separate?
4. What was your level of accuracy in correctly interpreting your partner's behaviors?
5. Why is the ability to separate the actual behavior from your interpretation of it important? Speculate about future situations in which this ability could come in handy for you.

C. Nonverbal Travels

Objective

To describe cultural variations in nonverbal behaviors that students have encountered.

Instructions

1. In order to make use of student experiences and backgrounds conduct a discussion on nonverbal differences across cultures (and co-cultures).

2. Put columns on the board of the different types of nonverbal communication (e.g., proxemics, chronemics, facial expressions, gestures) and encourage students to describe the variations they have encountered in their travels (or perhaps in their culture of origin). Be careful not to generalize one student's experience to all situations.

3. Compare and contrast these experiences to the descriptions in the text, and conduct a discussion about the importance of adjusting to nonverbal differences.

Discussion Questions

1. Which categories have the most variations?

2. Give examples of cultural misunderstandings that could occur because of these cultural variations.

3. How does understanding cultural difference relate to tolerance?

4. Why is it important to recognize that differences exist in nonverbal rules of different cultures?

5. When and why is it appropriate to adapt our nonverbal behavior when interacting with members of other cultures or subcultures?

D. The Rules of Touch (*Invitation to Insight,* text, p. 222)

Objective

To help students develop an awareness of how appropriate touch is governed by cultural and social rules.

Note   This exercise can trigger strong feelings from students about their own instances of both appropriate and inappropriate touch. Suggest to students that they use the language skills (e.g., "I" language) from Chapter 5 to voice their pleasure or displeasure to others in such situations.

Discussion Questions

1. How and why do the rules change due to gender?

2. What do you know about the rules and norms of touch in other cultures?

3. Give examples of misunderstandings that could occur as a result of cultural differences in touching behavior. Suggest ways to prevent, manage, or remedy such misunderstandings. .

E. Distance Makes a Difference (*Invitation to Insight,* text, p. 225)

Objective

To let students experience the differences distance can make when relating to other people.

Note   Often the room is not large enough to give the partners enough room so that they are not distracted by those lined up beside them. If this is the case, do the exercise in several groups so that there is at least an arm's length separating everyone.

Discussion Questions

1. How did personal space needs differ in this exercise?
2. At what point did you experience discomfort? To what degree, and why?
3. What do distance needs say about the nature of different relationships?

F. Relational Messages in Nonverbal Communication

Objective

To illustrate to students how nonverbal behavior conveys relational messages such as immediacy and respect.

Instructions

1. Choose three volunteers who are willing to come to the front of the room and give directions to separate locations across town.
2. Ask the volunteers to step into the hallway while you "give the class some hints about nonverbal behavior."
3. While the volunteers are outside of the classroom, tell students how to behave nonverbally as each volunteer gives directions. For the first volunteer, students should communicate that they don't care and are not paying attention through their nonverbal behavior (e.g., play with cell phone, flip through book, sleep, stare at ceiling, shift restlessly, whisper with a classmate). For the second volunteer, have half of the room behave as though they were not paying attention and half of the room behave as though they are really interested and are paying attention diligently. For the third volunteer, students should all behave respectfully, giving their full nonverbal attention to the volunteer.
4. Bring in each volunteer one at a time to give directions at the front of the room and then sit down. Indicate to them when they finish that you'll debrief them in a minute.
5. After all three volunteers have sat down thank them for participating, and give special thanks to the first volunteer who suffered through the disrespect of their classmates not paying attention. Assure them that it was for a good reason.
6. Ask each volunteer what they noticed about their classmates while they were giving directions. Ask each volunteer how they felt. Ask what messages were being communicated to them through the class members' nonverbals. Point out any observations you made (i.e. often the second volunteer tends to unconsciously shift his or her body and eye contact to the side of the room that is paying attention).

Discussion Questions

1. What are some other ways in which we convey relational messages through our nonverbals?
2. Have you ever been or would you ever want to be in a situation similar to the first volunteer's experience? How about the third? Explain.
3. Give some examples of other situations in which it might be important to be aware and convey nonverbally that we are paying attention or that we respect the speaker.
4. Which directions do you most remember? Often, it's the last one.

Note	Try to choose a student who you think might be a good sport or emotionally strong to be the first volunteer. Also, try to choose volunteers who you think might have good observation skills (so that they pick up on the messages the class is sending). Also, this activity can be a good segue into the listening chapter. Discuss why paying attention nonverbally can improve listening. Discuss when and why it's important to convey good listening skills nonverbally.

CHAPTER 7
LISTENING: MORE THAN MEETS THE EAR

Objectives

After studying the material in Chapter Seven of *Looking Out/Looking In,* you should understand:

1. The importance of listening in personal relationships and in the workplace.
2. The definition of listening.
3. The difference between hearing and listening.
4. The difference between mindless and mindful listening.
5. Five elements involved in the process of listening.
6. Seven types of ineffective listening.
7. The reasons why skilled listening can be challenging.
8. Four guidelines for listening better.
9. Three types of listening responses that can be used to better understand a speaker's message.
10. Four types of listening responses that can be used to offer a speaker your own assessment of the situation and to offer direction.
11. The factors involved in choosing the best listening response.

Specifically, you should be able to:

1. Identify your own reasons for improving your listening skills.
2. Identify your own ineffective listening behavior, including
   A) the circumstances in which you listen ineffectively.
   B) the ineffective listening styles you use in each set of circumstances.
   C) the reasons why you listen ineffectively in each set of circumstances.
   D) the consequences of your ineffective listening behaviors.
3. Use the skill of paraphrasing effectively to understand others and as a tool to help others.
4. Paraphrase another person by:
   A) using appropriate nonverbal attending behaviors
   B) fluently and concisely paraphrasing factual information
   C) fluently and concisely paraphrasing the speaker's thoughts and feelings
   D) expressing your statement tentatively, and making open-ended requests for the speaker to verify the accuracy of your paraphrase.
5. Craft listening responses that carefully follow the guidelines of effectiveness explained in the text.
6. Demonstrate your ability to use the following response:
   A) prompting
   B) questioning
   C) paraphrasing
   D) supporting
   E) analyzing

F) advising

G) judging

7. Choose the best listening response according to your goal and other factors described in the text.

Notes on Class and Student Activities

A. Listening Breakdowns (*Invitation to Insight,* text, p. 239)

Objective

To help students overcome common listening myths and understand the separate elements involved in the listening process.

Note	If students have a difficult time coming up with examples of how they failed at listening, let them start with examples of how others have failed in listening to them. Then guide the students back into self-awareness.

Discussion Questions

1. Which instances were more frequently representative of you? Less? Explain.

2. Which elements in the process are more difficult? Explain.

3. Which parts of the listening process do you most need to improve? Why?

4. What is the importance of understanding and improving all parts of the listening process?

B. Speaking and Listening with a "Talking Stick"(*Invitation to Insight,* text, p. 244)

Objective

To focus the student's attention on the benefits of talking less and listening more.

Note	1.	Encourage students to talk about anything of interest to them. What happened to them this morning may seem as important as serious world events.
	2.	After the exercise, a valuable discussion can come from students discussing times they have not felt listened to, and in turn, not listened themselves.

C. Classroom Listening

Objective

To guide students in developing effective listening questions for the large group setting.

Instructions

1. Conduct a discussion of classroom listening and responding styles.

2. Have students suggest questions they might ask during a lecture (have some of your "favorites" ready to get them started—e.g., "Professor Wiemann, don't you think paraphrasing sounds fake?").

3. Identify any counterfeit questions and suggest alternatives.

4. Contrast this type of listening to other types of listening.

D. Paraphrasing Practice
(*Skill Builder,* text, p. 253, and 7.3 in the *Student Activities Manual*)

Objective

To give students practice with paraphrasing.

Discussion Questions

See questions in the text or use 7.3 in the *Student Activities Manual* as a stimulus.

E. Listen to the Little Children

Objective

To give students practice with paraphrasing.

Note	Little children are usually much more forgiving and less evaluative as students practice this very difficult skill.

Instructions

1. Assign students to visit with a child under the age of ten (a sibling or other relative, or perhaps a neighbor or volunteer at a nursery school).
2. Tell them to ask questions about what the child is doing, interested in, or planning. Tell them to use a number of listening styles, but to particularly practice their paraphrasing skills.
3. Have students write a short report of what they learned or share this orally with the class.

Discussion Questions

1. How easy or difficult was it to use the skill of paraphrasing in this situation?
2. Did your understanding of the child's answers change after paraphrasing? If so, how?
3. How did the child(ren) respond to your paraphrasing?
4. How can paraphrasing improve other listening situations?

F. What Would You Say? (text, p. 260)

Objective

To give students practice with a variety of listening responses.

To show students their typical style of responding to another's problem, and to demonstrate the frequent ineffectiveness of the typical response styles.

Option

In a variation of the exercise, assign one or two students each of the typical response styles, having them react to another student who role-plays the problems listed.

Discussion Questions

1. In your opinion, which types of responses would lead to productive and unproductive outcomes?
2. Which type of listening response do you have a tendency to use most?
3. Which listening responses do you feel you need to improve, and why?

G. One-Way and Two-Way Communication

Objective

To demonstrate the advantages of checking back with the sender of a message (i.e., one-way vs. two-way communication).

Instructions

1. Copy the following notes and chart onto a chalkboard so that everyone can see them:

   ■ **ONE-WAY**
   — Low sender frustration, High receiver frustration
   — Low accuracy
   — Short time necessary

   ■ **TWO-WAY**
   — High sender frustration, Low receiver frustration
   — High accuracy
   — Long time necessary

ONE-WAY			TWO-WAY	
TIME:			TIME:	
NUMBER CORRECT			**NUMBER CORRECT**	
ESTIMATE	ACTUAL		ESTIMATE	ACTUAL
		5		
		4		
		3		
		2		
		1		
		0		

2. Select one member of the group to act as a sender. The sender's job will be to describe two simple drawings to the rest of the group.

3. Select two observers, one to note the sender's behavior in the exercise, and the other to note the behavior of the group members.

Note

1. Alert the observers to watch for certain behaviors: level of frustration, perceived confidence, and mistaken assumptions or misinterpretations. These observations will be helpful in the post-exercise discussion.

2. In the post-exercise discussion, make sure the students recognize all the characteristics of one-way and two-way communication.

4. Supply the group members with sheets of unlined 8½-by-11-inch paper.

5. Make sure everyone hears and understands the following directions: "In a minute, the sender will describe a simple set of figures that the group members should draw as accurately as possible. The group members should ask no questions or respond in any way to the sender's directions. The idea is to create a one-way communication situation."

6. The sender now stands or sits so that he or she can be heard but not seen by the group. The instructor then gives the sender a copy of the first drawing found here. (Actually, any simple drawing will work in this exercise. A variation is to have the

sender create his or her own drawing and describe it to the group. Remember, however, that the drawing should be quite simple. This exercise is hard enough this way!)

7. The sender should describe this drawing to the group as quickly and as accurately as possible. The instructor should make sure that the group members don't communicate with each other during this step. All should understand that a glance at another's drawing furnishes an additional source of information, thus destroying a one-way communication situation.

8. After the sender has finished, note the time that his or her description took and place it on the chart. Next, find out how many group members think they've drawn all five figures exactly, how many think they got four, three, and so on. Place the numbers in the appropriate spaces on the chart.

9. Now the sender should move so that he or she can see and be seen by the group. The instructor will give the sender the drawing he or she is to describe. This time, however, the group members should ask necessary questions to make sure they understand the drawing being described. This should be two-way communication. The only limitation on communication here is that the sender must use words only—no gestures—to describe the drawing to the group.

10. Remember, the goal is to have all group members reproduce the drawing perfectly, so everyone should feel free to ask plenty of questions.

11. Repeat step 8.

12. Now show the drawings one at a time to the group members so they can see how accurate their reactions are. The instructor should then record the accuracy of the group's drawings. For a figure to be correct, its size should be correct proportionately, and it should be positioned in the correct relationship to the preceding and following figures.

13. Now note the data the exercise has produced on your chart.

Discussion Questions

1. After looking it over, what assumptions might you make about one-way and two-way communication? Which takes longer? Which is more accurate?

2. Which is more frustrating for the sender? For the receiver?

3. What parallels does this exercise have in your everyday life? Does the exercise tell you anything about the way you listen?

4. Consider the efficiency of one-way and two-way communication. Remember, efficiency takes into account time, cost, and so on. Are there situations in society where one-way communication is used? Consider the military, police and fire departments, and so on. What precaution is taken to ensure effective communicating situations where time is so important?

Options

Instead of having students re-create a drawing, have them re-create a description of a detailed scene in a photograph or advertisement. Ask for 5 volunteers to leave the room and return one by one. The first volunteer looks closely at the picture while he describes it in as much detail as possible to the second volunteer who can not look at the picture, take notes, ask questions or check back with the first in any way. Ask the class to pay attention to what happens as each volunteer passes on what he/she heard to the next. Finally, have the last volunteer tell the class what's in the picture. The result is almost always a completely wrong or extremely reductive description.

Then, re-do the activity with a different, but similarly detailed picture. This time, allow two-way communication and contrast the differences between the first and second activity.

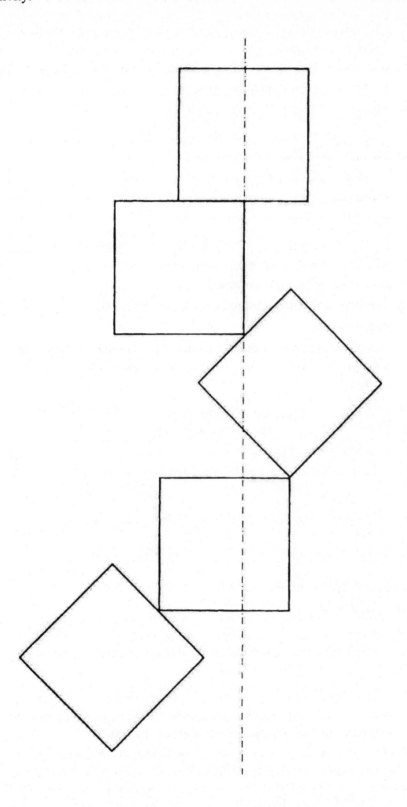

CHAPTER 8
COMMUNICATION AND RELATIONAL DYNAMICS

Objectives

After reading the material in Chapter Eight of *Looking Out/Looking In*, you should understand:

1. Eight factors that influence our choice of relational partners.
2. The concept of social exchange theory.
3. The ten stages of interpersonal relationships.
4. Three types of dialectical tensions.
5. Eight strategies for managing dialectical tensions.
6. Three characteristics of relationships.
7. Four types of relational transgressions.
8. Strategies for relational repair, including forgiveness.
9. The content and relational aspects of messages.
10. Four types of relational messages.
11. The concept of metacommunication.

Specifically, you should be able to:

1. Identify factors that have influenced your choice of relational partners.
2. Describe the development and/or decline of own relationships in terms of Knapp's model.
3. Describe how dialectical tensions operate in your relationships.
4. Consider ways to effectively manage dialectical tensions.
5. Consider how the characteristics of relationships apply to your own experiences.
6. Identify relational transgressions that have occurred in your own relationships.
7. Consider the effectiveness of strategies for repairing relational transgressions.
8. Identify the content and relational aspects of messages you deliver to others and of messages that are sent to you.
9. Use metacommunication to keep relationships healthy.

Notes on Class and Student Activities

A. How Fast Should We Go?

Objective

To help students describe what leads them to be attracted to certain people, and to evaluate how they approach intimacy.

Instructions

1. Ask students to describe what leads them to be attracted to certain people, and compare this to the attraction variables in the text.
2. Next, review the stages of coming together in the text, and have students evaluate how quickly they should go through each increasing stage of intimacy.

Option

Bring in personal ads from the newspaper to stimulate discussion of attraction variables.

Discussion Questions

1. To what extent are your strong, positive personal relationships based on the listed attraction variables?

2. Do you believe that knowing these attraction variables can influence the relationships you would like to make stronger? To what extent do you "fit" the attraction variables for those people that you wish you were attractive to?

3. How fast is too fast when you are becoming intimate with someone?

4. How can you better evaluate how fast to proceed in relationships?

B. Your Relational Stage (*Invitation to Insight,* text, p. 278–279) and Relational Stages (8.2 in the *Student Activities Manual*)

Objective

To increase the students' awareness of stages of relational development.

Note

1. Some students have a tendency to describe romantic relationships of even a short duration as "bonded." Encourage them to see the value of behaviors at each stage in building the relationship over time. Remind them that one behavior does not make the stage, but a pattern and consistency of types of behavior.

2. Another problem some students have with relational stages is that they think "the higher the better." Help them to see that mutual understanding of and satisfaction with the stage is a far better guide.

Discussion

The activity includes a number of discussion questions for use with groups.

C. Your Dialectical Tensions (*Invitation to Insight,* text, p. 283, and Discovering Dialectics, 8.1 in the *Student Activities Manual*)

Objectives

To increase students' knowledge of the tensions at work in relationships.

To help students consider more effective strategies to manage tensions in relationships.

Instructions

1. Have students make a column for each of the strategies for dealing with dialectical tensions.

2. Record how frequently each is used and in which types of situations.

Discussion

The activity includes a number of discussion questions for use with groups.

D. Maintaining Your Relationships (*Invitation to Insight,* text, p. 285)

Objective

To help students consider their effectiveness in maintaining important relationships.

Instructions

Conduct as small group activity. Return to large group for discussion. Explain the analogy between communication tools and carpentry tools: A carpenter uses tools to build, maintain, and repair structures just as we can use communication skills to build, maintain, and repair relationships. Make comparisons between simple tools that are easy to learn to use (e.g., screwdrivers and perception checking) and more complex tools that are more difficult to learn and use (e.g., compound miter saw and responding non-defensively to criticism).

Discussion Questions

1. What happens to structures when they aren't maintained and repaired? How does this metaphor apply to relationships?

2. Which of the five maintenance strategies do you use, if any? Which need work? Explain.

3. Make suggestions about specific communication skills and concepts that can be used strategically to maintain satisfying relationships (e.g., to achieve openness one can use listening skills and clear messages).

4. Segue into the topic of relational repair and discuss specific strategies.

E. Your Relational Transgressions (*Invitation to Insight,* text, p. 288)

Objective

To help students identify their own relational transgressions and consider strategies for repair.

Discussion Questions

1. What types of transgressions do you find necessary to repair? Explain.

2. What strategies for repair might work best for you? Explain.

3. Make specific suggestions for how you can repair your transgressions.

F. Is Your Relationship Worthwhile?

Objectives

To illustrate social exchange theory.

To help students examine their own relationships in terms of rewards and costs.

Instructions

1. Use as assignment or small group activity.

2. Ask students to diagram an important relationship using the social exchange equation [rewards – costs = outcome]. Have them describe whether the payoffs and efforts are tangible or intangible.

3. Lead a discussion about what was learned. Ask them about their outcomes and about whether they find this a useful way to consider the value of relationships.

CHAPTER 9
INTIMACY AND DISTANCE IN RELATIONAL COMMUNICATION

Objectives

After studying the material in Chapter Nine of *Looking Out/Looking In,* you should understand:

1. Four dimensions of intimacy.
2. Similarities and differences between masculine and feminine intimacy styles.
3. Cultural influences on intimacy.
4. The role of computer-mediated communication in creating and maintaining intimacy.
5. The limits of intimacy.
6. The definition of self-disclosure and the role it plays in relationships.
7. Four degrees of self-disclosure.
8. How the Johari window represents the relationship between self-disclosure and self-awareness.
9. The benefits and risks of self-disclosure.
10. Eight guidelines for self-disclosure.
11. Four alternatives to self-disclosure.
12. Five reasons for lying.
13. The effects of lying.
14. Three advantages to choosing equivocation.
15. The ethics of evasion.

Specifically, you should be able to:

1. Identify which dimensions of intimacy are present in your relationships.
2. Describe if and how computer-mediated communication has contributed to intimacy in your relationships.
3. Explain reasons why you do and do not self-disclose.
4. Describe the breadth and depth of relationships that are important to you.
5. Describe the levels of self-disclosure you engage in and how they affect your relationships.
6. Choose levels of self-disclosure that are appropriate for a given situation.
7. Identify alternatives to self-disclosure you use, and consider their effects.

A. Your IQ (Intimacy Quotient) (*Invitation to Insight,* text, p. 304)
Objective

To help students determine the levels of intimacy in their important relationships.

Note	Reinforce for students the many different types of intimacy (many think only of physical intimacy at first).

Discussion Questions (provided in activity)

B. Self-Disclosure Tales
Objective

To increase the students' awareness of the levels of self-disclosure others use with them, and how they use with self disclosure with others, and to evaluate the appropriate level of self-disclosure in relationships.

Note	Students should relate examples of times in which people self-disclosed too much or too little to them. If they are comfortable, they can also share times when they self-disclosed too much or too little. They should focus on different types of relationships (family, friends, romantic, work, etc.).

Discussion Questions

1. How do you notice reciprocity of self-disclosure at work in your relationship?
2. What level of self-disclosure is appropriate in this relationship versus others?
3. What should we do when others are disclosing inappropriately to us?
4. How can we better evaluate our own appropriate level of self-disclosure?

C. Appropriate Self-Disclosure (*Skill Builder,* text, p. 316, and Disclosure and Alternatives, 9.4 in the *Student Activities Manual*)
Objective

To examine the potential risks and benefits of self-disclosure.

Note	Have students compare the risks and benefits of disclosing in various situations. They can often reinforce for one another the guidelines for appropriate self-disclosure with their "war stories."

Discussion Questions

1. Which guidelines were most relevant when developing your self-disclosing message? Explain.
2. What do you see as the benefits and risks of disclosing this information? To self? To others? To the relationship?
3. Consider textbook options other than self-disclosure for this situation. What are the pros and cons of each?

D. Email, Chats, Texting, and Cell Phones
Objective

To help students examine the role of technology in relational intimacy.

Instructions

Ask students to make a list of computer-mediated forms of interpersonal communication, and then lead a discussion.

Discussion Questions

1. How often do we use these forms of technology to communicate interpersonally with others? Which ones do we tend to use more than others? What is the balance between FtF and CMC?
2. Would you agree with studies described in the text that say intimacy may develop more quickly through CMC? If so, why?

3. How does CMC affect your self-disclosure? Would you self-disclose as much in FtF interactions? Which form of technology allows for the most amount of self-disclosure? The least?

4. How are FtF interactions affected by previous self-disclosures through CMC?

5. What do you perceive to be the relational pros and cons of communicating with another through CMC? FtF?

6. What do you envision to be the future of interpersonal relationships as we continue to develop our reliance on technology to communicate with one another?

CHAPTER 10
IMPROVING COMMUNICATION CLIMATES

Objectives

After studying the material in Chapter Nine of *Looking Out/Looking In,* you should understand:

1. How confirming and disconfirming messages create positive and negative communication climates.
2. Three types of confirming messages.
3. Nine types of disconfirming messages.
4. How communication climates develop.
5. The relationship between a communicator's self-concept and his or her defensive reaction to a message.
6. How defense mechanisms operate when a communicator perceives attacking messages.
7. Nine defense mechanisms.
8. Six types of defense-arousing communication and six contrasting behaviors that lessen the level of threat and defensiveness.
9. How and why Gibb's defensive and supportive behaviors can minimize or increase defensive responses to your message.
10. The five parts of the clear message format and four guidelines for its use.
11. Eight ways to respond non-defensively to criticism.
12. How seeking more information from a critic and agreeing with the criticism can minimize a communicator's defensive responses.

Specifically, you should be able to:

1. Use feedback from significant others to discover the different types of confirming and disconfirming messages you presently send.
2. Identify the confirming and disconfirming messages of others.
3. Use confirming messages to convey to others that you value them.
4. Explain how and why the communication climates in your relationships developed.
5. Consider suggestions for improving the communication climates in your relationships.
6. Identify your unproductive defensive responses to perceived verbal attacks by describing:
   A) the defense mechanisms you commonly use.
   B) the circumstances in which you use them.
   C) the parts of your presenting self-image you are attempting to defend.
   D) the consequences of your defensive behavior.
7. Use feedback from significant others to discover your own usage of Gibb's supportive and defensive behaviors.
8. Identify the supportive and defensive behaviors of others and consider how they may contribute to communication climates.
9. Use Gibb's supportive behaviors to prevent defensiveness and convey face-honoring relational messages of respect.

10. Use clear messages to speak your mind in a clear but non-threatening way.

11. Respond non-defensively to the criticism of others by seeking additional information from your critic and/or agreeing with your critic.

Notes on Class and Student Activities

A. Evaluating Communication Climates (*Invitation to Insight,* text, p. 336)

Objective

To identify the communication climate in important relationships and to describe the confirming and disconfirming behaviors that help define this climate.

Note	One way to help the discussion along in this exercise is to allow some students to describe the negative (or disconfirming) behaviors that their partners use (because it is easier to criticize others) and again to describe the positive, confirming behaviors that their partners use (because they don't have to brag about themselves in this instance). As this discussion progresses, lead the discussion into the spiral effect of behaviors in relationships (Gibb), and the effects of the students own behaviors become more apparent.

B. Defense Mechanism Inventory (*Invitation to Insight,* text, p. 340, and Understanding Defensive Responses, 10.1 in the *Student Activities Manual*)

Objective

To encourage the student to reflect on the patterns of defensive behavior he or she may display and to encourage the student to create a plan for more satisfying behaviors.

Note	The Understanding Defensive Responses in the *Student Activities Manual* and Defense Mechanism Inventory are similar exercises. We believe they are both needed to help the student recognize his or her own defensive behaviors. It is better if some time elapses between these assignments. Discussion can then address changes that may have occurred in their abilities to identify their own defensiveness and to make plans to improve effectiveness.

C. Defensiveness Feedback (*Invitation to Insight,* text, p. 346)

Objective

To provide the student with more information about the patterns of his or her defensive behaviors.

Note	The instructor may wish to use the statements in the concluding remarks (question 6) as the topics for discussion.

D. Behaviors and Interpretations (*Skill Builder,* text, p. 349)

Objectives

To help students practice separating behaviors from the interpretations they give to them.

To help students practice being provisional about their interpretations of others' behaviors.

Discussion Questions

1. How difficult is it to separate your observation of behavior from your interpretation of it? Is it easier now than it was earlier in the class?
2. Why is it important to be tentative and provisional about your interpretations?

E. Name the Feeling (*Skill Builder,* text, p. 349)

Objectives

To encourage students to recognize the feelings they may have in the listed circumstances.

To evaluate the effect on the message based on expressing the feeling or not expressing the feeling.

Option

An interesting adaptation of this exercise is to have students come up with messages in which strong feelings existed but wouldn't, couldn't, or shouldn't be expressed. Compare and contrast these statements with the ones in the text. Sometimes class members will argue at this point that many more feelings should, could, or would be expressed if others only knew how to express them.

Discussion Questions

1. How difficult was it to come up with words to label the feelings you might experience in these situations?
2. What would be the impact of each message if feelings weren't expressed?
3. What barriers prevent clear expressions of feelings? What suggestions do you have about how to overcome these barriers?
4. Are there any situations in which feelings shouldn't be expressed? Explain.
5. What can we do to find out what others are feeling?

F. Putting Your Message Together (*Skill Builder,* text, p. 352)
and Writing Clear Messages (10.3 in Student Activities Manual)

Objectives

To enable the student to practice expressing effective clear messages.

To enable the student to gain confidence in communicating.

To enable the student to get feedback from his or her classmates.

Option

The instructor might wish to write these suggestions on the chalkboard or put them on a ditto, copies of which might be given to each student in the class.

Discussion Questions

1. What were some of the characteristics of effective messages?
2. Were the messages difficult to clarify and express? Why or why not?
3. What were some useful bits of feedback you received?

G. Pushing My Buttons

Objective

To identify the words and behaviors that trigger defensiveness.

Instructions

1. In groups, have students create lists of words and behaviors that trigger their defensiveness.

2. Lead them through a discussion about recognizing those triggers/buttons. Relate this back to chapter four's rational thinking, and help students dispute any irrational thoughts. This can be a good prelude to learning to cope with criticism.

H. "Yes, but . . ."

Objective

To identify common excuse-making that contributes to a defensive climate.

Instructions

1. In groups, have students think about the excuses that they and others give (for being late, out of money, unprepared, etc.).

2. Describe the ways that we give excuses, and illustrate how this contributes to defensiveness (for example, saying "Yes, I was ten minutes late" has a different effect than saying, "Yes, I was late, but the traffic was terrible.").

3. Have students discuss alternate ways of simply admitting what is true without giving excuses. This is also a good prelude to learning to cope with criticism.

I. Coping with Criticism (*Skill Builder,* text, p. 359) and Nondefensive Responses to Criticism (10.4 in the *Student Activities Manual*) and Coping with Criticism (10.5 in the *Student Activities Manual*)

Objective

To practice responding nondefensively to criticism.

Note	Picking some students who are "good sports" to role-play some of these situations in front of the class is a good illustration to class members of "real" people responding in this manner. Encourage students to role-play situations that are real to them so that the practice is especially meaningful. Sometimes it's fun and effective to first role play a defensive response, and then repeat the situation with non-defensive responses.

Discussion Questions

1. How easy or difficult was it to respond non-defensively?

2. Which types of responses are most difficult? Which types are most useful? Explain.

3. What outcomes can you envision from responding defensively? Non-defensively?

4. How easy or difficult might it be to respond non-defensively in real life? Explain. Do you have any suggestions for how we might remember to respond non-defensively in the moment?

CHAPTER 11
MANAGING INTERPERSONAL CONFLICTS

Objectives

After studying the material in Chapter Ten of *Looking Out/Looking In,* you should understand:

1. The definition of conflict.
2. That conflict is natural and inevitable, and can be beneficial.
3. Five individual styles of conflict.
4. How conflict styles indicate the relationship between concern for self and concern for the other party.
5. Four factors to consider when deciding on an approach to handling conflict.
6. Relational conflict patterns and rituals and how they contribute to or take away from constructive relationships.
7. How gender and culture affect the ways in which conflict is handled.
8. The steps to reaching win-win conflict solutions.
9. Questions and answers about the validity of the win-win negotiating style.

Specifically, you should be able to:

1. Identify the characteristics of the conflicts in your life, according to the text definition.
2. Describe your personal conflict style by:
    A)   identifying the individual conflict style(s) you most commonly use
    B)   evaluating the appropriateness of the style(s)
    C)   recognizing the consequences of the style(s).
3. Choose the best conflict style based on the factors for consideration suggested in the text.
4. Describe what you perceive to be others' conflict styles.
5. Identify the relational conflict styles, patterns of behavior, and conflict rituals that define your relationships.
6. Recognize the potential benefits of using the win-win method to handle your conflicts.
7. Use the win-win problem-solving method by
    A) identifying your unmet needs
    B) choosing the best time and place to resolve the conflict
    C) describing your problem and unmet needs clearly and assertively
    D) considering your partner's point of view
    E) negotiating a win-win solution whenever possible
    F) following up on the solution.

Notes on Class and Student Activities

A. Understanding Conflict Styles (*Invitation to Insight,* text, p. 382 and 11.1 in the *Student Activities Manual*)

Objectives

To illustrate how conflict styles can differ.

To help students apply the concept of conflict style to conflict management.

To guide students in discovering their own conflict styles.

Discussion Questions

1. Which styles seemed to produce the most satisfying outcome in each situation?
2. Which style best characterizes you?
3. Describe the pros and cons of your style.
4. Are there changes you wish to make about the way conflict is handled in your life? Explain.

B. Your Conflict Rituals (*Invitation to Insight,* text, p. 383)

Objective

To describe positive and negative conflict rituals.

Note	Because conflict rituals are unacknowledged patterns, they are often hard to recognize. Some students need help recognizing the role their behaviors play in the ritual (rather than just blaming the other person for the conflict).

Discussion Questions

1. How and why did these rituals develop?
2. How often, if at all, do you break from these rituals? And, in what way?
3. How satisfying, generally, are the outcomes of your conflict rituals?
4. Are there changes you wish to make about the way conflict is managed in your life? If so, how would you go about making changes?

C. Win-Win Problem Solving (11.4 in the *Student Activities Manual*) and Conflict Resolution Dyads (11.5 in the *Student Activities Manual*)

Objective

To apply win-win problem-solving to real situations in which the students are involved.

Option

Have students complete activity in small groups and then run an in-class discussion.

Discussion Questions

1. Were there difficulties in getting the other people involved in your conflict to try win-win problem-solving?
2. Which of the win-win problem-solving steps seemed the easiest? The most difficult?
3. What kinds of brainstorming ideas were generated? Can you think of more ideas now that you are away form the other people? Can the class think of ideas not generated already?

4. What degree of satisfaction do you have with your first attempt at this method? How could you change that degree of satisfaction?

5. What adaptations may need to be made in different situations to make conflict resolution work for you?

6. In general, what do you perceive to be the benefits of and barriers to using the win-win method effectively?

D. Diagram a Conflict

Objectives

To help students understand the concept of conflict.

To illustrate the parts of the conflict definition with real-life examples.

Instructions

1. Review the elements of the conflict definition in the text, using examples.

2. Have students (individually or in pairs) diagram a conflict in their own lives illustrating (either visually or verbally) each part of the definition. You might put thought-provoking questions on the board to help them sort through the parts. For example:

    • Expressed Struggle: When and how did both parties become aware of the conflict?

    • Perceived Incompatible Goals: What goals do each party have that are incompatible? Do you feel they are truly incompatible? Or can you see options for mutually satisfying solutions?

    • Perceived Scarce Resources: What are the resources in this conflict that either party may perceive as limited?

    • Interdependence: What, specifically, does one party depend on the other for, and vice-versa?

    • Interference from Other Party: Is your conflict a minor dispute or a full-fledged conflict? How have the parties acted to prevent each other from reaching their goals?

Discussion Questions

1. Did you learn anything new about your conflict from analyzing it in this way?.

2. What is your attitude toward conflict, in general?

3. What do you suppose the attitude of the other party might be?

4. How long has this conflict been present in this relationship? Have you taken any actions to resolve it previously? If not, how soon do you think you and/or the other party can address it?

5. How important are the goals of the other party to you? Can you envision a solution in which both of your needs and goals are met? Or are you mostly concerned with defending yourself? How about the other party?

6. Speculate about positive, constructive outcomes that may occur from handling this conflict effectively?

E. Play to Win

Objective

To demonstrate through a simulation exercise the behaviors different people exhibit when they are in a situation they perceive as conflict or competition or win-lose.

Instructions

1. Copy the following chart onto the chalkboard.

HOW TO SCORE POINTS	
WHEN VOTE IS	**GROUP'S SCORE**
X X X X	Each group gets +50 pt.
X X X Y	Groups voting X get –100 pt. Groups voting Y get +300 pt.
X X Y Y	Groups voting X get –200 pt. Groups voting Y get +200 pt.
X Y Y Y	Groups voting X get –300 pt. Groups voting Y get +100 pt.
Y Y Y Y	Each group gets –50 pt.

2. Review these instructions about how to score. Each of the four groups will cast either an X or Y vote in each round. When the vote is tabulated, one of the preceding five combinations will result, and each group will score accordingly. (At this point, there's apt to be some confusion and questions such as "What are we voting on?" Don't get bogged down here. Everyone will understand the process as you move along.)

3. Divide your class into four equal groups.

4. Each group should now move to a corner of the room so that the members can talk together without interruption. There should be no communication—verbal or nonverbal—among groups except when instructions permit. The group's first task is to decide on how it will make decisions: unanimous agreement, majority vote, decision of the leader, consensus, and so on.

5. Place this scoreboard where it can be easily seen.

ROUND	VOTE	GROUP I	GROUP II	GROUP III	GROUP IV
1					
2					
(N) 3					
4					
(N) 5	(2X)				
6					
(N) 7					
(N) 8					
9 (10X)					

6. Explain that the object of the game is for each group to score the greatest number of positive points possible. Note that there will be nine rounds of voting. In round 5 the scores will be doubled, and in round 9 they'll be multiplied by 10. The (N) that appears before rounds 3, 5, 7, and 8 means that the groups will be allowed to negotiate before voting in those rounds.

7. Take three minutes for each group to discuss how it will vote in round 1.

8. After the three minutes, the instructor will collect a ballot from each group. Tally the votes and score for round 1 on the scoreboard.

9. Repeat the same procedure for the remaining rounds. Before each N round, one negotiator from each team should come to the center of the room, and if they desire, negotiate the next vote or votes.

10. During negotiations, only negotiators can speak—group members must remain quiet so that they may hear negotiations. There will be time to discuss the vote in the groups after negotiations are completed.

11. After all rounds are completed, conduct a discussion about the exercise.

Discussion Questions

1. Who won the game?

2. If two groups with the same goal finished with a tie score, did they both win? Did both lose?

3. In this game, can there be more than one winner? Why?

4. Did the groups cooperate during the game, helping the others reach their goals, or did they compete by trying to "beat" everyone?

5. Did the simulation provide opportunities for the students to behave either cooperatively or competitively, or did the students add these as they went along?

6. What did the students' behavior in this exercise tell them about how they handle conflict in their lives?

Note   This game usually illustrates some common ways people act when going after something they want. Most groups assume that to reach the goal they've chosen, they must keep others from reaching theirs, when, in fact, the surest way to succeed is to work together so all groups can score well. As one woman said when shown how all the groups could have reached their goal by cooperating, "But there can't be winners unless there are losers!"

Part 3

Test Bank

CHAPTER 1
A FIRST LOOK AT INTERPERSONAL RELATIONSHIPS

1. Chapter One indicates that effective interpersonal communication is strongly linked to social happiness and career success.
   Answer: T   **Type: T**   **Pages: 8–9**   **Knowledge**

2. The only way we learn who we are is through communication.
   Answer: T   **Type: T**   **Page: 6**   **Knowledge**

3. A lack of social relationships may affect physical health and life span as dramatically as smoking or a lack of physical activity.
   Answer: T   **Type: T**   **Page: 6**   **Knowledge**

4. An example of a communication breakdown is when you have a fight with a friend.
   Answer: F   **Type: T**   **Page: 15**   **Analysis**

5. The ability to speak and listen effectively can mean the difference between succeeding and failing in a job.
   Answer: T   **Type: T**   **Page: 9**   **Knowledge**

6. Shared understanding and clarity are the most important goals in achieving successful communication.
   Answer: F   **Type: T**   **Page: 16**   **Knowledge**

7. The major difference between impersonal communication and interpersonal communication is the number of people involved.
   Answer: F   **Type: T**   **Page: 18**   **Analysis**

8. You can fill even your instrumental goals through communication.
   Answer: T   **Type: T**   **Page: 8**   **Knowledge**

9. An older professor who forgets what it was like to be a student when he teaches is an example of different environments in the classroom.
    Answer: T   **Type: T**   **Page: 11**   **Comprehension**

10. Communication competence is a trait that people either possess or lack.
    Answer: F   **Type: T**   **Page: 27**   **Knowledge**

11. Just as judges instruct juries to disregard some statements made in court, we can reverse or erase the effects of communication interactions in everyday life.
    Answer: F   **Type: T**   **Page: 15**   **Comprehension**

12. There is no such thing as the "same" message; words and behaviors are different each time they are spoken or performed.
    Answer: T   **Type: T**   **Page: 15**   **Knowledge**

13. It is impossible to repeat the same communication event.
    Answer: T   **Type: T**   **Pages: 15–16**   **Knowledge**

14. The transactional model of communication suggests that communicators usually send and receive messages simultaneously.
    Answer: T   **Type: T**   **Page: 10**   **Knowledge**

15. The transactional model represents communication as static—more like a gallery of still photographs than a motion picture film.
    Answer: F   **Type: T**   **Page: 12**   **Knowledge**

16. We are not communicating when we remain silent.
    Answer: F   **Type: T**   **Page: 15**   **Comprehension**

17. Socially isolated people are much more likely to die prematurely than those with strong social ties.
    Answer: T   **Type: T**   **Page: 6**   **Knowledge**

18. Transactional communication may be compared to dancing due to the involvement needed by each partner.
    Answer: T   **Type: T**   **Page: 12**   **Knowledge**

19. According to your text, impersonal communication should always be avoided.
    Answer: F   **Type: T**   **Pages: 23–24**   **Comprehension**

20. According to your text, effective communicators are able to establish warm relationships with everyone they encounter.
    Answer: F   **Type: T**   **Pages: 23–24**   **Analysis**

21. Your text argues that it is important to react in unique ways to every person we meet and respond to each as a unique individual.
    Answer: F   **Type: T**   **Page: 18**   **Synthesis**

22. Communication, as the term is used in your text, consists only of messages that a sender deliberately conveys.
    Answer: F   **Type: T**   **Page: 14**   **Comprehension**

23. It's impossible to stop communicating.
    Answer: T   **Type: T**   **Page: 14**   **Knowledge**

24. Of the communication models described in your text, the linear model most accurately describes the interpersonal communication process.
    Answer: F   **Type: T**   **Pages: 10–14**   **Application**

25. We disclose more to people in interpersonal relationships than in impersonal ones.
    Answer: T   **Type: T**   **Page: 20**   **Knowledge**

26. Too much communication can have negative outcomes.
    Answer: T   **Type: T**   **Page: 17**   **Knowledge**

27. Studies show that divorced men (before age 70) have the same risks health-wise (heart disease, cancer, strokes) as married men.
    Answer: F   **Type: T**   **Page: 6**   **Knowledge**

28. As the text points out, your goal should be to become a perfect communicator.
    Answer: F   **Type: T**   **Page: 33**   **Comprehension**

29. All you need to develop good communication skills is common sense.
    Answer: F   **Type: T**   **Pages: 28**   **Analysis**

31. Dyadic communication is communication involving two people.
    Answer: T   **Type: T**   **Page: 18**   **Knowledge**

32. Communication is so important that its quantity and quality can affect blood pressure and coronary health.
    Answer: T   **Type: T**   **Page: 6**   **Comprehension**

33. When people communicate, they are often both senders and receivers of messages at the same time.
    Answer: T   **Type: T**   **Page: 10**   **Knowledge**

34. Feeling sad when a close friendship changes or ends is an indicator that interpersonal relationships are irreplaceable.
    Answer: T   **Type: T**   **Page: 18**   **Knowledge**

35. According to your text, your goal should be to have as many interpersonal communication experiences as possible.
    Answer: F   **Type: T**   **Pages: 20-21**   **Comprehension**

36. According to your text, the axiom "the more communication the better" is true.
    Answer: F   **Type: T**   **Page: 17**   **Knowledge**

37. Your text promises that if you communicate skillfully enough, you should be able to solve every problem you encounter.
    Answer: F   **Type: T**   **Page: 17**   **Knowledge**

38. In impersonal communication we treat others as individuals.
    Answer: F   **Type: T**   **Page: 18**   **Knowledge**

39. Fortunately, just knowing about a communication skill makes us able to put it into practice.
     Answer: F   **Type: T**   **Page: 31**   **Comprehension**

40. According to Chapter One, interpersonal communication is the main way by which our social needs are met.
     Answer: T   **Type: T**   **Page: 8**   **Knowledge**

41. Almost all verbal messages have a content dimension as well as convey relational information.
     Answer: T   **Type: T**   **Page: 16**   **Comprehension**

42. Research has shown that CMC (computer-mediated communication) has had an overall negative effect on interpersonal relationships.
     Answer: F   **Type: T**   **Pages: 21–23**   **Comprehension**

43. Internet users have more social networks than non-users.
     Answer: T   **Type: T**   **Page: 21**   **Knowledge**

44. According to your text, CMC (computer-mediated communication) can actually promote and reinforce other forms of communication, such as face-to-face.
     Answer: T   **Type: T**   **Page: 21**   **Knowledge**

45. Living in a multicultural world has affected the way we communicate.
     Answer: T   **Type: T**   **Page: 34**   **Comprehension**

46. Occupation and sexual orientation are types of co-cultures.
     Answer: T   **Type: T**   **Page: 34**   **Knowledge**

47. Communicating successfully with people from different cultural backgrounds only requires using the same exact elements of competence we use with people in our own country.
     Answer: F   **Type: T**   **Pages: 34–35**   **Comprehension**

48. Judging others because of cultural differences may negatively effect our communication with them.
     Answer: T   **Type: T**   **Pages: 35–36**   **Knowledge**

49. Your text defines communication competence as effective communication where one's goals are achieved in a way that, ideally, maintains or enhances the relationship in which it occurs.
     Answer: T   **Type: T**   **Page: 25**   **Knowledge**

50. A competent communicator will choose the same way of responding to others, no matter what the situation, since the response was successful in the past.
     Answer: F   **Type: T**   **Page: 27**   **Knowledge**

51. Seeing a situation from multiple points of view is called self-monitoring.
     Answer: F   **Type: T**   **Page: 31**   **Knowledge**

52. An environment refers specifically to the physical location where someone is when communicating.
     Answer: F   **Type: T**   **Page: 11**   **Knowledge**

53. According to Chapter One, all of the following are attributes needed to communicate successfully with people from different cultures except
    a. motivation
    b. tolerance for ambiguity
    c. friendliness
    d. open-mindedness
    e. knowledge and skill
    Answer: c   **Type: M**   **Pages: 35–36**   **Knowledge**

54. In Chapter One Deborah Tannen claims that
    a. electronic mail can deepen the quality of relationships.
    b. electronic mail makes interpersonal communication more impersonal.
    c. everyone prefers face to face communication rather than electronic mail.
    d. relationships cannot be maintained using electronic mail.
    e. all of the above are claimed by Tannen.
    Answer: a   **Type: M**   **Page: 23**   **Knowledge**

55. In the Looking at Diversity reading in Chapter One, Daria Muse says that a big part of communicating well is
    a. speaking more than one language.
    b. staying true to your own communication style.
    c. understanding communication models.
    d. being able to choose a behavior based on the situation.
    e. having experiences in more than one culture.
    Answer: d   **Type: M**   **Page:30**   **Comprehension**

56. Psychologist Abraham Maslow suggests that the most basic human needs
    a. are invented by other psychologists.
    b. must be satisfied before we concern ourselves with other ones.
    c. are proof that animals ascended from lower animal forms.
    d. prove the existence of a superior being.
    e. are generated by others in interpersonal interaction.
    Answer: b   **Type: M**   **Page: 9**   **Knowledge**

57. All of the following elements are included in the transactional communication model introduced in Chapter One except
    a. message.
    b. environment.
    c. channel.
    d. sender.
    e. noise.
    Answer: d   **Type: M**   **Pages: 10–11**   **Knowledge**

58. All of the following are involved in learning to perform communication skills effectively except
    a. awareness.
    b. prowess.
    c. awkwardness.
    d. skillfulness.
    e. integration.
    Answer: b   **Type: M**   **Page: 31**   **Knowledge**

59. The environments that communicators occupy are
    a. fields of experience that affect how they understand others' behavior.
    b. gaps that make common understanding impossible.
    c. the places where they stand or sit when they communicate.
    d. the attitudes they have about nature.
    e. the space that they require to communicate effectively.

    Answer: a   **Type: M**   **Page: 11**   **Knowledge**

60. "Decoding" is the process whereby
    a. we put our thoughts into words.
    b. we make sense out of the messages sent by others.
    c. we engage others in conversation.
    d. we choose the appropriate way to send messages.
    e. we create new ways of teaching reading and communication to children.

    Answer: b   **Type: M**   **Page: 10**   **Knowledge**

61. Strategies you can use to develop a more mindful and competent style of intercultural communication include
    a. reading.
    b. passive observation.
    c. self-disclosure.
    d. talking to experts.
    e. All of the above.

    Answer: e   **Type: M**   **Page: 36**   **Knowledge**

62. Almost all messages have
    a. a content dimension.
    b. a relational dimension.
    c. both content and relational dimensions.
    d. no dimensions unless the communicators intend them to.

    Answer: c   **Type: M**   **Page: 16**   **Comprehension**

63. Which of the following factors might contribute to different environments?
    a. experience
    b. age
    c. income level
    d. ethnic group
    e. All of the above

    Answer: e   **Type: M**   **Page: 11**   **Knowledge**

64. What health threats can result from a lack of close relationships?
    a. more likely to experience a higher rate of accidents
    b. more susceptible to the common cold
    c. more likely to die prematurely
    d. b and c
    e. All of the above

    Answer: d   **Type: M**   **Page: 6**   **Knowledge**

65. The three types of noise that can block communication are
    a. loud, moderate, and soft.
    b. mass communicational, personal, and transactional.
    c. external, physiological, and psychological.
    d. sociological, psychological, and communicational.
    e. linear, interactional, and transactional.

    Answer: c   **Type: M**   **Page: 11**   **Knowledge**

66. Skillful, integrated communicators are characterized by
    a. a conscious focus on communicating effectively.
    b. a greater degree of sociability.
    c. communicating competently without needing to think constantly about how to behave.
    d. exposure to a wide range of communication styles.
    e. others helping them out.

    Answer: c   **Type: M**   **Page: 31**   **Comprehension**

67. Research has shown that competent communicators achieve effectiveness by
    a. using the same types of behavior in a wide variety of situations.
    b. developing large vocabularies.
    c. apologizing when they offend others.
    d. giving lots of feedback.
    e. adjusting their behaviors to the person and situation.

    Answer: e   **Type: M**   **Pages: 28–29**   **Synthesis**

68. An interpersonal relationship differs from an impersonal one because
    a. we share our thoughts and feelings.
    b. the other person's life affects ours.
    c. we are sad when the relationship changes or ends.
    d. we find the time spent in the relationship rewarding.
    e. All of the above

    Answer: e   **Type: M**   **Pages: 18–20**   **Knowledge**

69. Which of the following is considered a misconception of communication?
    a. Communication is unrepeatable.
    b. Words have meaning.
    c. Communication is irreversible.
    d. It's impossible not to communicate.

    Answer: b   **Type: M**   **Page: 16**   **Knowledge**

70. You want to let a close friend know how much she/he means to you in a way that is sincere and doesn't embarrass either of you. Following the advice on communication competence in your text, you would
    a. follow the approach that you saw another friend use successfully, assuming it would work for you.
    b. avoid sending any message until you were sure it would be well received.
    c. try to follow exactly the approach you used successfully with others in the past.
    d. react in the way that first occurred to you.
    e. consider a variety of alternatives, choosing the one that you think will be most successful under these circumstances.

    Answer: e   **Type: M**   **Pages: 28–29**   **Evaluation**

71. Maslow's hierarchy of needs is important to the study of interpersonal communication because
    a. we all have needs.
    b. we can't understand our needs without communication.
    c. communication is usually necessary to meet each level of need.
    d. communication was Maslow's greatest need.
    e. the need for communication is the sixth "hidden" need.
    Answer: c   **Type: M**   **Page: 9**   **Comprehension**

72. Noise in the communication process is
    a. more than one communicator talking at a time.
    b. the nonverbal behaviors that accompany communication.
    c. the process of maintaining direct eye contact or not.
    d. the process of translating thoughts into words.
    e. any force that interferes with effective communication.
    Answer: e   **Type: M**   **Page: 11**   **Knowledge**

73. Which of the following is most clearly an example of interpersonal communication?
    a. Jim buys a sweater from a sales clerk.
    b. Rich invites the team to a party.
    c. Royce asks Jane about her sick child.
    d. Trent pleads for the class to vote.
    e. Sue chats with the mailman.
    Answer: c   **Type: M**   **Pages: 18–21**   **Analysis**

74. The transactional model of communication is considered a more accurate model than previous ones because
    a. people send and receive messages simultaneously.
    b. we cannot isolate a single "act" of communication from the event that came before and after it.
    c. the communication created results from the way partners interact.
    d. None of the above
    e. All of the above
    Answer: e   **Type: M**   **Page: 10–11**   **Knowledge**

75. Some of the social needs we strive to fulfill by communicating are
    a. encoding and decoding.
    b. control and affection.
    c. empathy and sympathy.
    d. talking and listening.
    e. communicating both verbally and nonverbally.
    Answer: b   **Type: M**   **Page: 7**   **Comprehension**

76. Some of the characteristics that make relationships more interpersonal than impersonal are
    a. higher levels of self-disclosure and intimacy.
    b. intrinsic rewards and proximity.
    c. scarcity, disclosure, and intimacy.
    d. uniqueness, irreplaceability, and interdependence.
    Answer: d   **Type: M**   **Pages: 18–20**   **Comprehension**

77. Integrated communicators express themselves in skillful ways because
  a. their communication is a self-conscious act.
  b. they have had more experience.
  c. they have internalized effective behavior.
  d. skills are basic to communication.
  e. others help them out.
  Answer: c   **Type: M**   **Page: 31**   **Comprehension**

78. Effective communicators have been found to
  a. have a consistent set of five behaviors they can call up at will.
  b. have a wide range of behaviors from which to choose.
  c. exhibit behaviors that are predictable by their partners.
  d. exhibit unique behaviors more often than less effective communicators.
  e. frequently rehearse about 20 behaviors until they get them right for any interaction.
  Answer: b   **Type: M**   **Page: 28**   **Comprehension**

79. When you pay attention to your behavior in relationships, you are
  a. unlikely to pay attention to others.
  b. too uptight.
  c. probably ego–driven.
  d. self-monitoring.
  e. intrinsic.
  Answer: d   **Type: M**   **Page: 32**   **Knowledge**

80. Identity and communication are related in that we
  a. gain an idea of who we are from the way others communicate with us.
  b. are drawn to communicators who test and challenge our identity.
  c. find others' identities become our own through communication.
  d. control communication with our identity.
  Answer: a   **Type: M**   **Pages: 6–7**   **Comprehension**

81. Which is an example of "noise" as the term is defined in your text?
  a. someone tapping a pencil while you're trying to talk
  b. a headache that interferes with you listening
  c. feelings of anger directed toward a partner
  d. preoccupation with another topic during a lecture
  e. All of the above
  Answer: e   **Type: M**   **Page: 11**   **Application**

82. Which is an example of "psychological noise" as defined in your text?
  a. the sound of a lawn mower just outside your window
  b. the smell of smoke drifting into the room you are in
  c. feeling embarrassed about a mistake you made
  d. a light flickering on and off during a lecture
  Answer: c   **Type: M**   **Pages: 11–12**   **Application**

83. Which of the following would not be considered a co-culture?
    a. senior citizen
    b. a person who uses a wheel chair
    c. construction worker
    d. Muslim
    e. None of the above

    Answer: e   **Type: M**   **Page: 34**   **Knowledge**

84. Two friends communicating would most likely be
    a. taking turns sending and receiving messages.
    b. primarily sending messages.
    c. primarily receiving messages.
    d. sending and receiving messages at the same time.
    e. neither sending nor receiving messages.

    Answer: d   **Type: M**   **Page: 10**   **Application**

85. Research on the effects of computer–mediated communication (CMC) indicates that
    a. time online has lessened time spent with family members.
    b. the quality and quantity of interpersonal communication has increased.
    c. communication by CMC is more complex than personal contact.
    d. CMC is reducing interpersonal communication competencies.
    e. All of the above.

    Answer: b   **Type: M**   **Page: 23**   **Analysis**

86. A cognitively complex communicator
    a. considers an issue from several angles.
    b. feels and experiences another's situation.
    c. usually has a high IQ.
    d. observes behavior with detachment.
    e. thinks and reacts quickly.

    Answer: a   **Type: M**   **Page: 31**   **Knowledge**

87. When you call three of your friends in one night to avoid studying, you are communicating to fulfill
    the social need of
    a. escape.
    b. control.
    c. affection.
    d. companionship.
    e. pleasure.

    Answer: a   **Type: M**   **Page: 7**   **Application**

88. When Susan realizes during an office meeting that she's interrupted a co-worker twice, she
    demonstrates the skill of
    a. empathy.
    b. self-monitoring.
    c. cognitive complexity
    d. affinity
    e. metacommunication

    Answer: b   **Type: M**   **Page: 32**   **Application**

89. Which of the following is a channel for communication?
    a.   touching
    b.   writing
    c.   gesturing
    d.   talking
    e.   All of the above
    Answer: e   **Type: M**   **Page: 10**   **Comprehension**

92. Interpersonal relationships
    a.   develop unique qualities.
    b.   are mostly alike.
    c.   follow the same basic rules about how control is distributed between communicators.
    d.   have more relational talk than content talk.
    e.   are none of the above.
    Answer: a   **Type: M**   **Page: 18**   **Comprehension**

93. Getting others to behave in ways that we want is considered what type of goal ?
    a.   basic
    b.   social
    c.   instrumental
    d.   physical
    e.   self-actualization
    Answer: c   **Type: M**   **Page: 8**   **Knowledge**

93. Relational dimensions of a message
    a.   deal with one or more social needs.
    b.   make statements about how the parties feel toward one another.
    c.   are usually expressed nonverbally.
    d.   All of the above
    e.   None of the above
    Answer: d   **Type: M**   **Page: 16**   **Comprehension**

104. The ability to construct a variety of different frameworks for viewing an issue is termed
    a.   feedback framework.
    b.   cognitive complexity.
    c.   communication competence.
    d.   metacommunicating.
    e.   integration.
    Answer: b   **Type: M**   **Page: 31**   **Knowledge**

INSTRUCTIONS for questions 105–109: Match each of the statements below with the element of the communication model it illustrates most clearly.
    a.   external noise
    b.   environment
    c.   channel
    d.   decoding
    e.   psychological noise

105. You decide to schedule a face-to-face meeting with your professor instead of e-mailing him.
    Answer: c   **Type: Matching**   **Page: 10**   **Application**

106. Alex decides what Dana meant by that frown.
     Answer: d   **Type: Matching**   **Page: 10**   **Application**

107. Your friend's religion is different from yours, but you went to the same high school and college.
     Answer: b   **Type: Matching**   **Page: 11**   **Evaluation**

108. You are worried about how your child is doing at school while your boss is giving the quarterly report.
     Answer: e   **Type: Matching**   **Page: 11**   **Application**

109. A person behind you in the theater fiddles with a crackling cellophane candy wrapper.
     Answer: a   **Type: Matching**   **Page: 11**   **Application**

110. Describe an interpersonal communication incident from your experience, identifying at least five elements of the transactional model of communication shown in *Looking Out/ Looking In*.
     Answer: **Type: E**   **Pages: 10–14**   **Synthesis**

111. Using the characteristics described in "Communication Competence: What makes an effective communicator?" evaluate your communication competence in the context of one interpersonal relationship in which you are involved. Discuss the range of behaviors in which you engage, your ability to choose the most appropriate behavior, your skill in performing certain behaviors, and your commitment to the relationship. Be sure to discuss this relationally, involving the behaviors of the other person, and how you adapt or fail to adapt to them.
     Answer: **Type: E**   **Pages: 25–33**   **Synthesis**

112. Using your own experiences as examples, explain the difference between interpersonal communication and impersonal communication.
     Answer: **Type: E**   **Pages: 18–21**   **Application**

113. Identify the three different needs that are fulfilled by communicating. Provide examples for each from your own experience.
     Answer: **Type: E**   **Pages: 6–9**   **Application**

114. Explain the concept of "noise." First, define it according to its role in the transactional model of communication in Chapter One. Next, imagine you are being interviewed for a job. Name and give examples of each of the three types of noise described by your text that might be present during this interview experience.
     Answer: **Type: E**   **Page: 11**   **Evaluation**

115. Explain the principle, "communication is irreversible." Use personal examples to demonstrate how this principle has affected your own life.
     Answer: **Type E**   **Page: 15**   **Application**

116. Describe an interpersonal relationship that you are in that involves at least some degree of computer–mediated communication (CMC). List the limitations of CMC in maintaining this relationship. Lastly, describe the ways in which CMC enhances the quantity and/or quality of this relationship.
     Answer: T   **Type: E**   **Pages: 21–23**   **Application**

CHAPTER 2

COMMUNICATION AND IDENTITY: CREATING AND PRESENTING THE SELF

1. Identity management occurs only in face-to-face interactions.
   Answer: F   **Type: T**   **Page: 75**   **Knowledge**

2. Research indicates that computer-mediated communication (CMC) offers advantages for identity management.
   Answer: T   **Type: T**   **Page: 76**   **Knowledge**

3. The influence of significant others becomes less powerful as we grow older.
   Answer: T   **Type: T**   **Page: 48**   **Comprehension**

4. The self-concept is extremely resistant to change.
   Answer: T   **Type: T**   **Page: 53**   **Comprehension**

5. People who are confident that others support their presenting selves prefer CMC over face-to-face interaction.
   Answer: F   **Type: T**   **Pages: 76**   **Synthesis**

6. In many cases a self-concept is based on data which may have been true at one time, but are now obsolete.
   Answer: T   **Type: T**   **Page: 59**   **Knowledge**

7. The self-concept is extremely subjective, being almost totally a product of interaction with others.
   Answer: T   **Type: T**   **Pages: 45, 52**   **Comprehension**

8. People with high self-esteem tend to disapprove of others more than people with low self-esteem.
   Answer: F   **Type: T**   **Page: 54**   **Comprehension**

9. People who think highly of themselves are likely to think highly of others too.
   Answer: T   **Type: T**   **Page: 54**   **Knowledge**

10. Our concept of self is shaped by the culture in which we have been reared.
    Answer: T   **Type: T**   **Page: 56**   **Synthesis**

11. The self-concept is a relatively stable set of perceptions you hold of yourself.
    Answer: T   **Type: T**   **Page: 41**   **Knowledge**

12. The self-concept is a constantly changing set of perceptions that others have of you.
    Answer: F   **Type: T**   **Page: 41**   **Knowledge**

13. Personality traits are largely a result of genetics rather than of socialization.
    Answer: T   **Type: T**   **Page: 44**   **Knowledge**

14. We tend to resist revising our own self-concept even if the new self image is more positive.
    Answer: T   **Type: T**   **Page: 53**   **Comprehension**

15. All inaccurate self-concepts are overly negative.
    Answer: F   **Type: T**   **Page: 52**   **Knowledge**

16. It is possible to have a more favorable image of yourself than the objective facts or the opinions of others warrant.
    Answer: T   **Type: T**   **Page: 52**   **Knowledge**

17. The person you believe yourself to be in moments of honesty is called the presenting self.
    Answer: F   **Type: T**   **Page: 65**   **Knowledge**

18. The face you try to show to others is called the perceived self.
    Answer: F   **Type: T**   **Page: 65**   **Knowledge**

19. The text advises that we shouldn't acknowledge our strengths because we will develop overly positive, distorted self-concepts.
    Answer: F   **Type: T**   **Page: 53**   **Comprehension**

20. Most Western cultures have what is called a collective identity.
    Answer: F   **Type: T**   **Page: 56**   **Knowledge**

21. Nonverbal behaviors play a big role in managing impressions.
    Answer: T   **Type: T**   **Page: 72**   **Knowledge**

22. The process of identity management can result in dishonest behavior.
    Answer: T   **Type: T**   **Page: 76**   **Knowledge**

23. Most researchers agree that we are born with many of our personality traits.
    Answer: T   **Type: T**   **Page: 44–45**   **Knowledge**

24. According to your text, the self-concept influences much of our future behavior.
    Answer: T   **Type: T**   **Page: 64**   **Knowledge**

25. Luckily, communication from others does not affect our self-concept.
    Answer: F   **Type: T**   **Pages: 45-48**   **Comprehension**

26. You shouldn't listen to the "boosters" and "busters" others give you since your self-concept is only your view of yourself.
    Answer: F   **Type: T**   **Pages: 46–47**   **Comprehension**

27. All communication behavior is aimed at making impressions.
    Answer: F   **Type: T**   **Page: 69**   **Comprehension**

28. Cognitive conservatism is the tendency to cling to an existing self-concept, even when evidence shows that it is no longer the case.
    Answer: T   **Type: T**   **Page: 53**   **Knowledge**

29. Your personality determines how you feel about the way you relate to others.
    Answer: F   **Type: T**   **Page: 44**   **Knowledge**

30. The self-concept is a product of the positive and negative messages you have received throughout your life.
    Answer: T   **Type: T**   **Page: 46**   **Knowledge**

31. Opinions of family members or teachers early in your life have little impact on the formation of your self-concept.
    Answer: F   **Type: T**   **Page: 48**   **Comprehension**

32. Some individuals view themselves more favorably than what the real facts indicate.
    Answer: T   **Type: T**   **Page: 52**   **Knowledge**

33. In a culture such as China or Japan, speaking directly is considered desirable.
    Answer: F   **Type: T**   **Page: 56**   **Knowledge**

34. A competent communicator is able to call on different identities when necessary.
    Answer: T   **Type: T**   **Page: 66**   **Knowledge**

35. Being a male or female makes little difference in how others communicate with us.
    Answer: F   **Type: T**   **Page: 57**   **Knowledge**

36. Defensiveness can become a problem for someone who is presented with information that contradicts his/her self-perception.
    Answer: T   **Type: T**   **Page: 55**   **Knowledge**

37. The only type of self-fulfilling prophecy that can occur is when your own expectations influence your behavior.
    Answer: F   **Type: T**   **Page: 59**   **Knowledge**

38. According to your text, being a high self-monitor is preferable to being a low self-monitor.
    Answer: F   **Type: T**   **Page: 70**   **Knowledge**

39. Managing your identity can be useful when you are meeting someone at a party for the first time.
    Answer: T   **Type: T**   **Page: 71**   **Comprehension**

40. While your personality may help to shape the way you communicate, your self-concept determines how you feel about the way you relate to others.
    Answer: T   **Type: T**   **Page: 45**   **Knowledge**

41. Research described in your text about CMC (computer-mediated communication) suggests that
    a. it may be an advantage for creating a desired impression.
    b. it permits a responder to ignore a message rather than be unpleasant.
    c. it lacks the "richness" of many nonverbal channels.
    d. all of the above are supported by research.
    e. none of the above are supported by research.
    Answer: d   **Type: M**   **Pages: 75–76**   **Knowledge**

42. In the example of schoolchildren taken from the book *Pygmalion in the Classroom*
    a. the less intelligent children performed better than expected.
    b. the more intelligent children performed better than expected.
    c. the children teachers predicted would do better, did so.
    d. all the children performed the same because they had similar self-concepts.
    e. teachers improved their self-concepts by working with good children.

    Answer: c   **Type: M**   **Page: 60**   **Recall**

43. Self-fulfilling prophecies are
    a. negative predictions of our behavior, imposed by others.
    b. negative predictions of our behavior, imposed by ourselves.
    c. positive or negative predictions of our behavior, imposed by others and/or ourselves.
    d. almost always negative predictions, imposed by ourselves and/or others.
    e. none of the above.

    Answer: c   **Type: M**   **Pages: 58–60**   **Knowledge**

44. "Cipher in the Snow" is included in your text to illustrate
    a. the importance of honest self-appraisal.
    b. the impact of dishonest identity management.
    c. the way people construct multiple identities.
    d. the impact of significant others on self-concept
    e. all of the above.

    Answer: d   **Type: M**   **Pages: 49–50**   **Comprehension**

45. Which of the following is definitely not an example of a self-fulfilling prophecy?
    a. A child fails a test after hearing her teacher tell her mother that she never does well on tests
    b. A student who previously complained of stage fright loses his place during a class speech and can't go on.
    c. A husband reluctantly agrees, with reservations, to his wife's request that they spend the holiday visiting Disneyland. He has a terrible time.
    d. Both b and c above qualify as examples of self-fulfilling prophecies.
    e. All of the above qualify as examples of self-fulfilling prophecies.

    Answer: e   **Type: M**   **Pages: 58–60**   **Analysis**

46. All of the following are methods you could use to make your self-concept more realistic except:
    a. Share your perception of yourself with a friend.
    b. Try to engage in more accurate self-talk.
    c. Make an effort to recognize more "ego buster" messages.
    d. Pay less attention to your past and more attention to your present behavior.

    Answer: c   **Type: M**   **Pages: 61–63**   **Analysis**

47. All of the following are true of the self-concept except that
    a. it is objective.
    b. it is changing.
    c. it is, in part, a product of interaction with others.
    d. it is, in part, a product of our early childhood experience.
    e. it can be changed.

    Answer: a   **Type: M**   **Page: 52**   **Comprehension**

48. The term "self-concept" refers to
    a. the sum of one's physiological, social, and psychological attributes as perceived by an impartial observer.
    b. the way an individual believes others perceive her/him.
    c. the total of an individual's beliefs about his/her physical characteristics, intelligence, aptitudes, and social skills.
    d. the sum of one's psychological, social, and physical attributes as perceived by a significant other.
    e. none of the above.

    Answer: c   **Type: M**   **Pages: 41–42**   **Comprehension**

49. A "significant other" is best defined as
    a. a powerful adult.
    b. a person who has affected one's self-concept.
    c. a totally supportive person.
    d. an extremely negative influence.
    e. all of the above.

    Answer: b   **Type: M**   **Page: 48**   **Comprehension**

50. According to your text, "ego-boosters and busters" are
    a. examples of how people ruin their self-concepts by taking drugs.
    b. people or words that influence the self-concept positively or negatively.
    c. the two essential elements of self-concept development.
    d. ways to predict how children will become good or bad readers.
    e. intentionally vague labels we give to mask true self-concepts.

    Answer: b   **Type: M**   **Pages: 46–47**   **Knowledge**

51. The higher levels of anxiety about speaking out in countries such as China, Korea, and Japan indicate that
    a. shyness is a problem in some cultures.
    b. reticence is valued in these cultures.
    c. assertiveness has not been taught correctly.
    d. the individualistic identity is better than the collective one.
    e. children are not taught public speaking in these countries.

    Answer: b   **Type: M**   **Page: 56**   **Comprehension**

52. People who are high self-monitors
    a. are much more aware of their impression management behavior than others.
    b. express what they feel without paying much attention to the impression their behavior creates.
    c. are usually bad actors.
    d. are not usually good "people readers."
    e. are easier to "read" than low self-monitors.

    Answer: a   **Type: M**   **Page: 70**   **Comprehension**

53. The relatively stable set of perceptions you hold of yourself is called your
    a. self-concept.
    b. interpersonal self.
    c. perceptual bias.
    d. self-feedback.
    e. self-orientation.

    Answer: a   **Type: M**   **Page: 41**   **Knowledge**

54. A self-fulfilling prophecy is
   a. an accurate prediction about another's behavior, based on background knowledge.
   b. a prediction about one's own behavior, based on past experience.
   c. a prediction which affects the outcome of one's own or another's behavior.
   d. a mistaken prediction which fails to occur.
   e. none of the above.

   Answer: c   **Type: M**   **Page: 58**   **Comprehension**

55. In individualistic cultures, a view of the self would involve all of the following except
   a. self-sufficiency.
   b. high value on tradition.
   c. high value on equality.
   d. high value on change.
   e. personal credit or blame.

   Answer: b   **Type: M**   **Page: 56**   **Comprehension**

56. Someone who is a "significant other" is
   a. "socially" conscious.
   b. a person whose opinion we especially value.
   c. always a supportive person.
   d. a person with significant goals.

   Answer: b   **Type: M**   **Page: 48**   **Knowledge**

57. If you want to change your self-concept, you should
   a. have realistic expectations and perceptions.
   b. ask others to send you only positive messages.
   c. take yourself less seriously.
   d. It is not possible to change the self-concept.

   Answer: a   **Type: M**   **Pages: 61–63**   **Comprehension**

58. People who have low self-esteem
   a. are likely to approve of others.
   b. perform well when being watched.
   c. work harder for critical people.
   d. expect to be rejected by others.
   e. had traumatic childhoods.

   Answer: d   **Type: M**   **Page: 54**   **Comprehension**

59. People who have high self-esteem
   a. expect to be accepted by others.
   b. have less of a need to work hard for people who demand high standards.
   c. are unable to defend themselves against negative comments.
   d. don't perform well when being watched.

   Answer: a   **Type: M**   **Page: 54**   **Comprehension**

60. The kind of person you believe yourself to be is called the
    a. perceived self.
    b. desired self.
    c. presenting self.
    d. myth of self.
    e. transient self.

    Answer: a   **Type: M**   **Page: 65**   **Knowledge**

61. All of the following are examples of social comparison except
    a. being judged for a test based on other student's grades.
    b. thinking over how you have added muscle mass in the last four months.
    c. deciding to go on a diet after looking at models in a magazine.
    d. judging your fitness level in contrast to others in the gym.
    e. all of the above are examples of social comparison.

    Answer: b   **Type: M**   **Page: 48**   **Application**

62. "Reference groups" are
    a. people whose self-concepts we have influenced.
    b. individuals whose self-esteem has been diminished.
    c. groups against which a person compares him/herself.
    d. groups formed to improve shaky self-esteem.
    e. people who hang around the library.

    Answer: c   **Type: M**   **Page: 51**   **Knowledge**

63. According to your text, the word "can't" often serves to
    a. let others share control in the relationship.
    b. help us accept our limitations.
    c. create a self-fulfilling prophecy.
    d. express equality through our humanity.

    Answer: c   **Type: M**   **Page: 62**   **Analysis**

64. The tendency to seek and attend to information that conforms to an existing self-concept has been labeled
    a. reflected appraisal.
    b. significance posturing.
    c. the stability hypothesis.
    d. cognitive conservatism.
    e. the weak spine phenomenon.

    Answer: d   **Type: M**   **Page: 53**   **Knowledge**

65. The communication strategies people use to influence how others view them is the process of
    a. ego-video
    b. reflected appraisal
    c. manipulation
    d. social ethics
    e. identity management

    Answer: e   **Type: M**   **Pages: 63–64**   **Knowledge**

66. People who hold excessively negative self-evaluations of themselves may do so due to
   a. distorted feedback
   b. society's emphasis on perfection
   c. obsolete information
   d. social expectations
   e. all of the above
   Answer: e   **Type: M**   **Pages: 52–53**   **Knowledge**

67. Jill still thinks of herself as a struggling student although as a college student her GPA is a 3.5. This is an example of
   a. self-monitoring.
   b. self-fulfilling prophecy.
   c. cognitive conservatism.
   d. myth of perfection.
   e. distorted feedback.
   Answer: c   **Type: M**   **Page: 53**   **Knowledge**

68. People try to manage their identities in order to
   a. initiate a relationship.
   b. save another's face.
   c. get others to do something they want.
   d. none of the above.
   e. all of the above.
   Answer: e   **Type: M**   **Pages: 71–72**   **Knowledge**

69. All of the following are ways that can help in changing your self-concept except
   a. seeking advice from books and others.
   b. being realistic in how you perceive yourself.
   c. determineing what may be inaccurate feedback from others.
   d. being willing to change.
   e. compareing yourself against others.
   Answer: e   **Type: M**   **Pages: 61–62**   **Knowledge**

70. The characteristic ways you think and behave across a variety of situations describes your
   a. self-concept.
   b. personality.
   c. self-esteem.
   d. self-worth.
   e. none of the above.
   Answer: b   **Type: M**   **Page: 44**   **Knowledge**

71. When Joe hangs his framed medical degrees on his office wall he is managing his identity through
   a. appearance.
   b. manner.
   c. setting.
   d. image.
   e. role.
   Answer: c   **Type: M**   **Page: 75**   **Knowledge**

72. To say that identity management is collaborative means that
    a. both people communicating agree with each other.
    b. each person creates an identity in response to the other's behavior.
    c. each person creates a similar identity.
    d. both people decide on their identities together.
    e. none of the above.

    Answer: b   **Type: M**   **Page: 67–69**   **Knowledge**

73. The process whereby the self-concept develops due to the way we believe others see us is called
    a. reflected appraisal.
    b. social comparison.
    c. feedback.
    d. other-imposed prophecy.
    e. distortion.

    Answer: a   **Type: M**   **Page: 46**   **Knowledge**

74. An example of a presenting self is
    a. Jan is very attentive in class and asks questions about the material to her professor.
    b. Jan regularly calls her friends, remembers birthdays, and listens to friends' problems.
    c. Jan is never late for work, volunteers for work committees, and turns in work on time.
    d. all of the above
    e. none of the above

    Answer: d   **Type: M**   **Page: 65**   **Comprehension**

75. Psyching yourself up before a soccer game is an example of
    a. positive prediction.
    b. a self-imposed prophecy.
    c. other-imposed prophecy.
    d. anxiety reduction.
    e. none of the above.

    Answer: b   **Type: M**   **Page: 59**   **Knowledge**

76. Which of the following does not characterize identity management?
    a. Identity management is collaborative.
    b. We create multiple roles.
    c. People differ in their degree of identity management.
    d. Identity management is always deliberate.
    e. The situation can affect how we manage our identities.

    Answer: d   **Type: M**   **Pages: 66–70**   **Knowledge**

INSTRUCTIONS for questions 77–81: Match each description below with the most accurate term.
    a. reflected appraisal
    b. significant other
    c. cognitive conservatism
    d. presenting self
    e. perceived self

77. The private self you honestly believe you are.

    Answer: e   **Type: Matching**   **Page: 65**   **Knowledge**

78. The tendency to cling to an existing self-concept
    Answer: c   **Type: Matching**   **Page: 53**   **Knowledge**

79. A person whose opinion we especially value
    Answer: b   **Type: Matching**   **Page: 48**   **Knowledge**

80. Process of judging ourselves by the evaluations of others
    Answer: a   **Type: Matching**   **Page: 46**   **Knowledge**

81. The "face" you show to others
    Answer: d   **Type: Matching**   **Page: 65**   **Knowledge**

82. Pick the three most important communication-related "cant's" (using the exercise on page 63 in your text). Next, explain whether each item is really a "can't," a "won't," or a "don't know how." Next, describe how that item affects your relationship with the person in question. Finally, explain how happy or unhappy you are with each item and what, if anything, you could do to change it.
    Answer: **Type: E**   **Page: 63**   **Evaluation**

83. Barry Stevens's piece in the text titled "Will the Real Me Please Stand Up?" talks about a split between the basic spirit and that which is learned through experience—the social self. From your own background, explain the nature of this split, the struggle between different aspects of the self, and talk about its effect on your self-concept.
    Answer: **Type: E**   **Pages: 73–74**   **Synthesis**

84. Describe two people for whom you are a significant other. Describe your communication behavior with each of them, giving examples of how (a) you deliver "booster" and "buster" messages to each of them; (b) you create self-fulfilling prophecies that work for and against each of them; and (c) they allow your communication with them to affect their behavior.
    Answer: **Type: E**   **Pages: 46–61**   **Synthesis**

85. Describe a recent self-fulfilling prophecy which you have imposed upon yourself that affects your communication. In what cases have you imposed it? What have the results been? How realistic was the prophecy? Does answering these questions change how you'll talk to yourself in the future? How? Next, describe a self-fulfilling prophecy you have imposed upon another person. How did you communicate it (i.e., what messages did you send, and what channels did you use)? What effect did your prophecy have upon your partner? Does answering this question affect how you'll communicate with the other person in the future? How?
    Answer: **Type: E**   **Pages: 58–61**   **Evaluation**

86. Explain how you managed impressions with others in a recent important event in your life. Cite the reasons why you managed impressions and then evaluate the way you presented yourself.
    Answer: **Type: E**   **Pages: 72–76**   **Analysis**

87. Describe how you have managed your manner, appearance, and setting to create desired impressions in two different specific instances.
    Answer: **Type: E**   **Pages: 72–76**   **Application**

88. Exlain the concept of reflected appraisal. Choose two people in your life who have contributed to how you view yourself and how their communication contributed to who you are today.
    Answer: **Type: E**   **Pages 46–48**   **Application**

89. Explain the characteristic, "The self-concept is subjective." Discuss the reasons why a distorted self-concept can occur. Using personal examples, also discuss how your self-concept has been affected by distortion.

Answer: **Type: E**   **Pages: 52–53**   **Analysis**

CHAPTER 3

PERCEPTION: WHAT YOU SEE IS WHAT YOU GET

1. While culture has a great deal to do with our perception, it is understood that self-esteem and moods of a person do not.
   Answer: F   **Type: T**   **Pages: 94, 101**   **Knowledge**

2. A common perceptual tendency is to assume that others are similar to us.
   Answer: F   **Type: T**   **Page: 105**   **Knowledge**

3. The text argues that an ailment may have a strong impact on how you relate to others.
   Answer: T   **Type: T**   **Page: 94**   **Knowledge**

4. Total empathy is impossible to achieve.
   Answer: T   **Type: T**   **Page: 111**   **Knowledge**

5. Practicing empathy tends to make people more tolerant of others.
   Answer: T   **Type: T**   **Page: 110**   **Comprehension**

6. True empathy requires agreement with the other person.
   Answer: F   **Type: T**   **Page: 110**   **Knowledge**

7. Identical foods can actually taste different to various individuals.
   Answer: T   **Type: T**   **Pages: 93–94**   **Knowledge**

8. Sensory data can be different to different people.
   Answer: T   **Type: T**   **Pages: 93–94**   **Knowledge**

9. We are influenced more by subtle stimuli rather than obvious ones.
   Answer: F   **Type: T**   **Page: 104**   **Knowledge**

10. In our perceptions, we cling more strongly to first impressions, even when they are wrong.
    Answer: T   **Type: T**   **Page: 104**   **Knowledge**

11. Your text points out that people with high self-esteem are quicker to assume the worst possible motives on the part of others.
    Answer: F   **Type: T**   **Page: 101**   **Knowledge**

12. In perceiving others, we usually blame their problems on their personal qualities rather than on factors outside them.
    Answer: T   **Type: T**   **Page: 103**   **Knowledge**

13. Since we are the ones who experience reality, we have a complete idea of what that reality is.
    Answer: F   **Type: T**   **Page: 84**   **Comprehension**

14. It's simply impossible to be aware of everything, no matter how attentive we may be.
    Answer: T   **Type: T**   **Page: 84**   **Analysis**

15. Since stimuli that are intense often attract our attention, we're more likely to remember extremely talkative people than those who are quiet.
   Answer: T   **Type: T**   **Pages: 84–85**   **Knowledge**

16. Unchanging people or things become less noticeable, and thus occupy less of our attention than those that change.
   Answer: T   **Type: T**   **Page: 85**   **Comprehension**

17. Selection is an objective process.
   Answer: F   **Type: T**   **Pages: 84–85**   **Comprehension**

18. No two people perceive a given set of sense data identically.
   Answer: T   **Type: T**   **Pages: 84–85**   **Comprehension**

19. The sensory data we receive are the same for all of us; perceptual differences occur only after we begin to process those data.
   Answer: F   **Type: T**   **Pages: 84–85**   **Comprehension**

20. After using the "Pillow Method" you should typically conclude that the issue being considered is not important enough to worry about.
   Answer: F   **Type: T**   **Pages: 112–115**   **Comprehension**

21. The "halo effect" is a perceptual tendency which causes us to be more generous in our judgment of ourselves over others.
   Answer: F   **Type: T**   **Page: 104**   **Knowledge**

22. People's occupations have little bearing on their perception of the world.
   Answer: F   **Type: T**   **Page: 100**   **Knowledge**

23. Only women are affected by changes in mood.
   Answer: F   **Type: T**   **Page: 94**   **Comprehension**

24. The self-serving bias illustrates our tendency to judge others more charitably than ourselves.
   Answer: F   **Type: T**   **Page: 103**   **Knowledge**

25. Your text claims that there is nothing wrong with the generalizations we make, using our organization constructs, as long as they are accurate.
   Answer: T   **Type: T**   **Pages: 87–88**   **Knowledge**

26. Punctuation is the process of organizing a series of events to determine causes and effects.
   Answer: T   **Type: T**   **Page: 89**   **Knowledge**

27. According to your text, each of us experiences a different reality.
   Answer: T   **Type: T**   **Page: 84**   **Knowledge**

28. Silence is valued over talk in most Asian cultures.
   Answer: T   **Type: T**   **Page: 97**   **Knowledge**

29. The three phases of perception (selection, organization, and interpretation) can occur in differing sequences.
   Answer: T   **Type: T**   **Page: 92**   **Knowledge**

30. According to your text, unhappy spouses are more likely than happy ones to make negative interpretations of their mates' behavior.
    Answer: T   **Type: T**   **Page: 92**   **Knowledge**

31. Sympathy is the ability to experience the world from another's point of view.
    Answer: F   **Type: T**   **Page: 109**   **Knowledge**

32. One way in which we organize our impressions of others is by appearance.
    Answer: T   **Type: T**   **Page: 86**   **Knowledge**

33. It is never appropriate to make a generalization.
    Answer: F   **Type: T**   **Page: 87**   **Comprehension**

34. Stereotyping occurs when generalizations lose touch with reality.
    Answer: T   **Type: T**   **Page: 87**   **Knowledge**

35. One experiment from your text on prejudice perceptions showed that females were more likely than males, and whites more likely than blacks, to label an action as prejudiced.
    Answer: F   **Type: T**   **Page: 89**   **Knowledge**

36. Whether you are happy or unhappy with a partner will affect how you interpret that partner's behavior.
    Answer: T   **Type: T**   **Page: 92**   **Comprehension**

37. The process whereby people try to influence each other's perceptions and attempt to achieve a shared perspective is called negotiation.
    Answer: T   **Type: T**   **Page: 92**   **Knowledge**

38. A shared relational narrative is the reason that some couples say they are happily married when the facts would indicate otherwise.
    Answer: T   **Type: T**   **Page: 92**   **Comprehension**

39. The attitude that one's own culture is superior to other cultures is called ethnocentrism.
    Answer: T   **Type: T**   **Page: 97**   **Knowledge**

40. The process of attaching meaning to behavior is called assignation.
    Answer: F   **Type: T**   **Page: 103**   **Knowledge**

41. The skill of perception checking allows you to see if you are correct in your interpretation of another's behavior.
    Answer: T   **Type: T**   **Page: 106**   **Knowledge**

42. Perception checking can be a useful tool when you don't want to embarrass or directly threaten another person.
    Answer: T   **Type: T**   **Page: 107**   **Comprehension**

43. Position Four in the Pillow Method takes the perspective that the original issue should still be seen as very important.
    Answer: F   **Type: T**   **Page: 113**   **Knowledge**

44. In all societies, gender is considered one of the most important factors in determining how people perceive one another.
    Answer: T   **Type: T**   **Page: 99**   **Knowledge**

45. Philip Zimbardo's mock prison experiment, described in Chapter Three, illustrated the perceptual influence of _____ in the behavior changes noticed.
    a. hunger and fatigue
    b. biological cycles
    c. gender
    d. occupational roles
    e. culture
    Answer: d   **Type: M**   **Page: 100**   **Comprehension**

46. The Pillow Method is designed to
    a. persuade someone to accept your viewpoint.
    b. settle a dispute.
    c. minimize an issue.
    d. gain insight into another's viewpoint.
    e. punctuate the cause and effect of an argument.
    Answer: d   **Type: M**   **Page: 112**   **Comprehension**

47. The story in your text about six men from Indostan illustrates
    a. the phenomenon called "culture shock."
    b. the way people tend to punctuate a series of events differently.
    c. the "Pillow Method" applied to resolve a problem.
    d. different interpretations depending on point of view.
    e. self-serving bias.
    Answer: d   **Type: M**   **Page: 114**   **Comprehension**

48. All of the following would be included in a good definition of empathy except:
    a. It involves taking the other's perspective.
    b. It includes concern for the other person.
    c. It requires a sense of the other person's feelings.
    d. It can't be totally achieved.
    e. It involves agreeing with the other's position.
    Answer: e   **Type: M**   **Pages: 109–110**   **Knowledge**

49. A perception check includes
    a. a description of the behavior you have noticed.
    b. two possible interpretations of the behavior.
    c. a request for clarification about how to interpret the behavior correctly.
    d. all of the above.
    e. none of the above.
    Answer: d   **Type: M**   **Page: 106**   **Knowledge**

50. What's missing from this perception check? "When you didn't do the grocery shopping today like you usually do, I figured you weren't feeling good or were mad at me."
    a. It doesn't describe behavior.
    b. It has only one interpretation.
    c. It doesn't request clarification.
    d. It is too specific.
    e. Nothing is missing from this perception check.
    Answer: c   **Type: M**   **Page: 106**   **Application**

51. What's missing from this perception check? "I figure you're either upset with me or worried about your test. Is it something like that?"
    a. It doesn't describe behavior.
    b. It has only one interpretation.
    c. It doesn't request clarification.
    d. It is too wordy.
    e. Nothing is missing from this perception check.
    Answer: a   **Type: M**   **Page: 106**   **Application**

52. What's missing from this perception check? "When I saw you having lunch with Emily, I figured you liked her more than me. What's going on?"
    a. It doesn't describe behavior.
    b. It has only one interpretation.
    c. It doesn't request clarification.
    d. It is too wordy.
    e. Nothing is missing from this perception check.
    Answer: b   **Type: M**   **Page: 106**   **Application**

53. What's missing from this perception check? "When you didn't call me when you said you would, I thought you might have forgotten or were mad at me. What happened?
    a. It doesn't describe behavior.
    b. It has only one interpretation.
    c. It doesn't request clarification.
    d. It is too wordy.
    e. Nothing is missing from this perception check.
    Answer: e   **Type: M**   **Page: 106**   **Application**

54. How could you improve this perception-checking statement? "When you gave me an F on my essay, I figured you hated me. Right?"
    a. Describe behavior.
    b. Give another interpretation.
    c. Request clarification.
    d. Say less.
    e. It is great as a perception-checking statement just the way it is.
    Answer: b   **Type: M**   **Page: 106**   **Analysis**

55. All of the following are physiological factors shaping perception except:
    a.   the senses.
    b.   age and health.
    c.   fatigue.
    d.   ethnicity.
    e.   hunger.
    Answer: d   **Type: M**   **Pages: 93–94**   **Knowledge**

56. The recognition of a "figure" as standing out from a "ground" of other stimuli takes place during what phase of the perception process?
    a.   ideation
    b.   stimulation
    c.   verification
    d.   organization
    e.   sensation
    Answer: d   **Type: M**   **Page: 85**   **Knowledge**

57. All of the following perceptual factors influence the way we interpret behavior except:
    a.   relational satisfaction
    b.   assumptions about human behavior
    c.   androgynous style
    d.   past experience
    e.   expectations
    Answer: c   **Type: M**   **Page: 91**   **Comprehension**

58. Talk is viewed as desirable and useful for both task and social purposes in
    a.   Western culture.
    b.   Asian culture.
    c.   upper- and middle-class groups.
    d.   older people.
    e.   all of the above.
    Answer: a   **Type: M**   **Page: 97**   **Knowledge**

59. Which of the following statements is not true?
    a.   People agree about what smells good or bad.
    b.   People's sensitivity to temperature varies significantly.
    c.   Odors that please some people repel others.
    d.   Men have mood cycles of ups and downs.
    e.   All of the above are true.
    Answer: a   **Type: M**   **Pages: 93–94**   **Analysis**

60. We notice some stimuli over others in our environment because they are
    a.   mild.
    b.   singular.
    c.   contrasting or changing.
    d.   related to modular communication.
    Answer: c   **Type: M**   **Page: 85**   **Knowledge**

61. The steps in the perception process are
    a. initial, intermediate, final.
    b. assumption, experience, expectation.
    c. physical, psychological, experimental.
    d. selection, organization, interpretation.
    e. response, action, interaction.
    Answer: d   **Type: M**   **Pages: 84–92**   **Comprehension**

62. In order to understand another person's perception of a problem, it is necessary to
    a. assume that person's social role.
    b. spend time in that person's culture or subculture.
    c. experience that person's physiological differences.
    d. all of the above
    e. none of the above
    Answer: e   **Type: M**   **Page: 109**   **Synthesis**

63. Empathy is related to perception in that
    a. the more perceptive you are, the less empathetic you need be.
    b. the more perceptive you are, the easier it is to forget to be empathetic.
    c. empathy is facilitated by trying to perceive things from the other person's point of view.
    d. empathy and perception are both a result of self-fulfilling prophecies.
    Answer: c   **Type: M**   **Page: 109**   **Analysis**

64. Curt made a poor first impression on Carol as he first arrived, so throughout their evening date, despite his pleasant behavior, Carol continued to see him in an unfavorable light due to
    a. her feelings of empathy.
    b. the halo effect.
    c. her punctuation of the events of the evening.
    d. the narrative of the date.
    e. physiological factors influencing Carol's perception.
    Answer: b   **Type: M**   **Page: 104**   **Application**

65. All of the following are causes of inaccurate perception except
    a. we cling to first impressions.
    b. we're influenced by what is most obvious.
    c. we assume others are similar to us.
    d. we rate ourselves more negatively than others see us.
    e. we judge ourselves more charitably than others.
    Answer: d   **Type: M**   **Pages: 103–105**   **Comprehension**

66. Being able to pick out your sister's comments from a babble of voices at a party illustrates the organizational principle of
    a. figure-ground organization.
    b. alternative patterning.
    c. perceptual freezing.
    d. selection of empathetic other.
    e. attention to the irritating.
    Answer: a   **Type: M**   **Page: 85**   **Application**

67. An effective perception checking statement
    a.   tends to have a better chance of working in a low-context culture.
    b.   requires that your words match your behavior.
    c.   doesn't always require 3 parts.
    d.   all of the above
    e.   none of the above
    Answer: d   **Type: M**   **Pages: 105–107**   **Knowledge**

68. Shannon says that she works out in the evenings instead of the afternoons because Roger is always late coming home from work. Roger says he doesn't bother to rush home from work because Shannon is always working out. This process of organizing the series of events in different ways is called
    a.   punctuation.
    b.   interpretation.
    c.   perceptuation.
    d.   conjugation.
    e.   intrepidation.
    Answer: a   **Type: M**   **Pages: 89–90**   **Application**

69. The term that refers to men and women possessing a mixture of traits that have previously been considered exclusively masculine or feminine is
    a.   chauvinistic.
    b.   adaptable.
    c.   rhetorically sensitive.
    d.   androgynous.
    e.   analogous.
    Answer: d   **Type: M**   **Page: 99**   **Knowledge**

70. Using the skill of perception checking will help prevent
    a.   negative self-fulfilling prophecies.
    b.   physiological noise.
    c.   inaccurate decoding of messages.
    d.   excessive feedback.
    e.   none of the above.
    Answer: c   **Type: M**   **Pages: 105–106**   **Synthesis**

71. Exaggerated beliefs associated with a perceptual categorizing system are
    a.   role constructs.
    b.   self-judgments.
    c.   white lies.
    d.   subcultural translations.
    e.   stereotypes.
    Answer: e   **Type: M**   **Page: 87**   **Knowledge**

72. John is in the market for a new car and hopes to buy a Toyota Scion. It seems everywhere he goes lately he sees a Scion on the road. What does this exemplify in the process of selecting stimuli?
    a.   repetitious stimuli
    b.   motives
    c.   change in stimulation
    d.   intense stimuli
    e.   organization
    Answer: b   **Type: M**   **Page: 85**   **Application**

73. When Mary meets Ted at a party, she asks him what he does for a living. This is an example of classifying people by
    a. appearance.
    b. psychological traits.
    c. membership.
    d. social role.
    e. interaction style.
    Answer: d   **Type: M**   **Page: 86**   **Application**

74. Laura knows her friend Mary Ellen is going through a difficult time so she doesn't mind that Mary Ellen is particularly quiet at dinner. This is an example of what stage in the perception process?
    a. selection.
    b. organization.
    c. redefinition.
    d. interpretation.
    e. none of the above.
    Answer: d   **Type: M**   **Page: 91**   **Application**

75. The process whereby people try to influence each other's perceptions and attempt to achieve a shared perspective is called
    a. negotiation.
    b. narration.
    c. differentiation.
    d. relationship building.
    e. organization.
    Answer: a   **Type: M**   **Page: 92**   **Knowledge**

76. While on vacation with her family in Germany, Abigail criticized how Germans drove on the Autobahn compared to American freeway driving. According to the text, Abigail's attitude is considered
    a. prejudice.
    b. ethnocentrism.
    c. ethnicity.
    d. punctuation.
    e. self-serving bias.
    Answer: b   **Type: M**   **Page: 97**   **Application**

77. All of the following are schemes by which we classify people except
    a. social roles.
    b. psychological traits.
    c. membership.
    d. interaction style.
    e. beliefs.
    Answer: e   **Type: M**   **Page: 86**   **Knowledge**

78. All of the following is true about stereotyping except
    a. a set of characteristics is ascribed to most members of a category.
    b. it affects interracial communication.
    c. it affects only personal relationships.
    d. it doesn't always occur because of bad intentions.
    e. it is a result of exaggerated generalizations.

    Answer: c   **Type: M**   **Pages: 87–89**   **Knowledge**

79. Donna complains to Jim that the volume on the TV is too loud; Jim claims he can't hear the TV if he turns it down. What type of perceptual influence does this example illustrate?
    a. psychological
    b. cultural
    c. gender
    d. social
    e. physiological

    Answer: e   **Type: M**   **Pages: 93–94**   **Application**

80. When Lynn got caught speeding, Amy said she should have been more careful; later when Amy got caught speeding, she denied she was driving too fast. This is an example of what tendency in perception?
    a. We are influenced by the obvious.
    b. The self-serving bias
    c. We pay attention to others' negative characteristics.
    d. The halo effect.
    e. We assume others are similar to us.

    Answer: b   **Type: M**   **Page: 103**   **Application**

Instructions for questions 81–85: Match each of the descriptions below with the term it best describes:
    a. punctuation
    b. interpretation
    c. empathy
    d. attribution
    e. androgynous behavior

81. You feel sadness when your friend tells you his cat died.

    Answer: c   **Type: Matching**   **Page: 109**   **Application**

82. You exhibit both sensitivity and strength when faced with a difficult decision.

    Answer: e   **Type: Matching**   **Page: 99**   **Application**

83. You say you're late because your partner is never ready on time; your partner says she takes her time getting ready because you're always late.

    Answer: a   **Type: Matching**   **Pages: 89–90**   **Application**

84. You think all children are hyperactive.

    Answer: d   **Type: Matching**   **Page: 103**   **Application**

85. You figure your friend's smile means she's happy.

    Answer: b   **Type: Matching**   **Pages: 90–91**   **Application**

INSTRUCTIONS for questions 86–90: Match each of the descriptions below with the term it best describes.
    a.   self-serving bias
    b.   stereotypting
    c.   sympathy
    d.   narrative
    e.   selection

86. You believe that most of the elderly are slow drivers.
    Answer: b   **Type: Matching**   **Page: 87**   **Application**

87. You notice car advertisements more when you need a new car.
    Answer: e   **Type: Matching**   **Page: 85**   **Application**

88. You tell your friend you're sorry that he was robbed.
    Answer: c   **Type: Matching**   **Page: 110**   **Application**

89. You claim your roommates are lazy when they don't clean up, but when you fail to clean, it's because of your many commitments.
    Answer: a   **Type: Matching**   **Page: 103**   **Application**

90. Your interaction with your coworkers creates a shared perspective of your boss.
    Answer: d   **Type: Matching**   **Page: 92**   **Application**

INSTRUCTIONS for questions 91–97: Match each of the perceptual schema examples below with constructs that describe it.
    a.   appearance
    b.   social roles
    c.   interaction style
    d.   psychological trait
    e.   membership

91. Jeri thinks Alicia is a typical lawyer.
    Answer: b   **Type: Matching**   **Pages: 99–100**   **Application**

92. Bertha did not want to associate with the girl wearing a ring in her nose.
    Answer: a   **Type: Matching**   **Pages: 85–86**   **Application**

93. Darin decided LuAnn was insecure when he heard her ask for help twice.
    Answer: d   **Type: Matching**   **Pages: 85–86**   **Application**

94. John responded to Lisa's comment sarcastically.
    Answer: c   **Type: Matching**   **Pages: 85–86**   **Application**

95. "That's just what a Republican would say," Mario thought.
    Answer: e   **Type: Matching**   **Pages: 85–86**   **Application**

96. At the party Jerry spent more time talking to the tall blonde than her dark-haired friend.
    Answer: a   **Type: Matching**   **Pages: 85–86**   **Application**

97. Alexandria thought John was friendly from the first time they met.
    Answer: c   **Type: Matching**   **Pages: 85–86**   **Application**

INSTRUCTIONS for questions 98–102: Match each of the descriptions below with the term it best describes.
    a.   punctuation
    b.   interpretation
    c.   stereotyping
    d.   organization
    e.   selection

98. A student decides her instructor is "mean" when he answered her question a bit abruptly in class.
    Answer: d   **Type: Matching**   **Page: 85–86**   **Application**

99. Your friend comes into the room and slams the door, so you assume he is angry with you.
    Answer: b   **Type: Matching**   **Pages: 90–91**   **Application**

100. As you listen to a classmate give a speech you notice her saying "you know" and "um" many times.
    Answer: e   **Type: Matching**   **Pages: 84–85**   **Application**

101. She says she's forced to tell him over and over to pick up his things because he never listens to her. He says he has to "tune her out" because she is always complaining about something.
    Answer: a   **Type: Matching**   **Pages: 89–90**   **Application**

102. You think all Japanese are hard workers after doing an internship in a Japanese company.
    Answer: c   **Type: Matching**   **Page: 87**   **Application**

103. Identify a situation from your recent experience in which you disagree with another person due to differing physiological environments. Show how these different environments led to the disagreement.
    Answer: **Type: E**   **Pages: 93–95**   **Synthesis**

104. Describe the four perceptual accuracies/inaccuracies identified by researchers in Chapter Three. What role has each played/not played in the formation of your perceptions of three people important to you?
    Answer: **Type: E**   **Pages: 103–105**   **Application**

105. Apply the Pillow Method to an interpersonal issue which has recently affected you. Describe your thoughts and feelings at each position on the pillow.
    Answer: **Type: E**   **Pages: 111–116**   **Synthesis**

106. Your text identified a variety of influences on perception. Name two of these categories of influence and apply them to the situation described below in terms of their effect on your interpretation of the event.
    The situation: Imagine you've been walking down the street with another friend. You both are aware that three individuals have been walking behind you for some time. As you turn into a restaurant and sit down, the other three enter and take a booth directly behind you and your friend.
    Answer: **Type: E**   **Pages: 93–101**   **Application**

107. Consider a stereotype you might hold, either positive or negative. Using information from the text, explain what led you to have this specific stereotype and how your behavior and communication has been affected by it.

Answer: **Type: E**   **Pages: 87–89**   **Analysis**

108. Choose one of the following social roles—gender or occupational—then explain how this area has influenced your perceptions. Use examples from your own life in your discussion.

Answer: **Type: E**   **Pages: 99–101**   **Application**

109. Using the following problem, apply the Pillow Method to viewing the issue. Identify each position and explain each position clearly in relation to the scenario.
Problem: You and a friend have talked about taking a trip to Europe after college graduation. While planning the trip during senior year, you discover that your friend is insisting on taking an organized tour while you have always dreamed of backpacking through Europe and staying at hostels.

Answer: **Type: E**   **Pages: 111–116**   **Synthesis**

The following essay questions work best as "take-home" exams because of the time necessary to effectively complete them.

110. Imagine yourself a member of the opposite sex. Describe all the events of a particular day from the vantage point of your "new" sex. What clothes would you want to wear? How would you greet your friends? How would you eat? How would you play? How would your perceptions of the world change? Be very specific and use concrete examples as well as vocabulary items from this chapter.

Answer: **Type: E**   **Page: 99–100**   **Evaluation**

111. Describe a subculture to which you belong. Give examples and explain several misunderstandings you have had with members of another subculture. What do these misunderstandings indicate about the way in which you view the world? Use terms and theory from text.

Answer: **Type: E**   **Pages: 97–99**   **Evaluation**

CHAPTER 4
EMOTIONS: THINKING, FEELING, AND COMMUNICATING

1. Generally speaking, people are more likely to share negative emotions rather than positive emotions.
   Answer: F   **Type: T**   **Page: 130**   **Knowledge**

2. Historically, people were discouraged from expressing the level of anger that is currently tolerated by contemporary society.
   Answer: F   **Type: T**   **Page: 130**   **Knowledge**

3. Social rules discourage too much expression of negative emotion, but there are really no social limits to expressing positive emotions.
   Answer: F   **Type: T**   **Page: 130**   **Knowledge**

4. Men are more likely than women are to reveal their strengths..
   Answer: T   **Type: T**   **Page: 129**   **Comprehension**

5. Research indicates that people from warmer climates are more emotionally expressive than people from cooler climates.
   Answer: T   **Type: T**   **Page: 126**   **Knowledge**

6. Your text argues that the complete and open expression of emotions is one key to positive relationships.
   Answer: F   **Type: T**   **Page: 132**   **Comprehension**

7. Over-expression of emotion may create physiological ailments as much as under-expression of emotion.
   Answer: T   **Type: T**   **Page: 132**   **Knowledge**

8. When sharing your feelings, it's not necessary to accept responsibility for them because so often others cause them.
   Answer: F   **Type: T**   **Pages: 136, 138**   **Knowledge**

9. Fortunately, for people who want to hide their emotions, all the physical changes that accompany emotions are internal.
   Answer: F   **Type: T**   **Page: 122**   **Knowledge**

10. Some people fail to communicate their emotions clearly because they understate or downplay them.
    Answer: T   **Type: T**   **Page: 135**   **Knowledge**

11. Since collectivist cultures pay more attention to nonverbal behaviors, they are better at expressing both positive and negative emotions.
    Answer: F   **Type: T**   **Page: 126**   **Knowledge**

12. An event that generates facilitative self-talk for one person might stimulate debilitative thinking for someone else.
    Answer: T   **Type: T**   **Page: 143**   **Comprehension**

13. The mind has little influence on our emotional states.
    Answer: F   **Type: T**   **Page: 123**   **Comprehension**

14. The approach to handling emotions described in your text involves talking yourself out of feeling unnecessarily bad.
    Answer: T   **Type: T**   **Page: 161**   **Knowledge**

15. It is important to express all your emotions to all the important people in your life as soon as you experience those emotions.
    Answer: F   **Type: T**   **Page: 150**   **Knowledge**

16. Your text advises that when you feel a certain way, you should act on that feeling immediately.
    Answer: F   **Type: T**   **Page: 136**   **Knowledge**

17. All emotions are caused by self-talk.
    Answer: F   **Type: T**   **Pages: 141–142**   **Comprehension**

18. People will respect and like you more if you go out of your way to please them.
    Answer: F   **Type: T**   **Page: 145**   **Comprehension**

19. One of the primary reasons we don't express emotions is that we don't recognize when they occur.
    Answer: T   **Type: T**   **Page: 133**   **Comprehension**

20. Anger can be either a facilitative or debilitative emotion.
    Answer: T   **Type: T**   **Pages: 140–141**   **Comprehension**

21. Feelings are often recognized by nonverbal changes, such as blushing.
    Answer: T   **Type: T**   **Page:122**   **Knowledge**

22. It is always clear what emotion someone is experiencing if you closely observe his nonverbal behavior.
    Answer: F   **Type: T**   **Page: 122**   **Knowledge**

23. Members of collectivistic cultures discourage expression of negative emotions that might upset relationships in the group.
    Answer: T   **Type: T**   **Page: 126**   **Knowledge**

24. Even across cultures, men tend to say "I love you" more than women.
    Answer: F   **Type: T**   **Page: 129**   **Knowledge**

25. Social isolation and depression are problems that can result from the inability to constructively talk about emotions.
    Answer: T   **Type: T**   **Page: 124**   **Knowledge**

26. Academic background is the best predictor of the ability to detect and interpret emotional expressions.
    Answer: F   **Type: T**   **Page: 129**   **Knowledge**

27. Your personality makes little difference in the way you experience and communicate emotions.
    Answer: F   **Type: T**   **Page: 125**   **Knowledge**

28. When we experience mixed emotions, we generally communicate only one feeling—usually the most positive one.
   Answer: F   **Type: T**   **Page: 136**   **Knowledge**

29. Your text suggests that to feel better you should first talk about how you feel and then act on that feeling.
   Answer: F   **Type: T**   **Page: 133**   **Comprehension**

30. Expanding your emotional vocabulary is one suggestion your text makes for expressing your emotions.
   Answer: T   **Type: T**   **Page: 134**   **Knowledge**

31. According to cognitive psychologists, it is not events that cause people to feel bad, but rather the beliefs they hold about the events.
   Answer: T   **Type: T**   **Page: 142**   **Knowledge**

32. It rarely matters what channel to use when expressing an emotion (phone, e-mail, etc.) as long as you express yourself clearly and honestly.
   Answer: F   **Type: T**   **Page: 138**   **Comprehension**

33. One difference between facilitative emotions and debilitative emotions is whether you feel the emotion for a short or long period of time.
   Answer: T   **Type: T**   **Page: 141**   **Knowledge**

34. The fallacy of causation is based on the irrational belief that emotions are caused by others rather than by one's own self-talk.
   Answer: T   **Type: T**   **Page: 147**   **Knowledge**

35. Researchers have found that college students who can pinpoint the negative emotions they experience, such as anger, also have the best strategies for managing their emotions.
   Answer: T   **Type: T**   **Page: 133**   **Knowledge**

36. The "amygdale" refers to
   a. the threat alarm system in the brain.
   b. a type of emotional contagion.
   c. a reservoir of emotional memories
   d. nonverbal reactions expressed on the face.
   e. none of the above.
   Answer: a   **Type: M**   **Page: 141**   **Knowledge**

37. The "Looking at Diversity" reading about the ways Zuni and Anglo cultures deal with emotion expression indicates that
   a. Anglos don't show love as much as Zunis.
   b. Zunis emphasize listening over talking.
   c. Zunis encourage their children to freely express intense emotions.
   d. Zunis feel emotions less intensely than Anglos.
   e. all of the above were mentioned by the reading.
   Answer: b   **Type: M**   **Page: 128**   **Comprehension**

38. Social scientists generally agree that there are four components to the phenomena we label as "feelings." They are:
    a. physiological changes, nonverbal reactions, cognitive interpretations, and verbal expression.
    b. physical changes, mental recognition, and verbal description.
    c. sensing, organizing, interpreting, and encoding.
    d. verbal and nonverbal manifestations, physical depression, and catharsis.
    e. stimulus, proprioception, emotional contagion and response.
    Answer: a   **Type: M**   **Pages: 122–124**   **Comprehension**

39. Emotions that we experience are a result of
    a. our own temperaments.
    b. beliefs we hold.
    c. self-talk.
    d. emotional memories.
    e. all of the above.
    Answer: b   **Type: M**   **Page: 142**   **Comprehension**

40. Your text tells you that you should
    a. express all your emotions to your friends.
    b. try to recognize your emotions.
    c. be glad you have debilitative emotions.
    d. express only positive emotions.
    e. stop being so emotional.
    Answer: b   **Type: M**   **Page: 133**   **Comprehension**

41. According to your text, one reason people don't express feelings is
    a. they lack awareness of their emotions.
    b. it's a waste of time.
    c. interpretations are easier to understand.
    d. they are rarely asked to do so.
    e. many people rarely have feelings.
    Answer: a   **Type: M**   **Page: 133**   **Comprehension**

42. Research described in this chapter found that when subjects were coached to move their facial muscles in ways that appeared afraid, angry, disgusted, amused, sad, etc., the subjects responded
    a. as if they themselves were having these feelings.
    b. by showing the opposite feeling.
    c. by showing more intense feelings than the volunteers.
    d. with no emotion at all.
    e. with pity for the volunteers.
    Answer: a   **Type: M**   **Page: 123**   **Comprehension**

43. Many of our debilitative feelings come from
    a. our genetic make-up .
    b. our emotional memory .
    c. the beliefs we hold about events .
    d. a and c .
    e. All of the above are sources of debilitative feelings.
    Answer: e   **Type: M**   **Pages: 141–142**   **Knowledge**

44. Which of the following is true of debilitative feelings?
    a. They often last a long time.
    b. They keep you from functioning effectively.
    c. They are intense.
    d. They are a product of your beliefs.
    e. All of the above are true of debilitative feelings.
    Answer: e   **Type: M**   **Pages: 140–142**   **Comprehension**

45. People who subscribe to the fallacy of perfection believe
    a. everyone is perfect except them.
    b. there's no point in striving for perfection since it is unattainable.
    c. a worthwhile communicator should be able to handle any situation with complete confidence and skill.
    d. perfection requires much practice.
    e. only professors are perfect.
    Answer: c   **Type: M**   **Page: 144**   **Knowledge**

46. Which of the following is an example of falling for the fallacy of causation?
    a. "People at parties make me nervous."
    b. "If I ask her/him for a date the answer will probably be no."
    c. "I'm no good at anything!"
    d. "Everybody is against me."
    e. "I should be a better person."
    Answer: a   **Type: M**   **Page: 147**   **Application**

47. Which of the following does the text offer as a guideline for expressing emotions?
    a. The sooner a feeling is shared, the better.
    b. Try to avoid sharing negative feelings whenever possible.
    c. Share multiple feelings when appropriate.
    d. Let others know that they have caused you to feel a certain way.
    e. Try to avoid getting too emotional.
    Answer: c   **Type: M**   **Page: 135**   **Application**

48. All of the following are parts of the procedure for dealing with debilitative feelings except:
    a. Record your self-talk.
    b. Monitor your emotional reactions.
    c. Dispute your irrational beliefs.
    d. Identify the activating event.
    e. Analyze your motives.
    Answer: e   **Type: M**   **Pages: 149–150**   **Comprehension**

49. "I can't think of anything!" is an example of subscribing to the fallacy of
    a. overgeneralization.
    b. perfection.
    c. shoulds.
    d. causation.
    e. helplessness.
    Answer: a   **Type: M**   **Page: 146–147**   **Application**

50. "My roommate ought to be more understanding." This quote is an example of the fallacy of
   a. shoulds.
   b. causation.
   c. approval.
   d. perfection.
   e. helplessness.

   Answer: a   **Type: M**   **Page: 146**   **Application**

51. Which of the following is the best advice for expressing your emotions ?
   a. Accept responsibility for your own feelings.
   b. Express your feelings as soon as they occur.
   c. Recognize that feeling and acting out the feeling are the same.
   d. Express only primary feelings.
   e. Tell yourself you shouldn't feel bad.

   Answer: a   **Type: M**   **Page: 136**   **Evaluation**

52. According to your text, women are more likely than men to express all of the following emotions except their own
   a. vulnerability.
   b. loneliness.
   c. strength.
   d. fear.
   e. sadness.

   Answer: c   **Type: M**   **Page: 129**   **Comprehension**

53. When you believe that a worthwhile communicator should be able to handle every situation with complete confidence and skill, you are falling for the fallacy of
   a. perfection.
   b. causation.
   c. approval.
   d. shoulds.
   e. overgeneralization.

   Answer: a   **Type: M**   **Page: 144**   **Knowledge**

54. When you think it is not just desirable but vital to get the acceptance of virtually every person, you are falling for the fallacy of
   a. perfection.
   b. causation.
   c. approval.
   d. shoulds.
   e. overgeneralization.

   Answer: c   **Type: M**   **Page: 145**   **Knowledge**

55. When you believe that others cause your emotions rather than your own self-talk, you are falling for the fallacy of
    a. perfection.
    b. causation.
    c. approval.
    d. shoulds.
    e. overgeneralization.

    Answer: b   **Type: M**   **Page: 147**   **Knowledge**

56. When you believe that satisfaction in life is determined by forces beyond your control, you are falling for the fallacy of
    a. causation.
    b. helplessness.
    c. catastrophic expectations.
    d. approval.
    e. shoulds.

    Answer: b   **Type: M**   **Page: 147**   **Knowledge**

57. According to your text, the first step in minimizing your debilitative emotions is to
    a. monitor your emotional reactions.
    b. note the activating event.
    c. record your self-talk.
    d. dispute your irrational beliefs.
    e. confront the person who caused them.

    Answer: a   **Type: M**   **Page: 149**   **Knowledge**

58. Which of the following is an example of self-talk?
    a. I shouldn't have pushed so hard.
    b. I'll make her neurotic.
    c. I'll never be able to make her see my side.
    d. I can't get anyone to listen to me.
    e. All of the above might be examples of self-talk.

    Answer: e   **Type: M**   **Pages: 142–143**   **Application**

59. Frowning, sweating, and a sudden change in vocal pitch are all emotional changes classified as
    a. proprioceptive stimuli.
    b. nonverbal reactions.
    c. cognitive interpretations.
    d. physio-emotional changes.
    e. all of the above.

    Answer: b   **Type: M**   **Pages: 122**   **Knowledge**

60. An empty feeling in the pit of your stomach, tense muscles, and headaches are examples of the emotional component labeled
    a. nonverbal reactions.
    b. cognitive interpretations.
    c. physiological changes.
    d. rational-emotive therapy.
    e. environment.

    Answer: c   **Type: M**   **Page: 123**   **Comprehension**

61. Your text says we don't express our emotions very well or very frequently because
    a.   of social rules and roles.
    b.   others put us down.
    c.   we recognize so many emotions.
    d.   self-disclosure is already high enough.
    e.   of inadequate self-concepts.
    Answer: a   **Type: M**   **Pages: 130**   **Comprehension**

62. Which of the following is a better way of expressing emotion in the statement: "You're making me nervous"?
    a.   Say "I feel nervous when you drive over the speed limit."
    b.   Say "Your fast driving is not making me feel very safe."
    c.   Say "I feel like taking the keys."
    d.   All of the above could improve the statement.
    e.   No improvement is needed.
    Answer: a   **Type: M**   **Pages: 136, 138**   **Evaluation**

63. Facilitative feelings
    a.   are emotional counterfeits.
    b.   happen only when you feel good.
    c.   keep us from communicating effectively.
    d.   contribute to effective functioning.
    e.   are more common in other cultures.
    Answer: d   **Type: M**   **Page: 140**   **Comprehension**

64. Debilitative emotions
    a.   are emotional counterfeits.
    b.   happen only when you feel bad.
    c.   detract from effective functioning.
    d.   contribute to effective functioning.
    e.   none of the above
    Answer: c   **Type: M**   **Page: 140**   **Comprehension**

65. Two things that distinguish facilitative feelings from debilitative ones are
    a.   emotions and behavior.
    b.   interpretation and intention.
    c.   longevity and interpretation.
    d.   intention and intensity.
    e.   intensity and duration.
    Answer: e   **Type: M**   **Pages: 140–141**   **Knowledge**

66. Which of the following is an example of the fallacy of causation?
    a.   "My boss makes me so nervous that I can't do a good job."
    b.   "I'd better visit my parents though I'm really busy today."
    c.   "Bruce is making me crazy with his excuses."
    d.   both a and b above
    e.   a, b, and c above
    Answer: e   **Type: M**   **Page: 147**   **Application**

67. Self-talk
    a. can be facilitative or debilitative.
    b. can determine how you feel .
    c. includes identifying an event, your thought, and feeling.
    d. allows you to have control over how you feel.
    e. All of the above

Answer: e   **Type: M**   **Pages: 142–143**   **Comprehension**

68. The statement "Bob never has a good word to say about anyone" is an example of the fallacy of
    a. shoulds.
    b. approval.
    c. overgeneralization.
    d. causation.
    e. all of the above.

Answer: c   **Type: M**   **Pages: 146–147**   **Application**

69. Subscribing to the fallacy of catastrophic expectations can lead to
    a. self-fulfilling prophecies.
    b. erroneous perception checking.
    c. reflected appraisals.
    d. physiological noise.
    e. both c and d above.

Answer: a   **Type: M**   **Pages: 58, 148**   **Synthesis**

70. "I feel like quitting school" is an example of
    a. a feeling statement.
    b. an emotionally counterfeit statement.
    c. an emotional intention.
    d. a contextual emotion.
    e. a self-fulfilling prophecy.

Answer: b   **Type: M**   **Page: 134**   **Application**

71. Revealing multiple feelings means
    a. mixing up all the feelings you have.
    b. expressing more than one feeling.
    c. sharing what you feel and what your partner feels, too.
    d. all of the above.
    e. none of the above.

Answer: b   **Type: M**   **Pages: 135–136**   **Comprehension**

72. The best predictor of being able to detect and interpret emotional expressions is
    a. foreign travel
    b. academic background
    c. cultural similarity
    d. biological sex
    e. none of the above

Answer: d   **Type: M**   **Page: 129**   **Knowledge**

73. Gene is in a great mood when he calls Laura. However, she is in a funk from a stressful day at work. After a brief chat Gene hangs up the phone feeling discouraged. This is an example of
   a.   emotional recognition.
   b.   emotional memory.
   c.   emotional contagion.
   d.   emotional detachment.
   e.   none of the above.

   Answer: c   **Type: M**   **Page: 131**   **Application**

74. Which of the following is not characteristic of our emotions?
   a.   The mind plays an important role in determining emotional states.
   b.   Sometimes nonverbal behavior can cause an emotional state.
   c.   Bodily changes may occur, such as a churning stomach, as a result of experiencing an emotion.
   d.   Most people don't overstate the strength of their feelings.
   e.   None of the above

   Answer: d   **Type: M**   **Pages: 122–124**   **Comprehension**

75. Which of the following is not true about the effect of gender on emotions?
   a.   Women are more attuned to emotions than men, both within and across cultures.
   b.   Men are more likely to express feelings with men than with women.
   c.   Women are more likely to express both positive emotions and feelings of vulnerability than men.
   d.   Men are more likely to express their strengths than women.
   e.   All of the above are true about the effect of gender on emotions.

   Answer: b   **Type: M**   **Page: 129**   **Knowledge**

76. High affection communicators are
   a.   in better mental health.
   b.   less stressed.
   c.   happier.
   d.   more likely to be in satisfying romantic relationships.
   e.   all of the above.

   Answer: e   **Type: M**   **Page: 133**   **Knowledge**

77. Each of the following is an example of an emotionally counterfeit statement except
   a.   I feel like going to a movie.
   b.   I want to go to a play since I'm bored.
   c.   I feel we've been seeing too much of each other and want to break-up.
   d.   I feel that you are driving too fast.
   e.   All are emotionally counterfeit statements.

   Answer: b   **Type: M**   **Page: 134**   **Application**

78. A particularly powerful form of debilitative self-talk is
   a.   deliberation.
   b.   rumination.
   c.   obsessing.
   d.   emotional memorizing.
   e.   none of the above.

   Answer: b   **Type: M**   **Page: 143**   **Knowledge**

INSTRUCTIONS for questions 79–91: Match each of the statements below with the fallacy it most clearly represents.

   a.   fallacy of causation
   b.   fallacy of shoulds
   c.   fallacy of overgeneralization
   d.   fallacy of perfection
   e.   fallacy of helplessness

79. "Those interviewers made me so nervous."
       Answer: a   **Type: Matching**   **Page: 147**   Application

80. "You ought to keep in touch more."
       Answer: b   **Type: Matching**   **Page: 146**   Application

81. "I know he'll be crushed if I don't go out with him."
       Answer: a   **Type: Matching**   **Page: 147**   Application

82. "You never tell me how you feel."
       Answer: c   **Type: Matching**   **Pages: 146–147**   Application

83. "I lost my temper with Mac last night. I've had interpersonal communication; I know better."
       Answer: d   **Type: Matching**   **Page: 144**   Application

84. "I can't tell my boyfriend his smoking upsets me; he might break up with me.
       Answer: e   **Type: Matching**   **Pages: 147–148**   Application

85. "You're making me angry."
       Answer: a   **Type: Matching**   **Page: 147**   Application

86. "You should be more patient."
       Answer: b   **Type: Matching**   **Page: 146**   Application

87. "I'm such an idiot; I forgot my sister's birthday."
       Answer: c   **Type: Matching**   **Pages: 146–147**   Application

88. "I've always been quiet in class and I don't see myself changing now."
       Answer: e   **Type: Matching**   **Pages: 147–148**   Application

89. "There is nothing good or bad but thinking makes it so." Apply this Shakespeare quote to communication in one of your relationships. Give specific examples and describe details.
       Answer: **Type: E**   **Pages: 123–124,140–143**   Application

90. Give examples of cultural, gender, and social influences on emotional expression from your own life.
       Answer: **Type: E**   **Pages: 126–130**   Application

91. "When emotions begin to be shared, a relationship begins to deepen." How does this come about? Give two examples from your own experience that support this statement.
       Answer: **Type: E**   **Pages: 124–125**   **Analysis**

92. Identify at least three fallacies from the text you most commonly accept. Explain each fallacy and explain the potential harm each may cause if you fail to dispute it.
    Answer: **Type: E**   **Pages: 144–149**   **Analysis**

93. Explain the relationship between interpersonal perception as described in Chapter Three and the rational-emotive approach to emotions in Chapter Four.
    Answer: **Type: E**   **Pages: Ch 3 and 142–143**   **Synthesis**

94. Explain the concept of self-talk and how it can affect our emotions. Describe the self-talk process and provide an example from your own life where it has influenced your feelings.
    Answer: **Type: E**   **Pages: 142–143**   **Application**

95. Define and explain debilitative emotions, as well as the differences between them and facilitative emotions. Also, describe the process by which one can minimize the irrational thinking that can lead to debilitative emotions.
    Answer   **Type: E**   **Pages: 140–142, 149–150**   **Analysis**

The following essay question works best as a " take-home" exam because of the time necessary to effectively complete it.

96. What are the guidelines suggested in your text for expressing feelings? Describe how you can apply these guidelines to your life. Give specific examples.
    Answer: **Type: E**   **Pages: 132–138**   **Application**

CHAPTER 5
LANGUAGE: BARRIER AND BRIDGE

1. To be effective, an "I" statement must include all four elements, in the order described in your textbook.
    Answer: F   **Type: T**   **Page: 177**   **Knowledge**

2. "It's A Girl Thing For Women," suggests that the word "girl" is most often viewed by women as a derogatory term.
    Answer: F   **Type: T**   **Page: 167**   **Comprehension**

3. "The Many Meanings of 'I Love You'" in this chapter points out how several different interpretations of the phrase 'I love you' may be misinterpreted due to semantic rules.
    Answer: T   **Type: T**   **Page: 160**   **Comprehension**

4. Equivocal words are words that can be interpreted in more than one way.
    Answer: T   **Type: T**   **Page: 159**   **Knowledge**

5. Emotive words are words that sound as if they're describing something, but are really announcing the speaker's attitude toward it.
    Answer: T   **Type: T**   **Page: 174**   **Knowledge**

6. Linguistic relativism is a notion that holds that our cultural worldview is shaped and reflected by the language spoken by its members.
    Answer: T   **Type: T**   **Page: 188**   **Knowledge**

7. "I'm rather upset" is more powerful language than "I'm upset."
    Answer: F   **Type: T**   **Pages: 171–172**   **Comprehension**

8. A perfectly worded "I" statement delivered with total sincerity will ensure that the other person will not get defensive.
    Answer: F   **Type: T**   **Page: 178**   **Knowledge**

9. American Sign Language is considered a literal system of communication rather than symbolic. .
    Answer: F   **Type: T**   **Page: 158**   **Knowledge**

10. Syntactic rules govern the grammatical aspects of a language.
    Answer: T   **Type: T**   **Page: 162**   **Knowledge**

11. Relative words gain their meaning from comparison.
    Answer: T   **Type: T**   **Page: 159**   **Knowledge**

12. The U.S.   is a high-context language culture.
    Answer: F   **Type: T**   **Page: 185**   **Comprehension**

13. High-level abstractions can be useful as verbal shorthand between two people who know each other well.
    Answer: T   **Type: T**   **Page: 161**   **Knowledge**

14. All human languages are symbolic in nature.
   Answer: T   **Type: T**   **Pages: 157–158**   **Knowledge**

15. Much of the awkwardness that comes with first using "I" language is due to its unfamiliarity.
   Answer: T   **Type: T**   **Page: 178**   **Knowledge**

16. Inferential statements are conclusions arrived at from an interpretation of evidence.
   Answer: T   **Type: T**   **Page: 173**   **Comprehension**

17. Meanings are best found by studying the words people use, not by observing how people use them.
   Answer: F   **Type: T**   **Page: 159**   **Comprehension**

18. A formal language culture will have different vocabularies for different sexes, levels of social status, or degrees of intimacy.
   Answer: T   **Type: T**   **Page: 187**   **Comprehension**

19. "No" is so clear and short that it is one of the few words that is never misinterpreted.
   Answer: F   **Type: T**   **Page: 185**   **Analysis**

20. Asking questions may be a linguistic way to avoid making a declaration.
   Answer: T   **Type: T**   **Page: 176**   **Comprehension**

21. Statements that contain the word "is" ("Kyle is an active guy") may lead to the assumption that people are unchanging.
   Answer: T   **Type: T**   **Page: 161**   **Knowledge**

22. Women use more indirect and elaborate ways of talking than men do.
   Answer: T   **Type: T**   **Page: 183**   **Knowledge**

23. Research shows that linguistic differences are more often a function of gender roles than they are of biological sex.
   Answer: T   **Type: T**   **Page: 184**   **Comprehension**

24. Men discuss with other men the same conversation topics that women discuss with other women.
   Answer: F   **Type: T**   **Page: 181**   **Knowledge**

25. Your text confirms the stereotype that women are more likely to talk about feelings and relationships than men are.
   Answer: T   **Type: T**   **Page: 181**   **Knowledge**

26. Men and women report using language for different purposes.
   Answer: T   **Type: T**   **Pages: 181–182**   **Knowledge**

27. The process of static evaluation implies that people or things are unchanging.
   Answer: T   **Type: T**   **Page: 161**   **Knowledge**

28. Syntactic misunderstandings arise when people assign different meanings to the same words.
   Answer: F   **Type: T**   **Page: 159**   **Knowledge**

29. Low abstract language can lead to blanket judgments and stereotyping.
   Answer: F   **Type: T**   **Page: 161**   **Knowledge**

30. Communication researchers call the process of adapting one's speech style to match that of others convergence.
   Answer: T   **Type: T**   **Page: 170**   **Knowledge**

31. There are never times when equivocal language can be useful.
   Answer: F   **Type: T**   **Page: 159**   **Knowledge**

32. Pragmatic rules are stated rules that help us make sense of another's messages.
   Answer: F   **Type: T**   **Page: 166**   **Knowledge**

33. You rarely find convergence in cyberspace communication.
   Answer: F   **Type: T**   **Page: 171**   **Comprehension**

34. There are some occasions when less powerful forms of speech can enhance a speaker's effectiveness.
   Answer: T   **Type: T**   **Page: 172**   **Knowledge**

35. Researchers have found that "I/we" combinations have a good chance of being received favorably.
   Answer: T   **Type: T**   **Page: 180**   **Knowledge**

36. Low-context cultures use language to maintain social harmony.
   Answer: F   **Type: T**   **Page: 185**   **Knowledge**

37. One way in which language styles vary across cultures is whether they are elaborate or succinct.
   Answer: T   **Type: T**   **Page: 186**   **Knowledge**

38. After years of research, it has been concluded that names have little affect on how others think of us and the way we act.
   Answer: F   **Type: T**   **Page: 168**   **Knowledge**

39. Problems can arise when we label our opinions as facts.
   Answer: T   **Type: T**   **Page: 173**   **Comprehension**

40. "I" language offers a more accurate and less provocative way to express a complaint.
   Answer: T   **Type: T**   **Page: 177**   **Knowledge**

41. Communication scholars use the term "cooperation" to describe the way conversation operates when everyone involved uses the same set of pragmatic rules.
   Answer: F   **Type: T**   **Page: 166**   **Knowledge**

42. Speech can build and demonstrate solidarity with others.
   Answer: T   **Type: T**   **Page: 170**   **Knowledge**

43. Language can shape our perceptions of the world.
   Answer: T   **Type: T**   **Page: 168**   **Knowledge**

44. When a speaker uses powerful speech pattern he/she
    a. tends to be received more positively in culture like Mexico.
    b. stresses relational goals over content goals.
    c. may undermine relational goals to accomplish short term goals.
    d. will use very polite phrases and intensifiers.
    e. will be successful in all communication encounters.
    Answer: c   **Type: M**   **Page: 172**   **Knowledge**

45. "We" language
    a. may accomplish the goals of "I" language and sound less egotistical.
    b. should be avoided when expressing personal feelings and thoughts.
    c. can signal closeness and cohesiveness with others.
    d. can offend another person in some circumstances.
    e. All of these choices are correct
    Answer: e   **Type: M**   **Pages: 178–180**   **Knowledge**

46. "It's A 'Girl' Thing for Women" in Chapter Five illustrates
    a. that who uses the term "girl" determines the reaction to it.
    b. the use of "girl" is a sexist term.
    c. that "no" is more clear to women than to girls.
    d. how inexpressive the term "girl" is.
    e. how feminists have overreacted and banned the use of the term "girl."
    Answer: a   **Type: M**   **Page: 167**   **Comprehension**

47. The Sapir-Whorf hypothesis is the best known declaration of
    a. convergence.
    b. linguistic relativism.
    c. identity.
    d. emotive theory.
    e. pragmatism.
    Answer: b   **Type: M**   **Page: 189**   **Synthesis**

48. In a low-context language culture, you will notice
    a. indirect expression of opinions.
    b. use of silence admired.
    c. less reliance on explicit verbal messages.
    d. self-expression valued.
    e. ambiguity admired.
    Answer: d   **Type: M**   **Page: 185**   **Comprehension**

49. Succinctness in language is most extreme in cultures where
    a. silence is valued.
    b. the language system is limited.
    c. more than one language is spoken.
    d. verbal fluency is admired.
    e. the use of equivocation is high.
    Answer: a   **Type: M**   **Page: 186**   **Knowledge**

50. All of the following statements about gender and language are true except:
    a. Men's speech is more direct and task-oriented.
    b. Women's speech is more indirect and elaborate.
    c. Female speech often contains statements of sympathy and empathy.
    d. Women interrupt men more in mixed-sex conversations.
    e. Women are more likely to use more intensive adverbs than men.
    Answer: d   **Type: M**   **Pages: 181–182**   **Synthesis**

51. When we study semantic rules, we learn that
    a. words mean a lot in and of themselves.
    b. understanding occurs as a result of users agreeing on the same meanings for words.
    c. words typically can be interpreted in only one way.
    d. meanings rest more in words than in the people who use them.
    e. All of these choices are correct are true about semantic rules.
    Answer: b   **Type: M**   **Page: 159**   **Comprehension**

52. In cultures that stress formality in language,
    a. using correct grammar is most important.
    b. language use defines social position.
    c. the people talk less.
    d. there are fewer real friendships.
    e. the people are too stiff to really communicate.
    Answer: b   **Type: M**   **Page: 187**   **Comprehension**

53. Equivocal words
    a. have more than one commonly accepted definition.
    b. are low-level abstractions.
    c. mean the same to all people and are thus redundant.
    d. have meanings one person can guess at but another can't.
    e. have no known nonverbal signals to accompany them.
    Answer: a   **Type: M**   **Page: 159**   **Knowledge**

54. Which of the following is the least abstract definition of a successful college experience?
    a. a better understanding of Western civilization
    b. completion of the requirements listed on page 24 of the college catalog with a grade-point average of 2.0 or higher
    c. the ability to express oneself clearly, understand principles of the arts and sciences, and have some expertise in a chosen field of study
    d. both intellectual and social adjustment
    e. the ability to contribute to society
    Answer: b   **Type: M**   **Page: 161**   **Analysis**

55. A speaker's willingness to take responsibility for his/her thoughts or feelings can be indicated by the use of
    a. singular terms.
    b. "I" language.
    c. "you" language.
    d. consequence terms.
    e. euphemisms.
    Answer: b   **Type: M**   **Page: 176**   **Analysis**

56. "People from the East Coast are rude." Which of the following abstraction problems is illustrated by this statement?
    a. stereotyping
    b. confusing others
    c. confusing yourself
    d. being too frank
    e. bicoastalism
    Answer: a   **Type: M**   **Page: 161**   **Application**

57. Which of the following is a way to avoid the abstraction in the statement "I've got to be a better student"?
    a. "I'm going to spend two hours a day studying."
    b. "I'm going to try harder."
    c. "I'm going to get some help from some places on campus."
    d. "My mother and father will be happier if I'm a better student."
    e. "Instructors like students who try hard."
    Answer: a   **Type: M**   **Page: 161**   **Evaluation**

58. A behavioral description should include
    a. who is involved.
    b. in what circumstances the behavior occurs.
    c. the specific behaviors.
    d. All of these choices are correct.
    e. None of these choices are correct.
    Answer: d   **Type: M**   **Page: 177**   **Comprehension**

59. If I say "here the drink bring," I have violated a(n) _____ rule of our language.
    a. initial
    b. syntactic
    c. median
    d. semantic
    e. final
    Answer: b   **Type: M**   **Pages: 162–163**   **Knowledge**

60. Syntactic rules of language govern
    a. the grammar of a language.
    b. the ways in which speakers respond to symbols.
    c. the words that become slang.
    d. the creation of new tactics.
    e. the way that semanticists create meaning.
    Answer: a   **Type: M**   **Page: 162**   **Knowledge**

61. Making an inference is a reasonable thing to do relationally as long as
    a. you make a number of them.
    b. you wait for the other to infer also.
    c. the other person understands you.
    d. you identify the inference to the other person.
    e. you first describe the fact that led to the inference.
    Answer: e   **Type: M**   **Page: 173**   **Synthesis**

62. Which of the following statements is a fact?
    a. "It's clear you shouldn't have said that."
    b. "Fact number one: you said a dumb thing."
    c. "It's a fact that playing mind games always backfires."
    d. "I heard you say you weren't interested."
    e. "You should have thought about the result of saying you weren't interested before you opened
        your mouth."
    Answer: d   **Type: M**   **Page: 173**   **Knowledge**

63. If you take an "easy" class your friend recommended and find it "hard," you have had semantic
    problems due to
    a. euphemistic language.
    b. relative words.
    c. equivocal words.
    d. fiction terms.
    e. semantic distracters.
    Answer: b   **Type: M**   **Pages: 159–160**   **Knowledge**

64. Convergent speech patterns
    a. demonstrate superiority over others.
    b. express power and a sense of formality.
    c. demonstrate affiliation with one another.
    d. always utilize "I" statements instead of "you" statements.
    e. None of these choices are correct.
    Answer: c   **Type: M**   **Page: 170**   **Knowledge**

65. A friend told you there was a "good chance" that he would come to your party. When he didn't
    show up you were upset. The semantic problem you experienced was due to
    a. emotive language.
    b. relative language .
    c. equivocal words.
    d. euphemisms.
    e. semantic distracters.
    Answer: b   **Type: M**   **Pages: 159–160**   **Application**

66. A culture is unavoidably shaped and reflected by the language its members speak. This concept is
    a. high-context culture.
    b. low-context culture.
    c. cultural anthropology.
    d. cognitive determinism.
    e. linguistic relativism.
    Answer: e   **Type: M**   **Page: 188**   **Comprehension**

67. "Frank is lazy" is an example of which semantic problem?
    a. equivocation .
    b. relative language .
    c. abstraction
    d. static evaluation.
    e. none of the above.
    Answer: d   **Type: M**   **Page: 161**   **Application**

68. You think Erin is "arrogant." Your friend thinks she has a lot of "self-confidence." An argument over who is right would revolve around
    a. syntactic rules.
    b. relative terms.
    c. emotive language.
    d. sequential placement.
    e. linguistic determinism.
    Answer: c   **Type: M**   **Page: 174**   **Evaluation**

69. Misunderstandings that revolve around equivocal and relative language can all be clarified by
    a. clearer punctuation of perceptual events.
    b. more interpersonal and less impersonal communication.
    c. replacing abstract terms with concrete ones.
    d. static definitions.
    e. sequential placement.
    Answer: c   **Type: M**   **Pages: 159–162**   **Synthesis**

70. You tell a friend "I wish you'd be direct instead of hinting around," but your friend responds by denying that she/he hints. One way to help resolve the issue is to
    a. describe the hinting according to the dictionary.
    b. give a behavioral description of how your mother hints so your friend gets the idea.
    c. specifically describe the friend's hinting when it occurs.
    d. describe all at once the many times that the troublesome behavior occurs.
    e. None of these choices are correct will help resolve the issue.
    Answer: c   **Type: M**   **Pages: 161–162**   **Evaluation**

71. How could you increase the power of the statement "I, uh, think I'd be a little happier if you could make it on time. Okay?"?
    a. Revise the sequential placement.
    b. Use perception checking.
    c. Use more disclaimers.
    d. Add a tag question.
    e. None of the above increases the power of the statement.
    Answer: e   **Type: M**   **Pages: 171–172**   **Evaluation**

72. Which element of an "I" statement does this phrase represent? "I am having a really hard time concentrating when the TV volume is so loud."
    a. a description of the other person's behavior.
    b. a description of the speaker's feelings.
    c. the consequences of the other person's behavior.
    d. the speaker's interpretation of the other's behavior.
    e. None of these choices are correct, this is a "You" statement.
    Answer: c   **Type: M**   **Page: 177**   **Application**

73. Which element is not included in this "I" language statement? "When you hung up without saying where we'd meet, I felt confused and so I went to the wrong place."
    a. It doesn't describe the other person's behavior.
    b. It doesn't describe the speaker's feelings.
    c. It doesn't describe the consequences the other's behavior has for the speaker.
    d. It doesn't describe the speaker's interpretation of the behavior.
    e. This "I" language statement is fine just the way it is.
    Answer: d   **Type: M**   **Page: 177**   **Analysis**

74. Communication researchers call the process of adapting one's speech style to match that of others
    a. identity.
    b. convergence.
    c. divergence.
    d. semanticism.
    e. agreement.
    Answer: b   **Type: M**   **Page: 170**   **Knowledge**

75. Of the following statements, which is not characteristic of powerful speech?
    a. It can help candidates in job interviews.
    b. It often results in a favorable impression.
    c. It is always preferred over less powerful forms of speech.
    d. It gets different results in different cultures.
    e. All of these choices are correct are characteristic of powerful speech.
    Answer: c   **Type: M**   **Pages: 171–173**   **Comprehension**

76. Saying "You're a fantastic person" rather than "You're generous, helpful, and loyal" is an example of
    a. emotive language.
    b. static evaluation.
    c. abstraction.
    d. relative language.
    e. pragmatism.
    Answer: c   **Type: M**   **Page: 161**   **Knowledge**

77. Highly abstract language can lead to which of the following problems?
    a. stereotyping
    b. misunderstandings
    c. blanket judgments
    d. confusion
    e. All of these choices are correct
    Answer: e   **Type: M**   **Pages: 161–162**   **Comprehension**

78. What type of misunderstanding occurs when people assign different meanings to the same words?
    a. syntactic
    b. pragmatic
    c. semantic
    d. disruptive
    e. linguistic relativism
    Answer: c   **Type: M**   **Page: 159**   **Knowledge**

79. The grammar of a language is governed by
    a. semantic rules
    b. pragmatic rules
    c. syntactic rules
    d. relative rules
    e. None of these choices are correct

    Answer: c   **Type: M**   **Page: 162**   **Knowledge**

80. Of the following, what is not characteristic of pragmatic rules?
    a. They are almost always stated.
    b. They help us interpret messages in a given context.
    c. They aren't found in a dictionary.
    d. They govern how speech operates in everyday interaction.
    e. All of these choices are correct are characteristic of pragmatic rules.

    Answer: a   **Type: M**   **Pages: 165–166**   **Knowledge**

81. If a female employee is unsure how to interpret her older male boss's statement, "You look very nice in that sweater," it would be because of
    a. semantic rules.
    b. syntactic rules.
    c. pragmatic rules.
    d. abstract language.
    e. relative words.

    Answer: c   **Type: M**   **Pages: 165–166**   **Application**

82. Communicators who want to show affiliation with one another adapt their speech through
    a. rate of talking.
    b. choice of vocabulary.
    c. number of pauses.
    d. level of politeness.
    e. All of these choices are correct.

    Answer: e   **Type: M**   **Page: 170**   **Knowledge**

83. Statements that basically cancel the thought that precedes them are
    a. "it" statements.
    b. "but" statements.
    c. "we" statements.
    d. "I/we" statements.
    e. "you" statements.

    Answer: b   **Type: M**   **Page: 176**   **Knowledge**

84. Language styles vary across cultures
    a. in elaborateness or succinctness.
    b. in directness.
    c. in formality or informality.
    d. None of these choices are correct.
    e. All of these choices are correct.

    Answer: e   **Type: M**   **Pages: 185–187**   **Knowledge**

85. Of the following, what is not an element of a complete "I" statement?
    a. the other person's behavior.
    b. your feelings.
    c. the other person's intentions.
    d. your interpretations.
    e. the consequences the other person's behavior has for you.
    Answer: c   **Type: M**   **Page: 177**   **Knowledge**

INSTRUCTIONS for questions 86–94: Identify each of the following statements as fact or inference.
    a. inference
    b. fact

86. You are trying to hurt me.
    Answer: a   **Type: Matching**   **Page: 173**   **Evaluation**

87. You told Jimmy that I didn't want to go out with him.
    Answer: b   **Type: Matching**   **Page: 173**   **Evaluation**

88. Why are you mad at me? .
    Answer: a   **Type: Matching**   **Page: 173**   **Evaluation**

89. Jim wrote me a letter to help me get that job.
    Answer: b   **Type: Matching**   **Page: 173**   **Evaluation**

90. Your children are disruptive.
    Answer: a   **Type: Matching**   **Page: 173**   **Evaluation**

91. Your children interrupted me when I spoke.
    Answer: b   **Type: Matching**   **Page: 173**   **Evaluation**

92. The school board president was arrested for drunken driving.
    Answer: b   **Type: Matching**   **Page: 173**   **Evaluation**

93. Their new apartment is more comfortable than the old one.
    Answer: a   **Type: Matching**   **Page: 173**   **Evaluation**

94. You forgot my birthday.
    Answer: b   **Type: Matching**   **Page: 173**   **Evaluation**

INSTRUCTIONS for questions 95–98: Read the following statements and identify what type of language is being used in the underlined words or phrases. You will use some letters more than once.
    a. emotive language
    b. relative language
    c. equivocal language

95. John told me this restaurant was pretty <u>cheap</u> but I was surprised when I saw the prices on the menu.
    Answer: b   **Type: Matching**   **Pages: 159–160**   **Evaluation**

96. No one seemed to want to talk about the person who had the job before this. They just kept referring to the "<u>previous situation</u>."
    Answer: c   **Type: Matching**   **Page: 159**   **Evaluation**

97. It's a pretty good job and he told me that the pay was <u>average</u>.
   Answer: c   **Type: Matching**   **Page: 159**   **Evaluation**

98. The building where we had the interview wasn't much. I don't want to call it a <u>shack</u>. Let's just say
   it was an <u>economical structure</u>.
   Answer: a   **Type: Matching**   **Page: 174**   **Evaluation**

99. "Language is power." Discuss this statement, using (a) an explanation of the types of
   powerful/powerless language given in your text, and (b) examples of these types of language in your
   own life.
   Answer: **Type: E**   **Pages: 171–173**   **Analysis**

100. Using "I" language patterns from the text, create five "I" language statements you could actually
   deliver to people important in your life. Identify the four parts of each of your complete "I"
   statements.
   Answer: **Type: E**   **Pages: 176–177**   **Synthesis**

101. Compare and contrast your use of language with that of someone else you know, pointing out the
   similarities or differences in: 1) verbal communication style (direct/indirect, elaborate/succinct,
   formal/informal) and 2) worldview. Cite specific examples.
   Answer: **Type: E**   **Pages: 185–187**   **Synthesis**

102. Describe what abstract language is and how you use unnecessarily abstract language that causes
   communication problems. Give at least five examples. Tell how you could lower the level of
   abstraction in each of the examples you have given or provide reasons why the higher-level
   abstraction is justified and relationally beneficial.
   Answer: **Type: E**   **Pages: 161–162**   **Synthesis**

103. In your own words, explain the statement "meanings rest more in people than in words." Cite
   examples from your own experience.
   Answer: **Type: E**   **Pages: 158–167**   **Application**

104. According to your text, each language has its own unique style that distinguishes it from others.
   Explain the three ways verbal styles vary across cultures. Include examples in your discussion.
   Answer: **Type: E**   **Pages: 185–187**   **Analysis**

105. Three linguistic habits often cause disagreements: fact-opinion confusion, fact-inference confusion,
   and emotive language. Explain two of the habits and provide examples in your answer.
   Answer: **Type: E**   **Pages: 173–174**   **Analysis**

106. Your text identifies three areas where language shapes our perceptions: through naming and
   identity, affiliation, and power. Choose two areas and explain how they have shaped your
   perceptions.   Include specific examples in your discussion.
   Answer: **Type: E**   **Pages: 168–173**   **Synthesis**

The following essay question work best at "take-home" exams because of the time necessary to effectively complete them.

107. Tape-record two separate 10- to 15-minute conversations you have with a man and a woman who are important in your life. Describe these conversations briefly in terms of content and style. Compare the conversations and comment on any variables involved, using terms and research from your text that address the issue of gender and language.

      Answer: **Type: E**   **Pages: 181–184**   **Synthesis**

108. The text describes some ways in which men and women use language both differently and similarly. Cite a major research finding in each of the following areas and cite examples from your life that reflect these findings or contradict them: a) content, b) reasons for communicating, c) conversational style, and d) non-gender variables.

      Answer: **Type: E**   **Pages: 181–184**   **Synthesis**

CHAPTER 6

NONVERBAL COMMUNICATION: MESSAGES BEYOND WORDS

1. "The Way You Talk Can Hurt You?" reading in Chapter Six insists that it would be beneficial for men to change their vocal patterns to sound more cooperative and friendly in everyday interactions.
   Answer: F   **Type: T**   **Page: 219**   **Knowledge**

2. According to the text, you can not avoid communicating.
   Answer: T   **Type: T**   **Page: 198**   **Comprehension**

3. Nonverbal communication is usually specific and clear.
   Answer: F   **Type: T**   **Page: 205**   **Comprehension**

4. Nonverbal communication is not as effective at conveying thoughts or ideas as it is at conveying attitudes and feelings .
   Answer: T   **Type: T**   **Page: 199**   **Comprehension**

5. According to your text's definition of nonverbal communication, it follows that the way a person styles his/her hair is a nonverbal message.
   Answer: T   **Type: T**   **Page: 197**   **Analysis**

6. In social transactions, the higher status person is generally the more rigid, tense-appearing one, whereas the one with lower status is usually more relaxed.
   Answer: F   **Type: T**   **Page: 214**   **Knowledge**

7. Information about the status of two individuals in conversation can be communicated by not only their posture, but also eye contact and touch.
   Answer: T   **Type: T**   **Pages: 214, 217, 222**   **Synthesis**

8. In laboratory settings, subjects are better judges of positive facial expressions than they are of negative ones.
   Answer: T   **Type: T**   **Page: 206**   **Comprehension**

9. Gestures can be intentional or unintentional.
   Answer: T   **Type: T**   **Pages: 214, 216**   **Synthesis**

10. Research reveals that increased use of manipulators is often a sign of discomfort.
    Answer: T   **Type: T**   **Page: 216**   **Knowledge**

11. In many instances, the use of touch increases liking and boosts compliance.
    Answer: T   **Type: T**   **Page: 222**   **Knowledge**

12. Nonverbal messages convey relational information such as respect and friendliness .
    Answer: T   **Type: T**   **Page: 198**   **Knowledge**

13. Generally, facing someone directly signals your interest in that person.
    Answer: T   **Type: T**   **Page: 213**   **Knowledge**

14. Most communication scholars don't define American Sign Language as nonverbal communication.
    Answer: T   **Type: T**   **Page: 195**   **Knowledge**

15. Nonverbal communication can be very revealing, but it can have so many possible meanings that it's foolish to think your interpretation will always be correct.
    Answer: T   **Type: T**   **Page: 205**   **Comprehension**

16. Some people are more skillful than others at accurately decoding nonverbal behavior.
    Answer: T   **Type: T**   **Page: 206**   **Knowledge**

17. Your text defines nonverbal communication as any type of communication that isn't expressed by words .
    Answer: F   **Type: T**   **Page: 197**   **Comprehension**

18. Emotions show most clearly in different parts of the face.
    Answer: T   **Type: T**   **Page: 216**   **Knowledge**

19. According to your text, some researchers claim that over 90 percent of the emotional impact of a message comes from nonverbal sources.
    Answer: T   **Type: T**   **Page: 195**   **Knowledge**

20. Women's advantage over men in sensitivity to nonverbal cues likely has more to do with social status than with biological gender.
    Answer: T   **Type: T**   **Page: 209**   **Knowledge**

21. Stammering and saying "uh" are nonverbal behaviors termed disfluencies.
    Answer: T   **Type: T**   **Page: 218**   **Knowledge**

22. Paralinguistic elements always accompany the spoken word.
    Answer: T   **Type: T**   **Page: 218**   **Comprehension**

23. Many nonverbal behaviors are governed by cultural rules.
    Answer: T   **Type: T**   **Page: 210**   **Knowledge**

24. Silence or pauses count as nonverbal communication.
    Answer: T   **Type: T**   **Page: 218**   **Comprehension**

25. Patterns of eye contact are fairly consistent across cultures.
    Answer: F   **Type: T**   **Page: 211**   **Comprehension**

26. Emblems are nonverbal behaviors that have the same meaning to all members of a particular culture or co-culture.
    Answer: T   **Type: T**   **Page: 214**   **Knowledge**

27. It is possible to recognize paralinguistic messages, even if you don't understand the language being spoken.
    Answer: T   **Type: T**   **Page: 218**   **Comprehension**

28. According to research cited in your text, touch and health are not related.
    Answer: F   **Type: T**   **Page: 222**   **Knowledge**

29. Researchers have found that the face and eyes are capable of five basic expressions.
    Answer: F   **Type: T**   **Page: 216**   **Knowledge**

30. Pupil dilation can be a sign of interest.
    Answer: T   **Type: T**   **Page: 217**   **Knowledge**

31. Disfluencies are one type of paralanguage.
    Answer: T   **Type: T**   **Page: 218**   **Comprehension**

32. According to your text, people usually get more meaning from what others do than from what they say.
    Answer: T   **Type: T**   **Page: 195**   **Comprehension**

33. If you get within one foot of someone else in U.S. culture, you've invaded their intimate zone, according to researcher Edward T. Hall.
    Answer: T   **Type: T**   **Page: 226**   **Evaluation**

34. Messages about status can be conveyed through clothing and chronemics.
    Answer: T   **Type: T**   **Page: 224**   **Knowledge**

35. By making another person wait, you are sending messages about status, whether you intend to or not.
    Answer: T   **Type: T**   **Page: 228**   **Analysis**

36. Nonverbal cues are especially likely to carry weight when they contradict a speaker's words.
    Answer: T   **Type: T**   **Page: 204**   **Knowledge**

37. Deception studies have found that deceivers are more likely to be found out when they don't feel very strongly about the information being hidden.
    Answer: F   **Type: T**   **Page: 205**   **Knowledge**

28. If deceivers feel confident and not guilty, their deception is more likely to be found out.
    Answer: F   **Type: T**   **Page: 205**   **Knowledge**

29. Your text defines nonverbal communication as "messages expressed by nonlinguistic means."
    Answer: T   **Type: T**   **Page: 197**   **Knowledge**

30. Those with good nonverbal communication skills benefit in a number of areas, including career success and popularity.
    Answer: T   **Type: T**   **Page: 197**   **Comprehension**

31. Nonverbal communication plays a less important role in identity management than verbal communication.
    Answer: F   **Type: T**   **Page: 198**   **Knowledge**

32. Nonverbal behavior has a powerful effect in defining the status of a relationship.
    Answer: T   **Type: T**   **Page: 199**   **Comprehension**

33. Most text, instant, and e-mail messages are now able to present nonverbal cues about a speaker's feelings that are equivalent to face-to-face encounters.
    Answer: F   **Type: T**   **Page: 199**   **Comprehension**

34. Verbal and nonverbal communication are interconnected elements in every act of communication.
    Answer: T   **Type: T**   **Page: 201**   **Knowledge**

35. Accenting nonverbal behaviors match the thoughts and emotions the communicator is expressing verbally.
    Answer: F   **Type: T**   **Page: 202**   **Knowledge**

36. Changing your vocal intonation pattern is one way to regulate a conversation.
    Answer: T   **Type: T**   **Page: 202**   **Comprehension**

37. Signals of deception are called leakage.
    Answer: T   **Type: T**   **Page: 204**   **Knowledge**

38. Nonverbal messages are less ambiguous than verbal messages.
    Answer: F   **Type: T**   **Page: 205**   **Knowledge**

39. Since the face and eyes are probably the most noticed parts of the body, their nonverbal messages are easier to read than other parts of the body.
    Answer: F   **Type: T**   **Page: 216**   **Comprehension**

40. Awareness of the differences in nonverbal behavior between cultures has little affect on cultural tolerance and respect.
    Answer: F   **Type: T**   **Page: 210**   **Analysis**

41. Smiles and laughter have the same meanings to both Americans and Latinos.
    Answer: T   **Type: T**   **Page: 212**   **Comprehension**

42. Illustrators can stand on their own and often function as replacements for words.
    Answer: F   **Type: T**   **Page: 214**   **Knowledge**

43. Using too few gestures does not indicate a mixed message like using too many gestures does.
    Answer: F   **Type: T**   **Page: 216**   **Knowledge**

44. Paralanguage can influence the way a speaker is perceived by others.
    Answer: T   **Type: T**   **Pages: 219–220**   **Knowledge**

45. Communicators who pause and speak quietly are viewed just as confident as those who speak loudly and without hesitations.
    Answer: F   **Type: T**   **Page: 220**   **Knowledge**

46. When asked to determine a speaker's attitudes, listeners pay equal attention to paralanguage and the content of the words.
    Answer: F   **Type: T**   **Page: 218**   **Knowledge**

47. The far range of social distance is usually the distance used when salespeople and customers talk.
    Answer: F   **Type: T**   **Page: 226**   **Knowledge**

48. Our territory is the invisible bubble we carry with us wherever we go.
    Answer: F   **Type: T**   **Page: 227**   **Knowledge**

49. Since "beauty is in the eye of the beholder," physical attractiveness is not a general factor in how people are perceived.
    Answer: F   **Type: T**   **Page: 223**   **Comprehension**

50. Studies show that most people have about a 75% chance of accurately identifying someone who is lying.
    Answer: F   **Type: T**   **Page: 204**   **Knowledge**

51. In the excerpt from the Sherlock Holmes story in Chapter Six, Holmes points out that Watson
    a.   listens but fails to see.
    b.   sees but does not observe.
    c.   can't observe well because he doesn't communicate.
    d.   fails to solve cases because he pays too much attention to nonverbal messages.
    e.   watches but fails to listen.
    Answer: b   **Type: M**   **Page: 196**   **Knowledge**

52. "The Looking at Diversity" reading in Chapter Six ("Nonverbal Stereotyping") features a black man who says he is frequently
    a.   given more traffic tickets than white men in his age group.
    b.   is viewed as arrogant because of his posture and stride.
    c.   asked to speak to black groups because he knows how to behave nonverbally.
    d.   assumed to be a potential shoplifter.
    e.   suspected of violence because of his race.
    Answer: e   **Type: M**   **Page: 208**   **Knowledge**

53. "The Look of a Victim" story in this chapter points out that victims of assault may set themselves up as easy targets because of
    a.   their friendly facial expressions.
    b.   the way they walk.
    c.   their hairstyles.
    d.   eye contact with the attacker.
    e.   All of these choices are correct
    Answer: b   **Type: M**   **Page: 215**   **Knowledge**

54. Status can be conveyed nonverbally through
    a.   chronemics.
    b.   touch.
    c.   clothing.
    d.   posture.
    e.   All of these choices are correct
    Answer: e   **Type: M**   **Pages: 213–228**   **Synthesis**

55. Amanda wants to make a sale. According to the nonverbal information presented in Chapter 6, to get compliance from a customer she might try
    a. speaking in a rate much faster than her customer's
    b. lightly touching her customer.
    c. avoiding direct eye contact with her customer.
    d. keeping her facial expression as neutral as possible.
    e. None of these are correct are advisable to gain compliance.
    Answer: b   **Type: M**   **Page: 222**   **Application**

56. Studies of nonverbal communication across cultures reveal that
    a. smiles and laughter are a universal signal of positive emotions.
    b. sour expressions convey displeasure in some cultures and pleasure in others.
    c. the expression of feelings is discouraged in most cultures.
    d. all facial expressions are inborn.
    Answer: a   **Type: M**   **Page: 212**   **Synthesis**

57. The design and environment of rooms
    a. communicate information about the owner's personality.
    b. shape the interaction that takes place there.
    c. communicate information about the interests of the owner.
    d. b and c above
    e. All of these choices are correct
    Answer: e   **Type: M**   **Page: 227**   **Synthesis**

58. Kinesics is the study of
    a. personal distances.
    b. verbal and nonverbal behavior.
    c. body position and motion.
    d. environmental stress.
    e. clothing and color.
    Answer: c   **Type: M**   **Page: 213**   **Knowledge**

59. Proxemics is the study of
    a. the way people and animals use space.
    b. the way people use words to transmit messages.
    c. the way people use facial expressions.
    d. the way people use silence.
    e. the way people use vocal cues.
    Answer: a   **Type: M**   **Page: 225**   **Knowledge**

60. The many ways the voice communicates—including tone, speed, pitch, number and length of pauses, volume, etc.—are called
    a. paralanguage.
    b. vocalics.
    c. noncommunicators.
    d. nonvocals.
    e. proxemics.
    Answer: a   **Type: M**   **Page: 218**   **Knowledge**

61. The nonverbal researchers cited in your text claim that, when we consider the actual meaning involved in communication situations, verbal messages
    a. carry less meaning than nonverbal ones.
    b. carry more meaning than nonverbal ones.
    c. aren't really listened to.
    d. are too full of nonverbal signals.
    e. define the communication situation.
    Answer: a   **Type: M**   **Page: 195**   **Comprehension**

62. Nonverbally, women _____ more than men.
    a. make less eye contact
    b. smile less
    c. are less vocally expressive
    d. gesture more
    e. require more personal space
    Answer: d   **Type: M**   **Page: 209**   **Comprehension**

63. Studies of nonverbal posture behaviors have found that
    a. we are generally unaware of posture.
    b. different facial expressions help posture interpretation.
    c. we should use unambiguous postural cues.
    d. tension and relaxation of muscles can indicate status differences.
    e. posture is not important to body image.
    Answer: d   **Type: M**   **Page: 214**   **Comprehension**

64. All of the following statements are true except:
    a. The eyes can communicate positive and negative attitudes.
    b. Nonverbal messages of the face and eyes are the easiest to read.
    c. Even the pupils of the eyes can communicate messages.
    d. The eyes can indicate dominance and submission.
    e. The eyes send involvement messages.
    Answer: b   **Type: M**   **Page: 216**   **Knowledge**

65. All of the following are characteristics of nonverbal behavior except:
    a. Nonverbal skills are important.
    b. Nonverbal behavior is clear and unambiguous.
    c. Nonverbal communication is primarily relational.
    d. All nonverbal behavior has communicative value.
    e. Nonverbal communication serves many functions.
    Answer: b   **Type: M**   **Pages: 197–201**   **Knowledge**

66. All of the following are true about touch except:
    a. Touch can be of life-and-death importance to a child.
    b. Touch can signal a variety of relationships.
    c. Touch can be a way to communicate both negative and positive feelings.
    d. Touch can increase compliance.
    e. Touch in any of its forms can have positive effects.
    Answer: e   **Type: M**   **Pages: 220–223**   **Synthesis**

67. When our nonverbal behavior is unintentional,
    a. others disregard it.
    b. others attach more significance to it.
    c. others can't make interpretations based on it.
    d. others respond with their own unintentional behaviors.
    e. others recognize it and make interpretations based on it.
    Answer: e   **Type: M**   **Page: 198**   **Comprehension**

68. Edward T. Hall's Distance Zones are
    a. personal, impersonal, social, public.
    b. intimate, personal, social, public.
    c. intimate, non-intimate, social, public.
    d. open, blind, hidden, unknown.
    e. None of these are correct.
    Answer: b   **Type: M**   **Page: 226**   **Knowledge**

69. Most adaptors are
    a. unconscious.
    b. signs of deception.
    c. excitement cues.
    d. attempts to attract others.
    e. signs of vulnerability.
    Answer: a   **Type: M**   **Page: 216**   **Knowledge**

70. Using stammering or "uh, um, er" in conversation is the nonverbal behavior called
    a. affect displays.
    b. microexpressions.
    c. illustrators.
    d. disfluencies.
    e. macroexpressions.
    Answer: d   **Type: M**   **Page: 218**   **Knowledge**

71. The nonverbal term for brief flashes of emotion in the face is
    a. microexpressions.
    b. miniemotions.
    c. manipulators.
    d. disfluencies.
    e. multi-expressions.
    Answer: a   **Type: M**   **Page: 217**   **Knowledge**

72. If you see someone smiling, you could interpret this communication to mean
    a. the other is friendly.
    b. the other is happy.
    c. the other wants to communicate.
    d. the other is faking something.
    e. any of the above
    Answer: e   **Type: M**   **Page: 205**   **Application**

73. Facial expressions are
    a. the easiest nonverbal messages to decode accurately.
    b. often difficult to understand because of their rapid rate of change.
    c. rarely genuine and therefore impossible to decode.
    d. limited, relatively few emotions are shown in the face.
    e. usually more sincere if they last more than 10 seconds.
    Answer: b   **Type: M**   **Page: 216**   **Knowledge**

74. Nonverbal communication serves the functions of
    a. repeating and substituting.
    b. complementing and accenting.
    c. regulating and contradicting.
    d. All of these choices are correct.
    e. None of these are correct.
    Answer: d   **Type: M**   **Pages: 201–204**   **Knowledge**

75. When Joe nods his head up and down rather than saying "Yes," he is using a nonverbal behavior
    known as a(n)
    a. facilitator.
    b. interlocutor.
    c. emblem.
    d. nonverbalator.
    e. encoder.
    Answer: c   **Type: M**   **Page: 214**   **Application**

76. All of the following are true about nonverbal communication across cultures, except that
    a. distance patterns vary across cultures.
    b. patterns of eye contact vary around the world.
    c. emblems have precise and distinct meanings within cultural groups.
    d. interpretations of acceptable touch does not vary across cultures.
    e. smiles, laughter, and sour expressions are universal signals of positive or negative emotion.
    Answer: d   **Type: M**   **Pages: 210–212**   **Synthesis**

77. Research reveals that increased use of manipulators is often a sign of
    a. discomfort.
    b. power.
    c. shyness.
    d. dogmatism.
    e. inferiority.
    Answer: a   **Type: M**   **Page: 216**   **Comprehension**

78. Vocal intonation patterns, audible breaths, eye contact patterns, and nodding in a conversation are
    nonverbal behaviors that illustrate the nonverbal function of
    a. substituting.
    b. regulating.
    c. accenting.
    d. repeating.
    e. complementing.
    Answer: b   **Type: M**   **Page: 202**   **Application**

79. All of the following are true about the voice and communication except:
    a. Communicators who speak loudly and without hesitations are viewed as more confident than those who pause and speak quietly.
    b. Younger-sounding communicators whose language is accent-free are rated as more competent than older-sounding communicators.
    c. Some vocal factors influence the way a speaker is perceived.
    d. Accents that identify a speaker's membership in a group lead to more positive evaluations of that person if the group is a prestigious one.
    e. People with more attractive voices are rated more highly than those with less attractive voices.
    Answer: b   **Type: M**   **Pages: 218–220**   **Comprehension**

80. Nonverbal regulators can signal
    a. turn-taking.
    b. the desire to end a conversation.
    c. an invitation to respond.
    d. All of these choices are correct.
    e. None of these are correct.
    Answer: d   **Type: M**   **Page: 202**   **Knowledge**

81. Nonverbal evidence of lying is most likely to occur when the deceiver
    a. has no strong feelings about the deception.
    b. has not rehearsed the deception.
    c. does not feel anxious or guilty about the lies.
    d. has lack of emotional involvement with the deception.
    e. doesn't know people are watching.
    Answer: b   **Type: M**   **Pages: 204–205**   **Comprehension**

82. In nonverbal communication, studies of leakage deal with
    a. innate behaviors.
    b. illness behaviors.
    c. environmental issues.
    d. deception signals.
    e. perceptions of illness.
    Answer: d   **Type: M**   **Page: 204**   **Application**

83. All of the following are true about nonverbal communication except:
    a. Nonverbal communication is universal for all cultures.
    b. Nonverbal communication may function to contradict verbal messages.
    c. Nonverbal communication is more ambiguous than verbal communication.
    d. Nonverbal signals are much more powerful than verbal messages when they are delivered at the same time.
    e. Nonverbal messages aren't as deliberate as verbal messages.
    Answer: a   **Type: M**   **Pages: 210–211**   **Comprehension**

84. Nonverbal communication plays an important role in
    a. conveying emotions.
    b. identity management.
    c. defining the kinds of relationships we want to have with others.
    d. None of these are correct.
    e. All of these choices are correct.
    Answer: e   **Type: M**   **Pages: 198–199**   **Knowledge**

CHAPTER 6   NONVERBAL BEHAVIOR: MESSAGES BEYOND WORDS   197

85. The function of influencing the flow of verbal communication is called
    a. repeating
    b. complementing
    c. substituting
    d. accenting
    e. regulating
    Answer: e   **Type: M**   **Page: 202**   **Knowledge**

86. Lynn shrugs her shoulders in response to Lisa's question. Lynn is using a function of nonverbal communication known as
    a. regulating
    b. accenting
    c. substituting
    d. complementing
    e. repeating
    Answer: c   **Type: M**   **Page: 202**   **Application**

87. The lawyer pounded his fist on the table for emphasis. He is using a function of nonverbal communication known as
    a. regulating
    b. accenting
    c. substituting
    d. complementing
    e. contradicting
    Answer: b   **Type: M**   **Page: 202**   **Application**

88. An indicator of deception is
    a. inconsistency
    b. low rate of speech
    c. more speech errors
    d. higher vocal frequency
    e. All of these choices are correct may be indicators of deception.
    Answer: e   **Type: M**   **Page: 204**   **Knowledge**

89. All of the following statements are true about nonverbal gender differences except
    a. Women express more emotions via facial expressions than do men.
    b. Women interact at closer distances, with both men and women.
    c. Women make more eye contact than do men with conversational partners.
    d. Women are more likely to lean forward in conversations than men.
    e. Women gesture more than men.
    Answer: d   **Type: M**   **Page: 209**   **Knowledge**

90. Gina looked annoyed when she walked into the classroom and saw Megan sitting in the chair she usually sits in. The nonverbal communication Gina is demonstrating is
    a. kinesics
    b. personal space
    c. territoriality
    d. chronemics
    e. regulation
    Answer: c   **Type: M**   **Page: 227**   **Knowledge**

91. Edward T. Hall defines social distance as
    a.   0 to 18 inches
    b.   18 inches to 4 feet
    c.   4 feet to 12 feet
    d.   12 feet to 25 feet
    e.   25 feet and beyond
    Answer: c   **Type: M**   **Page: 226**   **Knowledge**

92. Edward T. Hall defines personal distance as
    a.   0 to 18 inches
    b.   18 inches to 4 feet
    c.   4 feet to 12 feet
    d.   12 feet to 25 feet
    e.   25 feet and beyond
    Answer: b   **Type: M**   **Page: 226**   **Knowledge**

93. Students who were shown interior home photos accurately identifed that the homes communicated
    a.   the homeowners' politeness
    b.   the homeowners' tenseness
    c.   the homeowners' artistic interests
    d.   family orientations
    e.   All of these choices are correct
    Answer: e   **Type: M**   **Page: 227**   **Knowledge**

94. One experiment mentioned in your text (ethnic groups identified emotions from photos) showed
    how ethnicity influenced the way subjects gauged others' emotional states. Of the following, what
    was not one of the results?
    a.   Blacks reported a greater frequency of anger expressions than did the Caucasian, Asian, and
         Hispanic subjects.
    b.   Caucasians perceived the display of several emotions as more appropriate than did the other
         groups.
    c.   Asians perceived the emotions in the photos as least appropriate.
    d.   Caucasians perceived the emotions in the photos as more intense than the black, Asian, and
         Hispanic subjects.
    e.   All of these choices are correct were results from the experiment.
    Answer: d   **Type: M**   **Page: 210**   **Knowledge**

INSTRUCTIONS for questions 95–100: Match each description below with the term it best describes.
    a.   chronemics
    b.   paralanguage
    c.   disfluenciesd.
    d.   proxemics
    e.   kinesics

95. Study of use and structure of time
    Answer: a   **Type: Matching**   **Page: 228**   **Knowledge**

96. Waving, shaking head or finger
    Answer: e   **Type: Matching**   **Page: 213**   **Knowledge**

97. Arriving early for an appointment.
    Answer: a   **Type: Matching**   **Page: 228**   **Knowledge**

98. A strong accent or husky voice.
    Answer: b   **Type: Matching**   **Page: 218**   **Knowledge**

99. "Uh," "um," "er."
    Answer: c   **Type: Matching**   **Page: 218**   **Knowledge**

100. Standing "at arm's length."
    Answer: d   **Type: Matching**   **Page: 225**   **Knowledge**

INSTRUCTIONS for questions 101–107: Match each nonverbal function with the description below it best describes. You will use some letters more than once.
    a.   substituting
    b.   contradicting
    c.   regulating
    d.   accenting
    e.   repeating

101. Richard fell silent and looked expectantly at Doreen.
    Answer: c   **Type: Matching**   **Page: 202**   **Application**

102. Lois snapped her fingers and shouted, "Hurry up! Get a move on!"
    Answer: d   **Type: Matching**   **Page: 202**   **Application**

103. Nathan suppressed a yawn and slumped in his chair while saying, "Sure I'm interested in hearing about your trip. I'm all ears."
    Answer: b   **Type: Matching**   **Page: 204**   **Application**

104. When asked if she wanted a refill on her coffee, Maria covered the cup with her hand and shook her head.
    Answer: a   **Type: Matching**   **Page: 202**   **Application**

105. When he was asked how old he was, Davie held up four fingers and announced proudly, "I'm four!"
    Answer: e   **Type: Matching**   **Page: 201**   **Application**

106. "Angry? No, *I'm NOT* angry!"
    Answer: b   **Type: Matching**   **Page: 204**   **Application**

107. Liz rolled her eyes while her mother complained about her messy room.
    Answer: a   **Type: Matching**   **Page: 202**   **Application**

108. Imagine that you have been commissioned to design a new campus center. What sort of communication should take place there? What kinds of furnishings and decorations would you suggest to increase the likelihood of this communication occurring? What messages would your choice of designs and decorations communicate?
    Answer: **Type: E**   **Pages: 227–228**   **Evaluation**

109. One characteristic of nonverbal communication is "all behavior has communicative value." Describe two incidents from your experience which illustrate both deliberate and unintentional meaning derived from nonverbal communication in these two incidents. Identify the nonverbal behaviors that occurred. Identify the meanings you did/did not intend to convey and the meanings that were conveyed from your perspective and that of your partner in each incident.
    Answer: **Type: E**   **Pages: 197–198**   **Analysis**

110. Using at least two of the types of nonverbal communication described in your text, and referring to your own experience, describe an incident which illustrates how nonverbal behavior can be ambiguous. How could you or the other person involved have reduced the ambiguity of that situation?
    Answer: **Type: E**   **Pages: 205–206**   **Application**

111. Nonverbal communication reveals attitudes about status. Using examples, describe how status might be communicated through five different types of nonverbal messages.
    Answer: **Type: E**   **Pages: 213–228**   **Synthesis**

112. One characteristic of nonverbal communication is that it serves many functions. Explain the functions of substituting, accenting, and regulating using specific examples for support.
    Answer: **Type: E**   **Pages: 201–202**   **Analysis**

113. One characteristic of nonverbal communication is that it is primarily relational. Discuss the three ways this occurs as explained in your text, using specific examples.
    Answer: **Type: E**   **Pages: 198–199**   **Analysis**

114: Gender has a strong influence on nonverbal communication. Explain the differences between men and women in this area.   Include your personal experiences in your discussion.
    Answer: **Type: E**   **Pages: 208–209**   **Analysis**

CHAPTER 7
LISTENING: MORE THAN MEETS THE EAR

1. According to research, most listeners retain 70 percent of a message for several weeks.
    Answer: F   **Type: T**   **Page: 239**   **Knowledge**

2. There is no single "best" listening style to use in all situations.
    Answer: T   **Type: T**   **Page: 260**   **Comprehension**

3. A good listener will always state her own opinion so the other person knows where she stands on the issue.
    Answer: F   **Type: T**   **Page: 259**   **Comprehension**

4. You should do more paraphrasing than any other type of listening.
    Answer: F   **Type: T**   **Page: 254**   **Comprehension**

5. We spend more time listening than in any other type of communication.
    Answer: T   **Type: T**   **Page: 233**   **Knowledge**

6. It's impossible to listen effectively all of the time.
    Answer: T   **Type: T**   **Page: 241**   **Knowledge**

7. During careful listening, your heart rate will quicken and your body temperature will rise.
    Answer: T   **Type: T**   **Page: 243**   **Knowledge**

8. Questioning is one type of listening response used to help others.
    Answer: T   **Type: T**   **Page: 249**   **Knowledge**

9. Since paraphrasing may not always be accurate, speaking tentatively allows the other person to make a correction.
    Answer: T   **Type: T**   **Page: 253**   **Knowledge**

10. Because of its lively, segmented bursts of information, contemporary mass media has helped develop a generation of better listeners.
    Answer: F   **Type: T**   **Page: 245**   **Knowledge**

11. Studies show that good listeners keep eye contact and react with appropriate facial expressions.
    Answer: T   **Type: T**   **Page: 238**   **Knowledge**

12. According to the text, the most helpful way of responding to a problem is to offer good, specific advice.
    Answer: F   **Type: T**   **Page: 248**   **Comprehension**

13. Speaking is an active process; listening is a passive activity.
    Answer: F   **Type: T**   **Page: 243**   **Comprehension**

14. Listening behaviors such as insulated listening, pseudolistening, and selective listening are often reasonable responses to a deluge of relatively worthless information.

Answer: T   **Type: T**   **Page: 240**   **Comprehension**

15. Because prompting involves using silences, it is not classified as a listening response.

Answer: F   **Type: T**   **Page: 248**   **Knowledge**

16. Prompting is a more passive listening style than advising.

Answer: T   **Type: T**   **Page: 248**   **Evaluation**

17. Even if you give accurate advice to a person, that advice may not be helpful.

Answer: T   **Type: T**   **Page: 258**   **Knowledge**

18. Accurate analysis of a problem may arouse defensiveness.

Answer: T   **Type: T**   **Page: 258**   **Knowledge**

19. When you use paraphrasing as a helping tool, your reflection should usually contain both thoughts and feelings.

Answer: T   **Type: T**   **Page: 251**   **Knowledge**

20. Questioning and paraphrasing are both forms of feedback.

Answer: T   **Type: T**   **Pages: 249–251**   **Synthesis**

21. Counterfeit questions are aimed at understanding others.

Answer: F   **Type: T**   **Page: 249**   **Comprehension**

22. Analyzing can be one way to help a speaker consider alternative meanings.

Answer: T   **Type: T**   **Page: 256**   **Knowledge**

23. Advice given in a respectful, caring way is always the best listening response to use when approached with another's problem.

Answer: F   **Type: T**   **Page: 258**   **Knowledge**

24. Of the many different elements in the listening process, hearing is the physiological dimension.

Answer: T   **Type: T**   **Page: 236**   **Comprehension**

25. According to your text, people usually try their best to listen but their effectiveness is limited primarily by biological factors.

Answer: F   **Type: T**   **Pages: 241–244**   **Comprehension**

26. When you are paraphrasing, you need to repeat what the speaker has said word for word.

Answer: F   **Type: T**   **Page: 251**   **Comprehension**

27. Factual information paraphrasing focuses on the ideas a speaker has expressed.

Answer: T   **Type: T**   **Page: 251**   **Comprehension**

28. Since all judging listening responses are negative, we should avoid them at all cost.

Answer: F   **Type: T**   **Page: 259**   **Comprehension**

29. You should rotate your styles of listening after one or two responses so that you don't become bored by any one style.

Answer: F   **Type: T**   **Pages: 262–263**   **Evaluation**

30. While an important factor in making relationships work, listening is still less important than speaking.
    Answer: F   **Type: T**   **Page: 233**   **Knowledge**

31. Studies show that business people believe that listening is important and they also do it well.
    Answer: F   **Type: T**   **Page: 234**   **Knowledge**

32. Hearing occurs when the brain reconstructs electrochemical impulses into a representation of the original sound and then gives them meaning.
    Answer: F   **Type: T**   **Pages: 234–235**   **Knowledge**

33. Mindless listening is never suggested because it shows lack of concern for the speaker.
    Answer: F   **Type: T**   **Page: 235**   **Knowledge**

34. Mindless listening can be a practical way to listen.
    Answer: T   **Type: T**   **Page: 235**   **Comprehension**

35. Whereas hearing is a physiological process, attending is a psychological one.
    Answer: T   **Type: T**   **Page: 236**   **Knowledge**

36. Research suggests that most people remember about 60 percent of what they hear immediately after hearing it.
    Answer: F   **Type: T**   **Page: 239**   **Knowledge**

37. The residual message is the part of the message that we actually remember.
    Answer: T   **Type: T**   **Page: 239**   **Knowledge**

38. Interruptions are one characteristic of stage-hogging.
    Answer: T   **Type: T**   **Page: 240**   **Knowledge**

39. Insulated listeners respond only to the parts of your remarks that interest them.
    Answer: F   **Type: T**   **Page: 240**   **Knowledge**

40. Listening is easier to do than speaking.
    Answer: F   **Type: T**   **Page: 243**   **Knowledge**

41. Rapid thought is a factor in why we don't listen better because we can understand speech faster than the other person speaks.
    Answer: T   **Type: T**   **Page: 241**   **Knowledge**

42. Listening is a natural ability and, therefore, no one needs training to improve.
    Answer: F   **Type: T**   **Page: 244**   **Knowledge**

43. A counterfeit tag question is one where the asker is looking for agreement, not information.
    Answer: T   **Type: T**   **Page: 249**   **Knowledge**

44. Supporting listening responses allow you to tell the other person how you think he/she feels.
    Answer: F   **Type: T**   **Page: 254**   **Knowledge**

45. Women, rather than men, tend to respond to others' problems by offering advice.

Answer: F   **Type: T**   **Pages: 260–262**   **Knowledge**

46. Women are more likely than men to give supportive responses when presented with another person's problems.

Answer: T   **Type: T**   **Page:260**   **Knowledge**

47. When considering what listening response style to choose, the best choice will always be your personal style.

Answer: F   **Type: T**   **Pages: 262–263**   **Comprehension**

48. The listening program described in Chapter Seven, "They Aid Customers by Becoming Good Listeners," cosmetologists were trained listening skills to
    a.   help customers clarify their thinking.
    b.   provide appropriate advice to their customers.
    c.   frame questions that help sell products.
    d.   constructively criticize customer's hair style choices.
    e.   All of these answer are correct

Answer: a   **Type: M**   **Page: 261**   **Comprehension**

49. In the Looking at Diversity reading in this chapter, Bruce Anderson
    a.   proposes solving inner city problems through listening.
    b.   discusses the advantages to listening to classical music.
    c.   defends his choice to lip-read over learning American Sign Language.
    d.   eliminate overly loud music that leads to hearing problems.
    e.   explains his experience with hearing disability.

Answer: e   **Type: M**   **Page: 237**   **Knowledge**

50. His supervisor asked Michael to generate a PowerPoint presentation for the Thursday team meeting. On Thursday, Michael showed up without the presentation. Which element of the listening process is where Michael's listening failed?
    a.   hearing
    b.   attending
    c.   understanding
    d.   remembering
    e.   any of above

Answer: e   **Type: M**   **Pages: 236–239**   **Analysis**

51. According to a study of college students and their communication activities, over 50 percent of their communication time was spent
    a.   writing.
    b.   speaking.
    c.   engaging in face-to-face listening.
    d.   reading.
    e.   engaging in listening to mass communication media.

Answer: c   **Type: M**   **Page: 233**   **Recall**

52. All of the following are ineffective listening styles mentioned in the text except
   a. ambushing.
   b. insulated listening.
   c. stage hogging.
   d. pseudolistening.
   e. signal listening.

   Answer: e   **Type: M**   **Page: 240**   **Knowledge**

53. Which best describes the relationship between our rate of hearing speech and the average rate of speaking?
   a. We speak at nearly the same rate we are able to listen.
   b. We can listen 4-6 times faster than an average person speaks.
   c. We are able to speak 2 times faster than an average person can listen.
   d. We are able to listen slightly faster than an average person speaks.
   e. We can listen twice as fast as an average person speaks.

   Answer: b   **Type: M**   **Page: 241**   **Knowledge**

54. The process of using questioning and paraphrasing messages is a type of
   a. linear communication.
   b. insensitive listening.
   c. selective perception.
   d. defensive behavior.
   e. perception checking.

   Answer: e   **Type: M**   **Pages: 249–251**   **Synthesis**

55. All of the following are reasons why it is difficult to listen all the time except:
   a. We hear so many verbal messages.
   b. We are often wrapped up in personal concerns.
   c. We comprehend words at a slower rate than people speak them.
   d. We have many physical distractions.
   e. We think speaking has more advantages than listening.

   Answer: c   **Type: M**   **Pages: 241–245**   **Comprehension**

56. Giving only the appearance of being attentive is termed
   a. pseudolistening.
   b. selective listening.
   c. defensive listening.
   d. insensitive listening.
   e. fake listening.

   Answer: a   **Type: M**   **Page: 240**   **Knowledge**

57. The advantage of paraphrasing to help is that
   a. you can help the problem-holder to sort out the problem.
   b. you can suggest the solution that's best for your partner.
   c. you can point out your partner's good ideas.
   d. you can share your own experiences and ideas.
   e. All of these answer are correct.

   Answer: a   **Type: M**   **Page: 251**   **Comprehension**

58. According to your text, advice is
    a. only to be used when paraphrasing fails.
    b. helpful when it is correct or accurate.
    c. best when preceded by your analysis of a situation.
    d. actually unhelpful at least as often as it is helpful.
    e. less helpful than either supporting or judging response styles.

    Answer: d   **Type: M**   **Page: 258**   **Synthesis**

59. Which is the best helping paraphrase response to the following statement? "My boss keeps kidding me about how we should have an affair. I don't know what to do. Sometimes I think he's just joking, and sometimes I think it's a real proposition."
    a. "Either way it's sexual harassment, which is illegal. You shouldn't let him get away with it!"
    b. "So you can't figure out his motives, is that it?"
    c. "You sound upset by this."
    d. "You sound worried and confused because you're not sure if he's coming on to you or not?"
    e. "That's a common problem these days. I can see why you're upset, and I don't blame you."

    Answer: d   **Type: M**   **Pages: 251–253**   **Analysis**

60. Imagine you've been listening for some time to a friend talk about whether or not to drop out of school. Which is the best helping paraphrase response?
    a. "You're confused because there are as many reasons to stay as there are to leave, right?"
    b. "Which alternative sounds best to you?"
    c. "When you're this confused, it's best to go with your heart."
    d. "You do sound mixed up. Maybe you ought to hold off making a decision for a while."
    e. "Tell me more. I think we can get to the bottom of this if we talk it out. I'm listening."

    Answer: a   **Type: M**   **Pages: 251–253**   **Analysis**

61. You meet a friend at the supermarket and ask how he is doing. He replies, "I'm OK for the most part, just stressed with all these finals." Which of the following is the best helping paraphrase response?
    a. "Yeah, I know what you mean."
    b. "So, you're stressed, huh?"
    c. "You'll be fine; you always get good grades."
    d. "Bet you're wishing you hadn't taken 18 units, huh?"
    e. "So, you're managing most things just fine, but will be relieved when finals are over?"

    Answer: e   **Type: M**   **Pages: 251–253**   **Analysis**

62. When you try to reflect the underlying message in a statement, you are engaging in
    a. judging.
    b. questioning.
    c. paraphrasing.
    d. prompting.
    e. pseudolistening.

    Answer: c   **Type: M**   **Page: 251**   **Comprehension**

63. Which of the following bodily changes occurs during careful listening?
    a. heart rate quickens
    b. respiration increases
    c. body temperature rises
    d. All of these answer are correct
    e. none of these answers are correct
    Answer: d   **Type: M**   **Page: 243**   **Comprehension**

64. Which of the following is the best helping paraphrase response to the following statement? "I'm really bummed out about my apartment situation."
    a. "So, you're bummed out, huh?"
    b. "Your apartment situation is bad?"
    c. "You're depressed because you haven't found a place to live yet?"
    d. "You should really get a new place; I agree."
    e. "It will all work out by next month."
    Answer: c   **Type: M**   **Pages: 251–253**   **Analysis**

65. Constructive criticism is a kind of listening response that falls into the category termed
    a. advising.
    b. judging.
    c. analyzing.
    d. supporting.
    e. questioning.
    Answer: b   **Type: M**   **Page: 259**   **Comprehension**

67. Your roommate gives the appearance of listening to you, but you can tell from her responses that her mind is elsewhere. You could call her listening style in this instance
    a. stage hogging.
    b. insulated listening.
    c. pseudolistening.
    d. defensive listening.
    e. ambushing.
    Answer: c   **Type: M**   **Page: 240**   **Application**

68. Which of the following is the best helping paraphrase response to the following statements? "I can't stand that class! The lectures are a waste of time, and the tests are full of nitpicking questions. I'm not learning anything."
    a. "Sounds like you're fed up with the class."
    b. "Sounds like you're thinking about dropping the class."
    c. "Sounds like the class has nit-picking tests and is a waste of time."
    d. "Sounds like you resent spending so much time on information you don't consider useful."
    e. "Sounds like you're fed up with school."
    Answer: d   **Type: M**   **Pages: 251–253**   **Application**

69. "I think that the reason you're so confused is that you're trying to make everyone else happy and forgetting your own happiness." This statement is what type of listening response?
    a.   supporting
    b.   advising
    c.   questioning
    d.   paraphrasing
    e.   analyzing

    Answer: e   **Type: M**   **Page: 256**   **Application**

70. "From what you've said, it sounds like you're mad at your boss for expecting you to drop your personal plans whenever he wants you to work. Is that right?" This statement is what type of response?
    a.   supporting
    b.   judging
    c.   questioning
    d.   paraphrasing
    e.   analyzing

    Answer: d   **Type: M**   **Page: 251**   **Application**

71. "Sure it's unfair. But you shouldn't let that stop you. Life is unfair, so you're crazy to let it bother you." This statement is what type of response?
    a.   supporting
    b.   judging
    c.   questioning
    d.   paraphrasing
    e.   parroting

    Answer: b   **Type: M**   **Page: 259**   **Application**

72. When choosing the best listening style, it is important to consider
    a.   the situation.
    b.   the other person.
    c.   your personal style.
    d.   both a and b above.
    e.   a, b, and c above.

    Answer: e   **Type: M**   **Pages: 262–263**   **Comprehension**

73. Sue listens carefully to her instructor as he discusses the upcoming exam since she hopes to get an A. This illustrates what step in the listening process?
    a.   hearing
    b.   attending
    c.   understanding
    d.   responding
    e.   remembering

    Answer: b   **Type: M**   **Pages: 236–238**   **Application**

74. All of the following are reasons why it's impossible to listen well all the time except
    a. message overload.
    b. rapid thought.
    c. lack of training.
    d. faulty assumptions.
    e. All all of these answer are correct are reasons.
    Answer: e   **Type: M**   **Pages: 241–245**   **Knowledge**

75. The residual message is
    a. the part of the message we respond to.
    b. the part of the message we understand.
    c. the part of the message we remember.
    d. usually stated first.
    e. usually stated last.
    Answer: c   **Type: M**   **Page: 239**   **Knowledge**

76. Making sense of a message is related to which element of listening?
    a. hearing
    b. attending
    c. understanding
    d. responding
    e. remembering
    Answer: c   **Type: M**   **Page: 238**   **Knowledge**

77. Are you finally off the phone is an example of a question that traps the speaker.
    a. makes a statement.
    b. carries a hidden agenda.
    c. seeks a 'correct' answer.
    d. is based on an unchecked assumption.
    Answer: b   **Type: M**   **Page: 249**   **Application**

78. "You didn't like that restaurant, did you?" is an example of a question that
    a. traps the speaker.
    b. makes a statement.
    c. carries a hidden agenda.
    d. seeks a correct' answer.
    e. is based on an unchecked assumption.
    Answer: a   **Type: M**   **Page: 249**   **Application**

79. According to Ellen Langer, when you give careful and thoughtful attention and responses to the messages you receive you are listening
    a. selectively.
    b. purposefully.
    c. mindfully.
    d. for factual information.
    e. for personal information.
    Answer: c   **Type: M**   **Page: 235**   **Knowledge**

80. "I'm here if you need me" is an example of what type of listening response?
    a. prompting
    b. supporting
    c. understanding
    d. judging
    c. helping
    Answer: b   **Type: M**   **Page: 254**   **Application**

81. One study of 195 critical incidents in banking and medical settings showed that a major difference between effective and ineffective listening was
    a. how well the message was understood.
    b. how easy it was to remember the message.
    c. whether the message was of importance to the listener.
    d. whether the message could be remembered.
    e. the kind of feedback offered.
    Answer: e   **Type: M**   **Page: 238**   **Knowledge**

82. "Your mother drives you nuts? Let me tell you about mine!" is an example of what type of ineffective listening?
    a. insensitive listening
    b. stage-hogging
    c. selective listening
    d. nsulated listening
    e. ambushing
    Answer: b   **Type: M**   **Page: 240**   **Application**

83. The most popular piece of language is
    a. advising
    b. questioning
    c. paraphrasing
    d. judging
    e. supporting
    Answer: b   **Type: M**   **Page: 249**   **Knowledge**

84. All of the following are factors to consider before you decide to paraphrase except
    a. whether the issue is complex enough.
    b. whether you have the necessary time and concern.
    c. whether you can withhold judgment.
    d. whether the other person's feelings might be hurt.
    e. whether your paraphrase is in proportion to other responses.
    Answer: d   **Type: M**   **Page: 254**   **Knowledge**

85. "Don't worry about it" is an example of what type of "cold comfort" message ?
    a. denying others the right to their feelings.
    b. inimizing the significance of the situation.
    c. focusing on 'then and there' rather than 'here and now.'
    d. casting judgment.
    e. none of these answers are correct.
    Answer: a   **Type: M**   **Page: 255**   **Knowledge**

INSTRUCTIONS for questions 86–109: Match each statement with the helping listening style it characterizes.

a. paraphrasing
b. judging
c. supporting
d. advising
e. analyzing

86. "That's a terrible idea!"
    Answer: b   **Type: Matching**   **Page: 259**   **Analysis**

87. "You ought to give it a try. You've got nothing to lose."
    Answer: d   **Type: Matching**   **Page: 258**   **Analysis**

88. "He's doing that because he doesn't think you'll care."
    Answer: e   **Type: Matching**   **Page: 256**   **Analysis**

89. "I think you're doing a terrific job."
    Answer: c   **Type: Matching**   **Page: 254**   **Analysis**

90. "Sure it's discouraging now, but it will be over soon."
    Answer: c   **Type: Matching**   **Page: 254**   **Analysis**

91. "So you're upset because Chris didn't pay you back?"
    Answer: a   **Type: Matching**   **Page: 250**   **Analysis**

92. "The best thing for you to do is break up with him."
    Answer: d   **Type: Matching**   **Page: 258**   **Analysis**

93. "Have you ever thought about just giving her what she wants?"
    Answer: d   **Type: Matching**   **Page: 258**   **Analysis**

94. "I can't believe it! He's really a jerk for saying that."
    Answer: b   **Type: Matching**   **Page: 259**   **Analysis**

95. "So you're hoping she'll call, but you're not sure what you'll say if she does?"
    Answer: a   **Type: Matching**   **Page: 250**   **Analysis**

96. "Of course you get pushed around. Tat's what happens when you don't tell people what you want."
    Answer: b   **Type: Matching**   **Page: 259**   **Analysis**

97. "You're on the right track now."
    Answer: b   **Type: Matching**   **Page: 259**   **Analysis**

98. "Sounds like you're mad at me for embarrassing you. s that right?"
    Answer: a   **Type: Matching**   **Page: 250**   **Analysis**

99. "You've always done fine in the past. on't worry; you can do it this time, too."
    Answer: c   **Type: Matching**   **Page: 254**   **Analysis**

98. "You'd be a lot happier if you stopped blaming everyone else for your problems."
    Answer: b   **Type: Matching**   **Page: 259**   **Analysis**

99. "It seems to me you're only doing that to get back at him for cheating on you."
    Answer: e   **Type: Matching**   **Page: 256**   **Analysis**

100. "Don't try so hard and you'll probably do better."
    Answer: d   **Type: Matching**   **Page: 258**   **Analysis**

101. "Let me see if I've got this right. You're mad because you like the idea of a curfew for teens, but it's hard to enforce?"
    Answer: a   **Type: Matching**   **Page: 2503**   **Analysis**

102. "The reason you're insecure is that money means a lot to you."
    Answer: e   **Type: Matching**   **Page: 256**   **Analysis**

103. "Don't give up. You'll get it this next time."
    Answer: c   **Type: Matching**   **Page: 254**   **Analysis**

104. So you're saying that you want to ask Kathy to the dance but you're afraid she'll turn you down?"
    Answer: a   **Type: Matching**   **Page: 250**   **Analysis**

105. "Have you tried just talking to her about it?"
    Answer: d   **Type: Matching**   **Page: 258**   **Analysis**

106. "I think you're still unsure of yourself because of all the moving you did as a child."
    Answer: e   **Type: Matching**   **Page: 256**   **Analysis**

107. ""That's a good idea".
    Answer: b   **Type: Matching**   **Page: 259**   **Analysis**

108. We have all been selective, insulated, defensive, insensitive, and ambushing listeners. Give an example of each type of listening from your own personal experience. Illustrate any misunderstandings that developed as a result of your listening behavior.
    Answer: **Type: E**   **Pages: 240–241**   **Analysis**

110. Chapter Seven lists seven different types of listening responses. Imagine a speaker says the following remarks to you. Write seven responses to this situation—an example of prompting, questioning, paraphrasing, supporting, analyzing, advising and judging. "This woman at work never speaks to me. I mean, I come in and say something like, 'Hi, how are you?' and she just stares at me. Rude, right? How can a person just ignore someone?"
    Answer: **Type: E**   **Pages: 248–259**   **Application**

111. Describe the style(s) of listening you use most often when helping others. How successful are these styles? What makes them successful or unsuccessful? What might you do to increase your effectiveness as a helpful listener?
    Answer: **Type: E**   **Pages: 248–259**   **Evaluation**

112. In your own words, describe what paraphrasing is and how it is used to help others solve their problems. Use real or hypothetical examples and concrete language to explain and illustrate your answer.
   Answer: **Type: E**   **Pages: 250–253**   **Synthesis**

113. Read the following three hypothetical situations and discuss for each which of the seven listening responses described in your text might suit the situation and other person best. Explain why your choices are more likely to be helpful than the other types of listening responses.
   Your employer is giving complicated directions for a task you must do.
   A friend storms into the room clearly furious over something that happened to her while she was at school today.
   Your brother comes to you about a job offer that he's trying to decide about accepting.
   Answer: **Type: E**   **Pages: 248–259**   **Application**

114. Recount an interpersonal situation in which you failed to listen effectively. Describe the factors which caused you to listen poorly. What could you have done to change those factors?
   Answer: **Type: E**   **Pages: 241–245**   **Evaluation**

115. There are five elements in the listening process. Discuss each with a full and detailed explanation.
   Answer: **Type: E**   **Pages: 236–239**   **Analysis**

116. Your text provides a number of reasons for why we don't listen better. Discuss each one of them and then identify/explain one or two that are main reasons for why you don't listen better.
   Answer: **Type: E**   **Pages: 241–245**   **Evaluation**

117. A Chinese Proverb says, "To be heard, there are times you must be silent." Thoughtfully explain what this means to you incorporating information from your text on listening.
   Answer: **Type: E**   **Pages: 245–246, 248–259**

CHAPTER 8
COMMUNICATION AND RELATIONAL DYNAMICS

1. Dialectical tensions arise when a relationship is new and tend to disappear after the first two years.
    Answer: F   **Type: T**   **Pages: 279, 282**   **Knowledge**

2. Of the three types of dialectical tensions, research indicates that young married couples report having the most difficulty with the openness versus privacy tension.
    Answer: F   **Type: T**   **Page: 281**   **Knowledge**

3. People with especially high or low self-esteem find "perfect" people more attractive than people who are competent but flawed.
    Answer: T   **Type: T**   **Page: 270**   **Knowledge**

4. According to Chapter Eight, we are usually attracted to people who are similar to us.
    Answer: T   **Type: T**   **Page: 268**   **Comprehension**

5. Small talk typically occurs during the initiating stage of an interpersonal relationship.
    Answer: F   **Type: T**   **Page: 274**   **Knowledge**

6. The experimenting stage of interpersonal relationships is characterized by small talk.
    Answer: T   **Type: T**   **Page: 274**   **Knowledge**

7. According to your text, we are more attracted to people who are good at what they do but admit their mistakes.
    Answer: T   **Type: T**   **Page: 270**   **Knowledge**

8. Reciprocal liking builds attractiveness.
    Answer: T   **Type: T**   **Page: 269**   **Knowledge**

9. Social circles merge and the relational partners take on a new relational identity in the intensifying stage of relationships.
    Answer: F   **Type: T**   **Page: 275**   **Comprehension**

10. Differentiation in relationships is always negative, since it is part of the "coming apart" process.
    Answer: F   **Type: T**   **Page: 276**   **Comprehension**

11. The circumscribing stage of interpersonal relationships involves total avoidance of the other.
    Answer: F   **Type: T**   **Page: 276**   **Comprehension**

12. The initiating stage of interpersonal relationships is usually brief.
    Answer: T   **Type: T**   **Page: 273**   **Comprehension**

13. Attraction to others is greatest when we perceive we are similar to them in a high percentage of important areas, like goals and beliefs.
    Answer: T   **Type: T**   **Page: 269**   **Comprehension**

14. Differences strengthen a relationship when they are complementary.
    Answer: T   **Type: T**   **Page: 269**   **Knowledge**

15. Dialectical tensions exist in relationships when two incompatible forces or pressures exist at the same time.
    Answer: T   **Type: T**   **Page: 279**   **Comprehension**

16. It is impossible to like someone without being immediate with them.
    Answer: F   **Type: T**   **Page: 290**   **Knowledge**

17. Immediacy only occurs through nonverbal behavior such as eye contact and facial expressions.
    Answer: F   **Type: T**   **Page: 290**   **Knowledge**

18. The person who exercises the greatest amount of conversational control doesn't always make the decisions in interpersonal relationships.
    Answer: T   **Type: T**   **Page: 291**   **Comprehension**

19. Metacommunication is communication about communication.
    Answer: T   **Type: T**   **Page: 291**   **Knowledge**

20. Affinity is defined as the degree to which people like or appreciate one another.
    Answer: T Type: T Page: 289 Knowledge

21. There are two types of relational control: decision control and conversation control.
    Answer: T   **Type: T**   **Page: 291**   **Knowledge**

22. Metacommunication is a destructive substitute for real communication.
    Answer: F   **Type: T**   **Page: 291**   **Comprehension**

23. Verbal metacommunication is a necessary ingredient in successful relationships.
    Answer: T   **Type: T**   **Page: 291**   **Knowledge**

24. Relational messages deal most commonly with control, immediacy, affection, or respect.
    Answer: T   **Type: T**   **Pages: 289–291**   **Knowledge**

25. Affinity messages can be either positive or negative.
    Answer: T   **Type: T**   **Page: 289**   **Knowledge**

26. Whereas affinity involves liking, respect involves esteem.
    Answer: T   **Type: T**   **Page: 290**   **Knowledge**

27. Liking or loving is a better predictor of relational satisfaction than respect.
    Answer: F   **Type: T**   **Page: 290**   **Knowledge**

28. All appropriate self-disclosure leads to liking.
    Answer: F   **Type: T**   **Page: 270**   **Knowledge**

29. The two key ingredients in successful self-disclosure are reciprocity and timing.
    Answer: T   **Type: T**   **Page: 270**   **Knowledge**

30. When we are trying to decide whether a relationship with another person is no longer "worth the effort," we are using the social exchange formula.
    Answer: T   **Type: T**   **Page: 271**   **Knowledge**

31. Asking someone, "What's your major?" is an example of uncertainty reduction in the experimenting stage.
    Answer: T   **Type: T**   **Page: 274**   **Knowledge**

32. The move from initiating to experimenting occurs at the same pace for both those communicating in cyberspace and face-to-face.
    Answer: F   **Type: T**   **Page: 274**   **Knowledge**

33. The intensifying stage is the time when individuals give up some characteristics of their old selves and develop shared identities.
    Answer: F   **Type: T**   **Page: 275**   **Knowledge**

34. Partners make fewer straightforward requests in the integrating stage than they did in earlier relational stages.
    Answer: T   **Type: T**   **Page: 275**   **Knowledge**

35. It is possible for a business partnership to move to a bonding stage.
    Answer: T   **Type: T**   **Page: 275**   **Comprehension**

36. In the stagnating stage, communication between members decreases in quantity and quality.
    Answer: F   **Type: T**   **Page: 276**   **Knowledge**

37. All relationships begin, progress, decline, and end in the same linear fashion based on Knapp's developmental stages.
    Answer: F   **Type: T**   **Page: 278**   **Knowledge**

38. The levels of connection and autonomy that we seek can change over time.
    Answer: T   **Type: T**   **Page: 279**   **Knowledge**

39. Some couples never experience distance in their relationship.
    Answer: F   **Type: T**   **Page: 280**   **Comprehension**

40. The dialectical tension strategy couples use when they choose one end of the dialectical spectrum at some times and the other end at other times is called segmentation.
    Answer: F   **Type: T**   **Page: 281**   **Knowledge**

41. The dialectical tension strategy whereby couples simultaneously accept opposing forces without trying to diminsh them is called integration.
    Answer: T   **Type: T**   **Page: 282**   **Knowledge**

42. Rules about self-disclosure vary between cultures.
    Answer: T   **Type: T**   **Page: 284**   **Knowledge**

43. Communication accounts for as much as 80 percent of the difference between satisfying and unsatisfying relationships.
    Answer: T   **Type: T**   **Page: 285**   **Knowledge**

44. One type of communication that helps maintain relationships is evaluation.
    Answer: F   **Type: T**   **Page: 285**   **Knowledge**

45. Trangressions are always intentional.
    Answer: F   **Type: T**   **Page: 286**   **Knowledge**

46. The only benefit of forgiving a transgression is that the relationship might be repaired.
    Answer: F   **Type: T**   **Pages: 287–288**   **Knowledge**

47. One study found that the two least forgivable offenses of dating partners were sexual infidelity and unjustified suspicion.
    Answer: F   **Type: T**   **Page: 288**   **Knowledge**

48. Almost all verbal messages have a content dimension as well as convey relational information.
    Answer: T   **Type: T**   **Page: 288**   **Comprehension**

49. Relational messages are frequently nonverbal.
    Answer: T   **Type: T**   **Page: 289**   **Comprehension**

50. Relational dimensions of messages make statements about how the parties feel toward one another.
    Answer: T   **Type:**   **Page: 288**   **Knowledge**

51. In Chapter Eight's "Looking At Diversity" reading, Matt DeLanoy talks about how communicating on the Internet makes it easier to meet people since he
    a.   is very shy.
    b.   is overweight.
    c.   stutters.
    d.   is physically disabled.
    e.   None of these choices are correct
    Answer: c   **Type: M**   **Page: 273**   **Knowledge**

52. According to the text, we are usually attracted to people who
    a.   like us.
    b.   are high self-disclosers.
    c.   are perfect.
    d.   approve of us even in ways we know are inaccurate.
    Answer: a   **Type: M**   **Page: 269**   **Comprehension**

53. According to Knapp's model of interaction stages, symbolic public gestures that show the world that a relationship exists usually occur in which stage in interpersonal relationships?
    a.   experimenting
    b.   intensifying
    c.   bonding
    d.   integrating
    e.   circumscribing
    Answer: c   **Type: M**   **Page: 275**   **Knowledge**

54. Which of the following does not typically occur in the intensifying stage of interpersonal relationships?
   a. The parties spend an increasing amount of time together.
   b. The parties begin to take on an identity as a social unit.
   c. The parties hint and flirt.
   d. Feelings are expressed nonverbally.
   e. The parties might take trips together.
   Answer: b   **Type: M**   **Page: 274**   **Synthesis**

55. Social exchange theory suggests that we often seek out people who can give us
   a. rewards greater than or equal to the costs we encounter in dealing with them.
   b. more self-esteem.
   c. relational rewards rather than physical ones.
   d. something in exchange for what we give them.
   e. both relational and physical things without demanding anything of us.
   Answer: a   **Type: M**   **Page: 271**   **Knowledge**

56. "Why don't you go ahead and visit your friends without me this weekend. I'll stick around and catch up on my studies." This statement typifies which relational stage?
   a. integrating
   b. differentiating
   c. bonding
   d. terminating
   e. intensifying
   Answer: b   **Type: M**   **Page: 276**   **Application**

57. When two opposing or incompatible forces exist simultaneously in an interpersonal relationship, the struggle to achieve these opposing goals creates what is called a
   a. collectivistic tension.
   b. differentiating end state.
   c. counterfeit goal state.
   d. dialectical tension.
   e. proximity problem.
   Answer: d   **Type: M**   **Page: 279**   **Knowledge**

58. Conflicting desires for both intimacy and the lack of it in an interpersonal relationship lead to the
   a. connection-autonomy dialectic.
   b. cohesion-revolt dialectic.
   c. predictability-novelty dialectic.
   d. openness-privacy dialectic.
   Answer: d   **Type: M**   **Page: 280**   **Knowledge**

59. The strategy where communicators respond to one end of the dialectical spectrum and ignore the other is
   a. denial
   b. disorientation
   c. alternation
   d. segmentation
   Answer: a   **Type: M**   **Page: 281**   **Knowledge**

60. Judith and Natalie work for the same employer and often have lunch together to talk about their current romances, problems with their families, and apartment headaches. Most Saturday afternoons they play tennis together. Which relationship stage do they seem to be in?
    a.   initiating
    b.   differentiating
    c.   bonding
    d.   intensifying
    e.   circumscribing

Answer: d   **Type: M**   **Page: 274**   **Application**

61. Molly makes an excuse not to attend a party she knows Jack is invited to. She's most likely in which stage with Jack?
    a.   initiating
    b.   avoiding
    c.   circumscribing
    d.   experimenting
    e.   bonding

Answer: b   **Type: M**   **Page: 276**   **Application**

62. In the "Accidental Tourist" Communication Transcript from your text, Macon and Muriel's discussion had problems because
    a.   they couldn't agree about the importance of math skills.
    b.   Macon didn't show enough immediacy cues like eye contact when talking.
    c.   Macon stuck only to the content level of the conversational messages.
    d.   Muriel and Macon communicated too much.
    e.   Macon wanted relational control over Muriel.

Answer: c   **Type: M**   **Page: 292**   **Analysis**

63. Almost every message has
    a.   content dimention
    b.   relational dimension
    c.   both a content and a relational dimension.
    d.   no dimensions unless the communicators intend them to.
    e.   an unintentional message.

Answer: c   **Type: M**   **Page: 288**   **Knowledge**

64. The relational dimension of a message
    a.   deals with one or more social needs.
    b.   makes statements about how the parties feel toward one another.
    c.   are usually expressed nonverbally.
    d.   All of these choices are correct.
    e.   None of these choices are correct.

Answer: d   **Type: M**   **Page: 288**   **Knowledge**

65. Your roommate says, "It's your turn to take out the trash" in a demanding tone of voice. If you want to find out the relational dimension of the message, you should
    a. remind your roommate nicely that you took the trash out last night.
    b. use perception checking to see if your roommate is upset with you.
    c. negotiate other ways of dealing with the trash problem.
    d. ask your roommate's friends to explain the real problem.
    e. point out how defensive your roommate sounds.
    Answer: b   **Type: M**   **Pages: 288–289**   **Application**

66. In any relationship, the power to determine what will happen in the relationship is a type of relational control called
    a. decision control.
    b. conversation control.
    c. distributional control.
    d. powerful control.
    e. context control.
    Answer: a   **Type: M**   **Page: 291**   **Knowledge**

67. Talking the most, interrupting the other person, and changing the topic most often are all common indicators of
    a. conversation control
    b. decision control
    c. powerful control
    d. context control
    e. distributional control
    Answer: a   **Type: M**   **Page: 291**   **Knowledge**

68. Whenever we discuss a relationship with another, we are
    a. arguing
    b. improving our relationship
    c. self-disclosing
    d. metacommunicating
    e. receiving double messages.
    Answer: d   **Type: M**   **Page: 291**   **Knowledge**

69. The degree to which the partners in an interpersonal relationship like or appreciate one another is called
    a. appreciation.
    b. self-respect.
    c. the communication of honesty.
    d. affinity.
    e. the like-love phenomenon.
    Answer: d   **Type: M**   **Page: 289**   **Knowledge**

70. The stage where a couple might come up with "our song" is
    a. initiating
    b. experimenting
    c. intensifying
    d. integrating
    e. bonding
    Answer: d   **Type: M**   **Page: 275**   **Knowledge**

71. The best predictor of whether a couple will be friends after reaching the terminating stage is
    a. whether they have children.
    b. whether they were friends before their emotional involvement.
    c. whether they went to counseling.
    d. whether communication was positive during the break-up.
    e. b and d

    Answer: e   **Type: M**   **Page: 277**   **Knowledge**

72. "I was feeling trapped" is communication that characterizes what dialectical tension?
    a. connection-autonomy
    b. openness-privacy
    c. predictability-novelty
    d. win-lose
    e. None of these choices are correct.

    Answer: a   **Type: M**   **Page: 279**   **Knowledge**

73. All of the following are strategies that couples use to kept their relationships satisfying except
    a. positivity.
    b. social networks.
    c. openness.
    d. constructive criticism.
    e. assurances

    Answer: d   **Type: M**   **Page: 285**   **Knowledge**

74. Of the following, what is not a category of relational transgressions?
    a. minor vs. significant
    b. one-time vs. incremental
    c. deliberate vs. intentional
    d. social vs. relational
    e. open vs. private

    Answer: e   **Type: M**   **Pages: 286–287**   **Knowledge**

75. John and Valerie have an agreement that he will call to tell her when he will be late from work so she won't worry. When he forgets, Valerie is upset because of what type of transgression?
    a. minor
    b. significant
    c. relational
    d. deliberate
    e. incremental

    Answer: c   **Type: M**   **Page: 286**   **Application**

76. The term used to describe messages that people exchange, verbally or nonverbally, about their relationship is
    a. microcommunication
    b. conversation
    c. discourse
    d. metacommunication
    e. miscommunication

    Answer: d   **Type: M**   **Page: 291**   **Knowledge**

77. Saying to your partner, "I wish you didn't use that tone of voice with me" is an example of
    a. metadata.
    b. relational transgression.
    c. the connection-autonomy dialectic.
    d. metacommunication.
    e. None of these choices are correct

    Answer: d   **Type: M**   **Page: 291**   **Application**

78. All of the following are true about similarity research except
    a. For the most part, we like people who are similar to us.
    b. Communication ability is more important to relational happiness than being similar.
    c. Being similar to others can boost your ego.
    d. Attraction is greatest when we're similar to others in areas like goals and beliefs.
    e. We tend to have stronger dislike for people who are similar to us but offensive.

    Answer: b   **Type: M**   **Pages: 268–269**   **Knowledge**

79. We are often attracted to people who
    a. we find physically attractive
    b. are different but can satisfy our needs.
    c. are similar to us.
    d. we interact with frequently.
    e. All of these choices are correct are true.

    Answer: e   **Type: M**   **Pages: 268–271**   **Knowledge**

80. The stage where partners act in old, familiar ways and no growth occurs is
    a. differentiation
    b. circumscribing
    c. stagnating
    d. avoiding
    e. terminating

    Answer: c   **Type: M**   **Page: 276**   **Knowledge**

81. One of the key differences between marriages that end in separation and those that are restored to their former intimacy is
    a. how long the couple remained in the integration stage.
    b. how much metacommunication occurs.
    c. the types of relational transgressions that happened.
    d. the communication that occurs when the partners are unsatisfied.
    e. None of these choices are correct.

    Answer: d   **Type: M**   **Page: 276**   **Knowledge**

82. According to your text, the process of getting to know others by gaining more information about them is called
    a. initiating
    b. approach behavior
    c. networking
    d. uncertainty reduction
    e. All of these choices are correct.

    Answer: d   **Type: M**   **Page: 274**   **Knowledge**

83. Susan is getting tired of the Friday night routine of eating out at the same restaurant with her husband. She is struggling with what dialectical tension?
    a. connection-autonomy
    b. openness-privacy
    c. predictability-novelty
    d. alternation-segmentation
    e. None of these choices are correct

    Answer: c   **Type: M**   **Pages: 280–281**   **Application**

84. A couple on their second marriage each share many feelings with each other, but they keep most details of their previous marriages private. They are managing the openness-privacy dialectic with the strategy of
    a. denial
    b. alternation
    c. segmentation
    d. balance
    e. recalibration

    Answer: c   **Type: M**   **Page: 281**   **Application**

85. Relationships
    a. are constantly changing.
    b. need ongoing maintenance to keep them satisfying.
    c. are affected by culture.
    d. typically progress from one stage to another.
    e. All of these choices are correct are true about relationships.

    Answer: e   **Type: M**   **Pages: 273–285**   **Synthesis**

87. The best chance of repairing damaged relationship requires
    a. sincere apology.
    b. an acknowledgement that the transgression was wrong.
    c. some type of compensation.
    d. a. and b.
    e. All of these choices are correct

    Answer: e   **Type: M**   **Page: 287**   **Knowledge**

88. The benefit of forgiveness is
    a. less emotional distress.
    b. less aggression.
    c. improvement of cardiovascular functioning.
    d. restoration of the damaged relationship.
    e. All of these choices are correct are beneficial.

    Answer: e   **Type: M**   **Pages: 287–288**   **Knowledge**

89. One type of relational transgression is
    a. unfaithfulness.
    b. verbal hostility.
    c. rage.
    d. criticism in front of others.
    e. All of these choices are types of relational transgressions.

    Answer: e   **Type: M**   **Page: 286**   **Knowledge**

INSTRUCTIONS for questions 90–94: Match the statement below with the relational stage it best describes.

    a. avoiding
    b. circumscribing
    c. experimenting
    d. integrating
    e. differentiating

90. Relational partners attempt to reduce uncertainty and to decide if the relationship is worth pursuing.
    Answer: c   **Type: Matching**   **Page: 274**   **Knowledge**

91. Relational partners begin to share identities and their social circles merge.
    Answer: d   **Type: Matching**   **Page: 275**   **Knowledge**

92. Relational partners begin to withdraw from one another to avoid disagreement
    Answer: b   **Type: Matching**   **Page: 276**   **Knowledge**

93. Relational partners create physical distance between one another and make excuses to reduce contact.
    Answer: a   **Type: Matching**   **Page: 276**   **Knowledge**

94. Relational partners shift from "we" orientation and use more "me" messages.
    Answer: e   **Type: Matching**   **Pages: 275–276**   **Knowledge**

95. Pick two people you know, one with whom you want to strengthen your relationship and one to whom you are not particularly attracted. Using the interpersonal attraction variables in the text, analyze the reasons why you want/don't want to form a relationship with each person.
    Answer: **Type: E**   **Pages: 268–270**   **Analysis**

96. Define the four types of relational messages and illustrate each of them with examples from your life.
    Answer: **Type: E**   **Pages: 289–291**   **Application**

97. Describe each of Knapp's relational stages, those of "coming together" and "coming apart." Use a personal relationship and explain the stage(s) that you have gone through including the communication used to reflect each stage.
    Answer: **Type: E**   **Pages: 272–278**   **Application**

98. Identify a dialectical tension in one of your interpersonal relationships. Explain how this tension has affected the relationship and identify/explain the strategy (or strategies) you use to manage the dialectical tension.
    Answer: **Type: E**   **Pages: 279–282**   **Application**

99. Similarity is considered a significant reason for why we form relationships. Explain in detail the various findings of similarity research as they apply to our attraction to others.
    Answer: **Type: E**   **Pages: 268–269**   **Comprehension**

100. One characteristic of relationships is that they are constantly changing. Explain this principle and include experiences from one of your own significant relationships in your discussion.
    Answer: **Type: E**   **Pages: 282–283**   **Application**

101. Explain why relationships require maintenance and the five strategies couples use to help maintain them.

Answer: **Type: E**   **Page: 285**   **Comprehension**

102. Define a relational transgression and provide some types of transgressions. Also, explain the three categories of transgressions.

Answer: **Type: E**   **Pages: 285–287**   **Comprehension**

103. Discuss how messages include both a content and relational dimension. Provide specific examples in your explanation.

Answer: **Type: E**   **Pages: 288–289**   **Comprehension**

CHAPTER 9

INTIMACY AND DISTANCE IN RELATIONAL COMMUNICATION

1. Your text suggests that while benevolent lies are common, the truth is always the best course of action.
    Answer: F   **Type: T**   **Pages: 323–324**   **Synthesis**

2. Self-disclosure must be frequent to be effective.
    Answer: F   **Type: T**   **Page: 305**   **Comprehension**

3. Cliches, the outer circle of the self-disclosure model in your text, are the most revealing type of communication.
    Answer: F   **Type: T**   **Page: 307**   **Knowledge**

4. The most revealing level of self-disclosure usually involves talking about feelings.
    Answer: T   **Type: T**   **Page: 307**   **Knowledge**

5. A well-documented conclusion from research is that one act of self-disclosure usually begets another.
    Answer: T   **Type: T**   **Page: 309**   **Knowledge**

6. When we self-disclose to strangers, it is usually for reciprocity or impression formation.
    Answer: T   **Type: T**   **Page: 311**   **Comprehension**

7. The strongest factor on why people disclose seems to be how well they know the other person.
    Answer: T   **Type: T**   **Page: 311**   **Knowledge**

8. In interpersonal relationships, the rule is: The more self-disclosure the better.
    Answer: F   **Type: T**   **Page: 307**   **Comprehension**

9. Since they are honest and true, comments to another, like "I've always thought you were a bit flaky," have constructive effects in self-disclosure.
    Answer: F   **Type: T**   **Page: 314**   **Comprehension**

10. It is quite possible to have a wide range of satisfying relationships without having much intimacy at all.
    Answer: T   **Type: T**   **Page: 299**   **Knowledge**

11. Intimacy can come from intellectual sharing alone.
    Answer: T   **Type: T**   **Page: 298**   **Comprehension**

12. Physical intimacy is obviously the best type of relational intimacy.
    Answer: F   **Type: T**   **Page: 298**   **Evaluation**

13. Lies may help us avoid embarrassment.
    Answer: T   **Type: T**   **Page: 317**   **Comprehension**

14. Couples are happiest when their levels of openness are roughly equal.
    Answer: T   **Type: T**   **Page: 314**   **Comprehension**

15. Hints are more direct than equivocal statements.
    Answer: T   **Type: T**   **Page: 323**   **Comprehension**

16. Research shows that most lies are told for the benefit of the recipient.
    Answer: F   **Type: T**   **Page: 318**   **Comprehension**

17. All self-disclosure leads to liking or attractiveness.
    Answer: F   **Type: T**   **Page: 314**   **Comprehension**

18. Your text makes the case that hints, benign lies, and equivocations are sometimes ethical alternatives to telling the truth.
    Answer: T   **Type: T**   **Page: 323**   **Synthesis**

19. Self-disclosure of personal thoughts and feelings may be inappropriate and risky in the work setting.
    Answer: T   **Type: T**   **Page: 313**   **Application**

20. Most self-disclosure is reciprocal.
    Answer: T   **Type: T**   **Page: 309**   **Comprehension**

21. You should avoid making disclosing statements that contain negative messages.
    Answer: F   **Type: T**   **Page: 313**   **Comprehension**

22. The best way to develop a positive interpersonal relationship is usually to begin that relationship by revealing a great amount of highly personal information about yourself.
    Answer: F   **Type: T**   **Page: 313**   **Knowledge**

23. People sometimes self-disclose to create a good impression.
    Answer: T   **Type: T**   **Page: 311**   **Knowledge**

24. According to the text, real self-disclosure does not involve attempts at control of the other.
    Answer: F   **Type: T**   **Page: 311**   **Comprehension**

25. The "Blind" window of the Johari model represents things about yourself that another may know about you, but you do not.
    Answer: T   **Type: T**   **Page: 308**   **Knowledge**

26. The "Unknown" window of the Johari model represents things about yourself that another knows, but you do not.
    Answer: F   **Type: T**   **Pages: 308–309**   **Comprehension**

27. The social penetration model represents both the breadth and the depth of your self-disclosure with another person.
    Answer: T   **Type: T**   **Page: 305**   **Knowledge**

28. Just because we have revealed many different kinds of facts to another doesn't mean that we have an intimate relationship.
    Answer: T   **Type: T**   **Page: 307**   **Comprehension**

29. Constant self-disclosure is a useful goal for those of us trying to improve a relationship.
    Answer: F   **Type: T**   **Page: 313**   **Comprehension**

30. Not all self-disclosure draws people closer.
    Answer: T   **Type: T**   **Page: 314**   **Synthesis**

31. Research shows that deception threatens relationships.
    Answer: T   **Type: T**   **Page: 319**   **Knowledge**

32. Some lies are designed to make the relationship grow.
    Answer: T   **Type: T**   **Page: 317**   **Knowledge**

75. If faced with a choice to tell a face-saving lie or deliver an equivocal message, most people will tell the lie.
    Answer: F   **Type: T**   **Page: 321**   **Knowledge**

76. Research supports that the quality of self-disclosure is not linked to marital satisfaction.
    Answer: F   **Type: T**   **Page: 311**   **Comprehension**

77. By definition, an intimate relationship must exhibit all four intimacy dimensions.
    Answer: F   **Type: T**   **Page: 299**   **Comprehension**

78. Male-male relationships involve less disclosure than male-female relationships.
    Answer: T   **Type: T**   **Page: 299**   **Knowledge**

79. Recent research has shown that men achieve intimacy through shared activities.
    Answer: T   **Type: T**   **Page: 300**   **Knowledge**

80. Because men share less personal information and feelings than women, they are not capable of achieving the type of intimate relationships that women have.
    Answer: F   **Type: T**   **Page: 300**   **Comprehension**

81. Emotional expression is the only way to develop close relationships.
    Answer: F   **Type: T**   **Page: 300**   **Comprehension**

82. Studies show that people from the United States are more disclosing than members of any culture studied.
    Answer: T   **Type: T**   **Page: 301**   **Knowledge**

83. Within the United States, the amount of disclosure is the same from one group to another.
    Answer: F   **Type: T**   **Page: 301**   **Knowledge**

84. Because cultures like Japan and Taiwan are collectivist, people there communicate the same with members of "in-groups" and "out-groups" alike.
    Answer: F   **Type: T**   **Page: 301**   **Comprehension**

85. Some studies show that relational intimacy may develop more quickly through computer-mediated communication than face-to-face.
    Answer: T   **Type: T**   **Page: 302**   **Knowledge**

86. Focusing on having intimate communication daily will lead to extremely satisfying relationships.
    Answer: F   **Type: T**   **Page: 302**   **Comprehension**

87. The most intimate relationships are those in which disclosure is great in both breadth and depth.
    Answer: T   **Type: T**   **Page: 305**   **Knowledge**

88. "Talking a problem out" can be helpful in clarifying your beliefs, opinions, thoughts , attitudes and feelings.
    Answer: T   **Type: T**   **Page: 309**   **Knowledge**

89. Reciprocity usually occurs on a turn-by-turn basis.
    Answer: F   **Type: T**   **Page: 309**   **Knowledge**

90. One good measure of happiness is how well the level of disclosure matches the expectations of communicators.
    Answer: T   **Type: T**   **Page: 313**   **Knowledge**

91. Silence is never an appropriate alternative to self-disclosure because it indicates a lack of interest in the relationship.
    Answer: F   **Type: T**   **Page: 316**   **Comprehension**

92. One study of deception determined that the average lie rate was 5 fibs every 10 minutes of conversation.
    Answer: F   **Type: T**   **Page: 317**   **Knowledge**

93. Equivocation can prevent the teller from feeling guilty.
    Answer: T   **Type: T**   **Page: 322**   **Knowledge**

94. In the Chapter Nine "Communication Transcript," Ramon discloses to his boss, Julie. Which of the following guidelines for self-disclosure did Ramon seem to ignore as he talked with her ?
    a.   Ask yourself if the risk of disclosure is reasonable.
    b.   Determine if the self-disclosure is relevant to the situation at hand.
    c.   Decide if the other person is important to you.
    d.   Select the appropriate amount and type of self-disclosure.
    e.   Ramon ignored all of the guidelines.
    Answer: d   **Type: M**   **Page: 315**   **Analysis**

95. According to your text, all of the following are reasons to be somewhat deceitful in relationships except
    a.   to guide social interaction.
    b.   to empower others.
    c.   to save face.
    d.   to avoid conflict.
    e.   to expand or reduce relationships.
    Answer: b   **Type: M**   **Pages: 317–318**   **Synthesis**

96. You've just delivered a speech to your classmates which none of them liked very much. According to your text, which of the following is the response you are most likely to hear when you ask them how you did?
   a. "You did a great job."
   b. "I'm nervous about my speech tomorrow."
   c. "I don't think it was a very good speech."
   d. "You made some interesting points."
   e. None of these answers are correct.

   Answer: d   **Type: M**   **Page: 321**   **Application**

97. The Johari Window is an important device to help explore the role
   a. coding plays in communication.
   b. interpretation plays in clarifying understanding.
   c. feedback plays in negative relationships.
   d. self-disclosure plays in communication.
   e. affection needs play in strong relationships.

   Answer: d   **Type: M**   **Page: 309**   **Knowledge**

98. According to the text, which of the following is good advice about self-disclosure?
   a. Wait for the other person to open up before you do.
   b. The more self-disclosure, the better.
   c. Self-disclosure is most productive when delivered in a constructive manner.
   d. Most relationships are characterized by almost constant amounts of self-disclosure.
   e. It's best to accompany each piece of negative self-disclosure with a compliment to soften any hurt.

   Answer: c   **Type: M**   **Pages: 309–314**   **Synthesis**

99. The social penetration model by Altman and Taylor
   a. shows ways in which a relationship can be more or less intimate.
   b. suggests how relationships can operate on superficial or more personal levels.
   c. defines a relationship in terms of its breadth and depth.
   d. helps identify why certain relationships are strong or weak.
   e. All of these answer are correct

   Answer: e   **Type: M**   **Page: 305**   **Analysis**

100. To qualify as self-disclosure, a statement must
   a. involve feelings.
   b. be intentional, significant, and not otherwise known.
   c. be reciprocated by the same type of statement from a partner.
   d. involve intimate information.
   e. be shared privately.

   Answer: b   **Type: M**   **Pages: 304–305**   **Comprehension**

101. "I've never been out of this state" is an example of self-disclosure at which of the following levels?
   a. cliche
   b. fact
   c. opinion
   d. feeling
   e. interpretation

   Answer: b   **Type: M**   **Page: 307**   **Application**

102. "It's nice to meet you" is an example of self-disclosure at which of the following levels?
     a. cliche
     b. fact
     c. opinion
     d. feeling
     e. interpretation
     Answer: a   **Type: M**   **Page: 307**   **Application**

103. "I'm worried that you won't follow through on your commitment" is an example of self-disclosure at which of the following levels?
     a. cliche
     b. fact
     c. opinion
     d. feeling
     e. interpretation
     Answer: d   **Type: M**   **Page: 307**   **Application**

104. "I don't think you're telling the truth" is an example of self-disclosure at which of the following levels?
     a. cliche
     b. fact
     c. opinion
     d. feeling
     e. interpretation
     Answer: c   **Type: M**   **Page: 307**   **Application**

105. Quadrants of the Johari Window are
     a. open, narrow, blind, unknown.
     b. open, hidden, blind, unknown.
     c. broad, narrow, blind, unknown.
     d. open, hidden, neutral, unknown.
     e. open, closed, neutral, unknown.
     Answer: b   **Type: M**   **Pages: 308–309**   **Knowledge**

106. Which of the following best fits the definition of self-disclosure?
     a. telling your romantic partner about your feelings toward him/her
     b. telling your college teacher about past grades
     c. telling your mother your weight
     d. telling your family physician about your health
     e. telling anyone anything about you
     Answer: a   **Type: M**   **Pages: 305–306**   **Application**

107. When the target of self-disclosure is a friend, the most frequent reason people give for volunteering personal information is
     a. to get to know the other better.
     b. relationship maintenance and enhancement.
     c. defensiveness reduction.
     d. self-validation.
     e. manipulation.
     Answer: b   **Type: M**   **Page: 311**   **Knowledge**

108. With strangers as the target of self-disclosure, the most common reason people give for disclosing is
    a. defensiveness reduction.
    b. manipulation.
    c. reciprocity.
    d. relationship maintenance.
    e. relationship enhancement.
    Answer: c   **Type: M**   **Page: 311**   **Knowledge**

109. "This was a rotten idea" is an example of self-disclosure at which of the following levels?
    a. cliche
    b. fact
    c. opinion
    d. feeling
    e. interpretation
    Answer: c   **Type: M**   **Page: 307**   **Application**

110. All of the following are dimensions of intimacy except
    a. physical
    b. emotional
    c. shared activities
    d. intellectual
    e. All of these answer are correct are dimensions.
    Answer: e   **Type: M**   **Pages: 298–299**   **Knowledge**

111. An intimate relationship
    a. may only exhibit one or two dimensions.
    b. can be achieved by sharing activities.
    c. can be created through exchanging important feelings.
    d. can come from exchanging ideas.
    e. All of these answer are correct are true.
    Answer: e   **Type: M**   **Page: 299**   **Comprehension**

112. One study of a randomly selected group of e-mail users showed that their electronic relationships were similar to traditional friendships in what way?
    a. interdependence
    b. breadth
    c. commitment
    d. depth
    e. All of these answer are correct are ways they were similar.
    Answer: e   **Type: M**   **Page: 299**   **Knowledge**

113. Research of male and female intimacy styles shows that
    a. differences are not as great as originally thought.
    b. women disclose more than men.
    c. women disclose more personal information than men.
    d. men grow close by doing things together.
    e. All of these answer are correct are true.
    Answer: e   **Type: M**   **Pages: 299–300**   **Knowledge**

114. An individualistic culture like the United States, compared to a collectivistic culture,
    a. discloses the same no matter what group is being disclosed to.
    d. rarely shows emotions.
    c. is not considered a very romantic culture.
    d. acts more familiar with strangers and discloses more personal information.
    e. shies away from public displays of affection.
    Answer: d   **Type: M**   **Page: 301**   **Knowledge**

115. Some studies show that computer-mediated communication
    a. always ensures intimacy.
    b. enhances verbal, emotional, and social intimacy in friendships.
    c. is harmful to sustaining intimacy.
    d. results in one level of self-disclosure.
    e. None of these answers are correct are true.
    Answer: b   **Type: M**   **Page: 302**   **Knowledge**

116. The process of deliberately revealing information about oneself that is significant and would not normally be known by others is
    a. social penetration.
    b. equivocation.
    c. self-disclosure.
    d. intimacy.
    e. reciprocity.
    Answer: c   **Type: M**   **Page:304**   **Knowledge**

117. According to the Altman and Taylor model, the dimension of self-disclosure where information shared moves from being impersonal to more personal is called
    a. breadth.
    b. social penetration.
    c. variety.
    d. depth.
    e. Equivocation.
    Answer: d   **Type: M**   **Page: 305**   **Knowledge**

118. What makes the disclosure in some messages deeper than others?
    a. Some revelations are more significant than others.
    b. Communicators have reached the level of sharing feelings.
    c. Some revelations are considered very private.
    d. None of these answers are correct are reasons.
    e. All of these answer are correct are reasons.
    Answer: e   **Type: M**   **Pages: 306–307**   **Comprehension**

119. Saying "I love my family" versus "I love you" exemplifies that some disclosures are deeper than others in terms of
    a. being personal.
    b. significance.
    c. how private they are.
    d. reciprocity.
    e. believability.
    Answer: b   **Type: M**   **Page: 306**   **Application**

120. "I really like Mark" is an example of self-disclosure at which of the following levels?
     a.   cliché
     b.   fact
     c.   opinion
     d.   feeling
     e.   interpretation
     Answer: c   **Type: M**   **Page: 307**   **Application**

121. The strongest factor in why we disclose is
     a.   how much control we might have over the other person.
     b.   how well we know the other person.
     c.   how strong our need is to get something off our chest.
     d.   how strong our need is for validation.
     e.   the likelihood there will be reciprocity.
     Answer: b   **Type: M**   **Page: 311**   **Knowledge**

122. When deciding how much to disclose, you should consider
     a.   if the other person is important to you.
     b.   whether the amount and type of disclosure is appropriate.
     c.   whether you have a moral obligation to do so.
     d.   whether the disclosure is relevant to the situation.
     e.   All are factors to consider.
     Answer: e   **Type: M**   **Pages: 313–314**   **Knowledge**

123. Saying to a friend, "I've always thought you weren't too bright," might show you didn't consider
     what guideline for self-disclosure?
     a.   Is the disclosure clear?
     b.   Will the effect of the disclosure be constructive?
     c.   Is the disclosure relevant?
     d.   Is the type of disclosure appropriate?
     e.   Do you have a moral obligation to disclose?
     Answer: b   **Type: M**   **Page: 314**   **Application**

124. Of the following, what is not considered a benefit of self-disclosure?
     a.   self-validation
     b.   catharsis
     c.   identity management
     d.   reciprocity
     e.   increased likeability
     Answer: e   **Type: M**   **Pages: 309–311**   **Knowledge**

125. Of the following, what is not considered a risk of self-disclosure?
     a.   loss of influence
     b.   negative impression
     c.   decrease in number of relationships
     d.   fear of disapproval
     e.   decrease in relational satisfaction
     Answer: c   **Type: M**   **Page: 312**   **Knowledge**

126. All of the following are alternatives to self-disclosure except
    a.   lying
    b.   silence
    c.   evasion
    d.   equivocation
    e.   hinting
    Answer: c   **Type: M**   **Pages: 316–323**   **Knowledge**

127. A benevolent lie
    a.   is considered unmalicious.
    b.   is never appropriate for someone who has morals.
    c.   will generally hurt another.
    d.   will only be considered helpful in extreme situations.
    e.   None of these answers are correct are true.
    Answer: a   **Type: M**   **Page: 317**   **Comprehension**

128. In one study of 130 subjects who kept track of the truthfulness of their everyday, conversational statements,
    a.   25 percent of these statements proved to be totally honest.
    b.   38.5 percent of these statements proved to be totally honest.
    c.   55.5 percent of these statements proved to be totally honest.
    d.   66 percent of these statements proved to be totally honest.
    e.   75 percent of these statements proved to be totally honest.
    Answer: b   **Type: M**   **Page: 317**   **Knowledge**

129. One experiment determined that the average lie rate was
    a.   3 fibs for every 10 minutes of conversation.
    b.   5 fibs for every 10 minutes of conversation.
    c.   7 fibs for every 10 minutes of conversation.
    d.   1 fib for every 5 minutes of conversation.
    e.   10 fibs for every 15 minutes of conversation.
    Answer: a   **Type: M**   **Page: 317**   **Knowledge**

130. When Kathy told John, "I'm just not ready for a serious relationship right now," instead of saying, "I'm not attracted to you," she was
    a.   lying
    b.   equivocating
    c.   hinting
    d.   placating
    e.   self-disclosing
    Answer: b   **Type: M**   **Page: 321**   **Application**

131. Equivocating can be advantageous because it
    a.   can save face for both the sender and receiver.
    b.   provides an alternative to lying.
    c.   spares the receiver from embarrassment.
    d.   spares the teller from feeling guilty.
    e.   All of these answer are correct are true.
    Answer: e   **Type: M**   **Pages: 321–322**   **Knowledge**

132. If someone says, "I really have to go. I should be studying for a test tomorrow," he/she would be lying in order to
    a. guide social interaction.
    b. save face.
    c. reduce interaction with another.
    d. avoid tension.
    e. show you're in control of a situation.
    Answer: c   **Type: M**   **Pages: 317–318**   **Application**

133. Of the following, what is not considered an effect of lying?
    a. Once lied to, you may need to redefine previous messages from the liar.
    b. Deception is more acceptable depending on the liar's motives.
    c. A lie will be considered a transgression if it is exploitive.
    d. The importance of the information lied about is a key factor in provoking a relational crisis.
    e. All of these answer are correct can be effects.
    Answer: e   **Type: M**   **Page: 319**   **Knowledge**

134. According to your text, hinting
    a. is less direct than an equivocal statement.
    b. aims to get a desired response from others.
    c. is not considered an alternative to lying.
    d. is not considered face-saving.
    e. doesn't depend on the other's ability to pick up the unexpressed message.
    Answer: b   **Type: M**   **Page: 323**   **Knowledge**

135. "I'm pretty sure that smoking isn't permitted here," is an example of
    a. lying.
    b. equivocating.
    c. hinting.
    d. self-disclosure.
    e. social penetration.
    Answer: c   **Type: M**   **Page: 323**   **Application**

136. A lie may be considered acceptable when
    a. the lie is mutually advantageous.
    b. it helps us avoid embarrassment.
    c. we expect another to lie.
    d. we've asked another to lie.
    e. All of these answer are correct are considered acceptable.
    Answer: e   **Type: M**   **Pages: 324–325**   **Knowledge**

INSTRUCTIONS for questions 137–141: Match the statement below with the term it best describes.
    a. self-disclosure
    b. cliche
    c. Johari Window
    d. social penetration
    e. fact

137. Model to explore the role of self-disclosure in relationships
     Answer: c   **Type: Matching**   **Page: 308**   **Knowledge**

138. Model to examine breadth and depth of relationships
     Answer: d   **Type: Matching**   **Page: 305**   **Knowledge**

139. "How are you doing? Fine!"
     Answer: b   **Type: Matching**   **Page: 307**   **Knowledge**

140. Voluntarily revealing personal information
     Answer: a   **Type: Matching**   **Page: 304**   **Knowledge**

141. "This is my third attempt to finish this race."
     Answer: e   **Type: Matching**   **Page: 307**   **Knowledge**

142. Referring to the reasons for deceit outlined in your chapter, analyze a current relationship you are in according to the degrees of truthfulness and deceit. Are you satisfied with the level of honesty? Explain your answer.
     Answer: **Type: E**   **Pages: 317–321**   **Analysis**

143. Using the social penetration model in your text, describe the breadth and depth of one important interpersonal relationship you have. Explain why you are satisfied/unsatisfied with this relationship.
     Answer: **Type: E**   **Pages: 305–306**   **Synthesis**

144. Discuss the four dimensions of intimacy in a relationship that is important to you. Explain your satisfaction with the intimacy or distance in each area. Relate any other factors (change, independence, culture, gender, etc.) that affect your intimacy in this relationship.
     Answer: **Type: E**   **Pages: 298–299**   **Evaluation**

145. Relate the four levels of self-disclosure—clichés, facts, opinion, and feelings—to the following four stages of relationships—experimenting, integrating, differentiating and stagnating. Discuss the level of self-disclosure that is most and least likely at each of these four stages.
     Answer: **Type: E**   **Page: 307**   **Synthesis**

146. Draw a Johari Window describing your relationship with an important person in your life. Comment on which parts of yourself you keep in the "hidden" area, and explain your reasons for doing so. Describe the benefits and costs of not disclosing these parts of your personality. Next, look at the size of the "blind" area model. Is the blind area large or small because of the amount of feedback you get from the other person, or because of the way you react to the feedback you do get? How would a window describing your partner's relationship with a mutual friend look similar to yours? Different? Explain. Are you satisfied with the kind of relationship your windows describe? If not, what could you do to change it?
     Answer: **Type: E**   **Pages: 308–309**   **Evaluation**

147. Your text described five reasons people tell lies. Provide examples of lies you have told or have been told to you that illustrate three of the different reasons for lying. Discuss whether or not each of these lies was a "benevolent lie" or not and why.
     Answer: **Type: E**   **Pages: 317–318**   **Synthesis**

148. Discuss the differences between masculine and female intimacy styles. Include research findings from your text to support your discussion.

   Answer: **Type: E**   **Pages: 299–300**   **Comprehension**

149. Discuss the various benefits and risks of self-disclosure. Provide examples from your own life where you have experienced both the benefits and risks.

   Answer: **Type: E**   **Pages: 309–312**   **Evaluation**

CHAPTER 10
IMPROVING COMMUNICATION CLIMATES

1. Defensiveness is often a self-perpetuating cycle.
   Answer: T   **Type: T**   **Page: 335**   **Synthesis**

2. Once a progressive spiral has been established in a relationship, it is likely to continue indefinitely.
   Answer: F   **Type: T**   **Page: 336**   **Knowledge**

3. When you respond non-defensively to criticism, you can agree with the truth of what the critic is saying.
   Answer: T   **Type: T**   **Page: 357**   **Knowledge**

4. The most damaging kind of disconfirming response is disagreeing with the other person.
   Answer: F   **Type: T**   **Page: 331**   **Knowledge**

5. The clear message format should always be used in the order given in your text for best results.
   Answer: F   **Type: T**   **Page: 351**   **Analysis**

6. It's okay to reword the clear message format to suit your own particular style of speaking.
   Answer: T   **Type: T**   **Page: 351**   **Analysis**

7. You shouldn't have to repeat the clear message format if you express yourself clearly in the first place.
   Answer: F   **Type: T**   **Page: 351**   **Analysis**

8. Messages shaping the communication climate of a relationship can be both verbal and nonverbal.
   Answer: T   **Type: T**   **Page: 334**   **Comprehension**

9. Endorsement is the strongest type of confirming message.
   Answer: T   **Type: T**   **Page: 331**   **Knowledge**

10. The Gibb categories define behaviors that improve or hurt the communication climate.
    Answer: T   **Type: T**   **Page: 340**   **Comprehension**

11. Stating your intentions is an important element of a clear message.
    Answer: T   **Type: T**   **Page: 350**   **Knowledge**

12. Tangential responses are one type of disconfirming message.
    Answer: T   **Type: T**   **Page: 334**   **Knowledge**

13. Just recognizing the other person isn't enough to be considered confirming.
    Answer: F   **Type: T**   **Page: 331**   **Evaluation**

14. Acknowledgment is more confirming than recognition.
    Answer: T   **Type: T**   **Page: 331**   **Evaluation**

15. Incongruent responses contain two messages that seem to deny or contradict each other.
    Answer: T   **Type: T**   **Page: 334**   **Knowledge**

16. Since ambiguous responses leave your partner unsure of your position, they would likely be interpreted as disconfirming.
    Answer: T   **Type: T**   **Page: 334**   **Comprehension**

17. Whereas acknowledging others means you are interested in their ideas, endorsement means that you agree with them.
    Answer: T   **Type: T**   **Page: 331**   **Knowledge**

18. Perception makes little difference in determining whether a message is disconfirming.
    Answer: F   **Type: T**   **Page: 331**   **Comprehension**

19. We often reduce cognitive dissonance by using defense mechanisms.
    Answer: T   **Type: T**   **Page: 338**   **Comprehension**

20. When coping with criticism, it isn't a good idea to ask what else is wrong because it just brings up too much material to handle at one time.
    Answer: F   **Type: T**   **Page: 356**   **Comprehension**

21. A controlling message can be verbal or nonverbal.
    Answer: T   **Type: T**   **Pages: 341–342**   **Comprehension**

22. Behavior that fits into Gibb's category of "strategy" attempts to manipulate the other into doing what you want.
    Answer: T   **Type: T**   **Page: 342**   **Knowledge**

23. What Gibb describes as "spontaneity" means saying the first thing that comes into your mind.
    Answer: F   **Type: T**   **Page: 342**   **Comprehension**

24. A supportive climate usually results from the expression of empathy.
    Answer: T   **Type: T**   **Page: 343**   **Comprehension**

25. When you decide to acknowledge an accurate criticism, an apology is also necessary.
    Answer: F   **Type: T**   **Page: 359**   **Knowledge**

26. Being ignored is less disconfirming than being dismissed or attacked.
    Answer: F   **Type: T**   **Page: 331**   **Knowledge**

27. A communication climate has to do with the way people feel about each other as they carry out activities.
    Answer: T   **Type: T**   **Page: 329**   **Knowledge**

28. The most common form of acknowledgement is listening.
    Answer: T   **Type: T**   **Page: 331**   **Knowledge**

29. Satisfied couples communicate a 5 to 1 ratio of positive to negative messages.
    Answer: T   **Type: T**   **Page: 330**   **Knowledge**

30. The emotional tone of a relationship is called the communication climate.
    Answer: T   **Type: T**   **Page: 329**   **Knowledge**

31. A spiral is always negative.
    Answer: F   **Type: T**   **Page: 336**   **Knowledge**

32. Once engaged in a negative spiral, it is impossible for a couple to recover.
    Answer: F   **Type: T**   **Page: 336**   **Comprehension**

33. When others confront us with attacks on our presenting self, we are likely to become defensive.
    Answer: T   **Type: T**   **Page: 337**   **Knowledge**

34. If an attack to our presenting self is justified, we will not react defensively.
    Answer: F   **Type: T**   **Page: 337**   **Comprehension**

35. An inconsistency between two conflicting pieces of information, attitudes or behavior is called displacement.
    Answer: F   **Type: T**   **Page: 337**   **Knowledge**

36. Compensation is the invention of logical but untrue explanations of behavior that is unacceptable to the self.
    Answer: F   **Type: T**   **Page: 339**   **Knowledge**

37. Another word to describe Gibb's defensive behavior of neutrality is indifference.
    Answer: T   **Type: T**   **Page: 343**   **Knowledge**

38. Asking for more information from your critics as a way to respond nondefensively means you need to be prepared to accept the comments.
    Answer: F   **Type: T**   **Page: 353**   **Comprehension**

39. One advantage of paraphrasing a critic's comments is that the intensity of the attack may be reduced.
    Answer: T   **Type: T**   **Page: 355**   **Knowledge**

40. Research suggests that agreeing with a fact when criticized is highly effective in restoring a damaged reputation with the critic.
    Answer: T   **Type: T**   **Page: 357**   **Knowledge**

41. It's impossible to honestly accept the other person's point of view while maintaining your own position.
    Answer: F   **Type: T**   **Page: 357**   **Knowledge**

42. Intention statements can communicate
    a. where you stand on an issue.
    b. requests of others.
    c. descriptions of how you plan to act in the future.
    d. a, b, and c above.
    e. only interpretations of behavior.
    Answer: d   **Type: M**   **Pages: 350–351**   **Comprehension**

43. Which of the following is an accurate feeling statement?
    a. "I feel like you're angry at me."
    b. "I feel like going home now."
    c. "I feel angry when you laugh at me."
    d. "I feel you ought to be more careful."
    e. All of these answers are correct are feeling statements.
    Answer: c   **Type: M**   **Page: 349**   **Evaluation**

44. All of the following are disconfirming messages except
    a. interrupting the other person.
    b. giving ambiguous responses.
    c. ignoring the other person.
    d. using a problem-oriented approach.
    e. responding with clichés.
    Answer: d   **Type: M**   **Pages: 331–334**   **Synthesis**

45. All of the following are behavioral descriptions except
    a. "I notice you're frowning."
    b. "I saw you walk out of the party."
    c. "Your behavior shows me you're angry."
    d. "You've shouted the last three times we've discussed money."
    e. "You haven't said 'I love you' in over a week."
    Answer: c   **Type: M**   **Page: 347**   **Application**

46. Which of the following is an interpretation?
    a. "I got an A on my history paper."
    b. "Sue only cares about herself."
    c. "I sure appreciate your help."
    d. "Would you tell me what you mean by that?"
    e. All of these answers are correct are interpretations.
    Answer: b   **Type: M**   **Page: 348**   **Application**

47. A consequence statement can describe
    a. what happens to you, the speaker.
    b. what happens to the person you're addressing or to others.
    c. why you're bothered or pleased by another's behavior.
    d. what happens without moralizing about it.
    e. All of these answers are correct.
    Answer: e   **Type: M**   **Page: 350**   **Synthesis**

48. All of the following are defense mechanisms except
    a. verbal aggression.
    b. compensation.
    c. displacement.
    d. apathy.
    e. endorsement.
    Answer: e   **Type: M**   **Pages: 338–340**   **Comprehension**

49. The most visible way disconfirming messages reinforce one another, as when one attack leads to another and another, is termed a(n)
    a.   escalatory conflict spiral.
    b.   de-escalatory conflict spiral.
    c.   cognitive dissonance reaction.
    d.   impervious dyad.
    e.   pillow-talk incident.
    Answer: a   **Type: M**   **Page: 336**   **Knowledge**

50. The text suggested that you may react non-defensively to criticism by
    a.   asking for a "time-out."
    b.   guessing about the specifics of a critic's remarks.
    c.   criticizing yourself.
    d.   giving the reasons for your behavior.
    e.   telling the critic to stop.
    Answer: b   **Type: M**   **Page: 354**   **Comprehension**

51. Your instructor tells you how poor your writing ability is and how wrong it is for you not to work harder on it. That instructor used the Gibb category of
    a.   description.
    b.   evaluation.
    c.   problem orientation.
    d.   equality.
    e.   provisionalism.
    Answer: b   **Type: M**   **Page: 341**   **Application**

52. According to research findings about defensiveness, when one person in a dyad acts in a defensive manner
    a.   a counterattack is appropriate.
    b.   the partner will be supportive.
    c.   a defensive spiral usually results.
    d.   perceptions are not realistic.
    e.   self-disclosure usually takes place.
    Answer: c   **Type: M**   **Page: 335**   **Knowledge**

53. The elements of a clear message are
    a.   feeling, interpretation, assertion, and consequence.
    b.   behavior, interpretation, feeling, assertion, and intention.
    c.   behavior, assertion, aggression, and interpretation.
    d.   behavior, interpretation, feeling, consequence, and intention.
    e.   assertion, aggression, negotiation, interpretation, and intention.
    Answer: d   **Type: M**   **Pages: 347–351**   **Synthesis**

54. Another term which describes the Gibb defensive category of neutrality would be
    a.   understanding.
    b.   aggressive perception.
    c.   positive/negative balance.
    d.   displaced loyalty.
    e.   indifference.
    Answer: e   **Type: M**   **Page: 343**   **Knowledge**

54. Evaluative language is also described as
    a. "me" language.
    b. "it" language.
    c. "you" language.
    d. "neutral" language.
    e. "supportive" language.
    Answer: c   **Type: M**   **Page: 341**   **Knowledge**

55. The term that describes the quality of a personal relationship is
    a. mood.
    b. tone.
    c. climate.
    d. environment.
    e. foundation.
    Answer: c   **Type: M**   **Page: 329**   **Knowledge**

56. Defensiveness is the process of protecting your
    a. interpretations.
    b. sense data.
    c. perceived self.
    d. presenting self.
    e. None of the above answers are correct
    Answer: d   **Type: M**   **Page: 337**   **Knowledge**

57. Gibb's categories provide a useful way for us to examine our
    a. self-concept.
    b. patterns of self-disclosure.
    c. defensive and supportive behaviors.
    d. manipulative behaviors.
    e. perceptual differences.
    Answer: c   **Type: M**   **Page: 340**   **Comprehension**

58. The communication climate in a relationship is determined by the
    a. roles each person has in the relationship.
    b. similarities of the parties.
    c. degree to which each person feels valued.
    d. amount of self-disclosure that occurs.
    e. listening and perceptual skills that each individual brings to the relationship.
    Answer: c   **Type: M**   **Page: 329**   **Knowledge**

59. A confirming response may
    a. criticizes the other.
    b. agree with or acknowledge the other.
    c. reveals deception.
    d. recognizes manipulation.
    e. controls the other.
    Answer: b   **Type: M**   **Page: 331**   **Comprehension**

60. People who act in accordance with Gibb's category of equality communicate that
    a. everyone is equal in every way.
    b. while they may have greater talent in some areas, all have just as much worth as human beings.
    c. all human beings are created with the capacity to be equal in all areas.
    d. All of these answers are correct
    e. None of the above answers are correct
    Answer: b   **Type: M**   **Page: 345**   **Comprehension**

61. "I know that isn't going to work under any circumstances" is an example of the Gibb defensive category of
    a. evaluation.
    b. control.
    c. superiority.
    d. certainty.
    e. strategy.
    Answer: d   **Type: M**   **Page: 345**   **Application**

62. Communicators can resolve cognitive dissonance by
    a. revising the self-concept in the face of criticism.
    b. avoiding the dissonant information.
    c. distorting the dissonant information.
    d. attacking the source of dissonant information.
    e. All of these answers are correct.
    Answer: e   **Type: M**   **Pages: 338–340**   **Comprehension**

63. Jenny says, "Beth, I'm really upset about how we divide the cooking chores." Beth retorts, "Speaking of cooking, my secretary brought in great cookies today." Beth's response is an example of a(n)
    a. impervious response.
    b. interrupting response.
    c. irrelevant response.
    d. impersonal response.
    e. tangential response.
    Answer: e   **Type: M**   **Page: 334**   **Application**

64. Robin asks her boss if she can take Friday afternoon off to clear up some legal problems. Her boss replies, "Seems like everybody has problems these days." The boss's reply is an example of a(n)
    a. impervious response.
    b. interrupting response.
    c. irrelevant response.
    d. tangential response.
    e. impersonal response.
    Answer: e   **Type: M**   **Page: 334**   **Application**

65. Molly asks her mother if she'll help her go through her wardrobe to see what needs to be thrown out. Her mother replies, "Throwing out things is a great idea; help me with cleaning out this refrigerator, won't you?" This reply is an example of a(n)
    a. impervious response.
    b. interrupting response.
    c. irrelevant response.
    d. tangential response.
    e. impersonal response.

Answer: d   **Type: M**   **Page: 332**   **Application**

66. Julie calls Stephanie to invite her to a party, leaving the message on Stephanie's voicemail. After two days, Stephanie still hasn't returned Julie's call. Julie might interpret this as what type of response?
    a. impervious.
    b. interrupting.
    c. irrelevant.
    d. tangential.
    e. impersonal.

Answer: a   **Type: M**   **Page: 331**   **Application**

67. "You are such a couch potato" is an example of what Gibb defense-arousing behavior?
    a. evaluation.
    b. control.
    c. strategy.
    d. neutrality.
    e. superiority.

Answer: a   **Type: M**   **Page: 341**   **Application**

68. Which of the following statements is the best supportive alternative to the accusation, "You just don't try hard enough."
    a. "You should try harder."
    b. "You give up too easily."
    c. "I'm worried you'll fail with two D's."
    d. "You should study two hours every night."
    e. "It's time we had a talk about trying."

Answer: c   **Type: M**   **Page: 347**   **Analysis**

69. Ambiguous responses
    a. are conversational "take aways."
    b. are unrelated to what the other person has just said.
    c. ignore the other person's attempt to communicate.
    d. contain messages with more than one meaning.
    e. interrupt the other person.

Answer: d   **Type: M**   **Page: 336**   **Knowledge**

70. Disconfirming responses loaded with clichés and other statements that never truly respond to the speaker are called
    a. impervious.
    b. interrupting.
    c. irrelevant.
    d. tangential.
    e. impersonal.
    Answer: e   **Type: M**   **Page: 334**   **Knowledge**

72. Agreeing with a critic's perception of your behavior involves
    a. telling the critic she/he's right.
    b. agreeing with the critic's right to see things his/her way.
    c. agreeing with the specifics of the criticism.
    d. All of these answers are correct.
    e. None of the above answers are correct.
    Answer: b   **Type: M**   **Page: 358**   **Application**

73. Which of the following is a non-defensive response to the criticism, "You've really messed up that account now"?
    a. "Tell me what, in your mind, I did that upset you."
    b. "Not taking Mr. Kimble to dinner endangers the account?"
    c. "So you're upset that the account may be lost?"
    d. "Losing that account might really hurt our department?"
    e. All of these answers are correct respond non-defensively to that criticism.
    Answer: e   **Type: M**   **Pages: 353–359**   **Analysis**

74. An inconsistency between two conflicting pieces of information about one's self, attitudes, or behavior is called
    a. a defensive spiral.
    b. a supportive spiral.
    c. cognitive dissonance.
    d. an ambiguous response.
    e. intrapersonal conflict.
    Answer: c   **Type: M**   **Page: 337**   **Knowledge**

75. Psychological devices that resolve dissonance by maintaining a positive presenting image are called
    a. reaction formations.
    b. confirming responses.
    c. defense mechanisms.
    d. self-fulfilling prophecies.
    e. climate adjusters.
    Answer: c   **Type: M**   **Page: 338**   **Comprehension**

76. If others start criticizing you, one productive way to respond is to
    a. tell them to stop the criticism.
    b. point out that criticism is not productive.
    c. criticize them to show them how it feels.
    d. ask for more specifics about what the criticism involves.
    e. just back off; there's no effective way to deal with this kind of "no-win" situation.
    Answer: d   **Type: M**   **Page: 353**   **Comprehension**

77. You can often respond non-defensively to criticism by agreeing
    a.   with the critic's truthful statements.
    b.   with the critic's judgment.
    c.   with the critic's perception of the situation.
    d.   both a and b above
    e.   both a and c above
    Answer: e   **Type: M**   **Pages: 357–358**   **Comprehension**

78. All of the following are non-defensive responses to criticism recommended by your text except
    a.   asking for more details about the criticism.
    b.   paraphrasing the speaker's comments.
    c.   asking about the consequences of your behavior.
    d.   accepting the speaker's comments, even if you disagree.
    e.   guessing about the details of the criticism.
    Answer: d   **Type: M**   **Pages: 353–356**   **Knowledge**

79. Defensive counterattacks can take the form of
    a.   verbal aggression and sarcasm.
    b.   description and neutrality.
    c.   facilitation and compromise.
    d.   assertion and aggression.
    e.   All of these answers are correct.
    Answer: a   **Type: M**   **Page: 338**   **Knowledge**

]

80. If you emphasize how good you are in sports when someone criticizes your academic performance, you've used the defensive reaction called
    a.   displacement.
    b.   rationalization.
    c.   repression.
    d.   regression.
    e.   compensation.
    Answer: e   **Type: M**   **Page: 339**   **Application**

82. Communication climates are a function of
    a.   the way people feel about one another.
    b.   the tasks people perform.
    c.   individual personality characteristics.
    d.   Gibb's functional theories.
    e.   time, place, and context.
    Answer: a   **Type: M**   **Page: 329**   **Comprehension**

83. Jim's boss at the bank criticizes the way Jim handled a new account. Jim says nothing to his boss, but he's very short-tempered with his roommate that evening. Which defense mechanism is Jim most likely using?
    a.   apathy
    b.   displacement
    c.   verbal aggression
    d.   regression
    e.   repression
    Answer: b   **Type: M**   **Page: 340**   **Application**

84. A defense mechanism that is characterized by a pretense of not caring is called
    a.   repression.
    b.   displacement.
    c.   compensation.
    d.   apathy.
    e.   None of the above answers are correct.
    Answer: d   **Type: M**   **Page: 340**   **Knowledge**

85. Just for fun, you flirted with an attractive person at a party last night. You know your partner is hurt,
    so you arrange a dinner at a favorite restaurant. You are most likely using the defense mechanism of
    a.   verbal aggression.
    b.   compensation.
    c.   rationalization.
    d.   apathy.
    e.   displacement.
    Answer: b   **Type: M**   **Page: 339**   **Application**

86. A reciprocating communication pattern in which each person's message reinforces the other's is called a(n)
    a.   conflict.
    b.   defense mechanism.
    c.   face-threatening act.
    d.   attack.
    e.   spiral.
    Answer: e   **Type: M**   **Page: 335**   **Knowledge**

87. "I'd love to go out with you, but I can't; I have so much going on in my life right now," is an
    example of
    a.   regression.
    b.   apathy.
    c.   compensation.
    d.   rationalization.
    e.   avoidance.
    Answer: d   **Type: M**   **Page: 339**   **Application**

88. Acting as if you don't understand something or changing the subject is an example of what type of
    dissonant information avoidance?
    a.   apathy.
    b.   displacement.
    c.   repression.
    d.   regression.
    e.   compensation.
    Answer: c   **Type: M**   **Page: 339**   **Knowledge**

89. Saying, "That's the way the cookie crumbles," is an example of what Gibb defense-arousing behavior?
    a.   control
    b.   strategy
    c.   certainty
    d.   evaluation
    e.   neutrality
    Answer: e   **Type: M**   **Page: 343**   **Application**

90. All of the following are defense-arousing behaviors except
    a. neutrality
    b. control
    c. superiority
    d. strategy
    e. spontaneity
    Answer: e   **Type: M**   **Pages: 341–345**   **Knowledge**

91. The clear message format
    a. should be worded to suit your own style of communication.
    b. may require you to repeat a part to ensure the other person's understanding.
    c. may be delivered in mixed order of the elements.
    d. can combine two or more elements in a single phrase.
    e. All of these answers are correct.
    Answer: e   **Type: M**   **Page: 351**   **Knowledge**

92. Paraphrasing is valuable in responding to critics because
    a. the intensity of the attack is often reduced when a complaint is acknowledged.
    b. the critic knows then that he/she is right.
    c. important information can be learned.
    d. All of these answers are correct.
    e. a. and c.
    Answer: e   **Type: M**   **Page: 355**   **Knowledge**

93. A spiral
    a. is a reciprocating communication pattern.
    b. can be escalatory or de-escalatory.
    c. rarely goes on indefinitely.
    d. reinforces the principle that "what goes around comes around."
    e. All of these answers are correct.
    Answer: e   **Type: M**   **Pages: 335–337**   **Knowledge**

94. When Jim suggests to Bob that there might be another way to approach handling a problem instead of enforcing his way of handling it, he is being _____ rather than _____.
    a. spontaneous, strategic.
    b. provisional, certain.
    c. equal, superior.
    d. empathetic, neutral.
    e. descriptive, evaluative.
    Answer: b   **Type: M**   **Page: 345**   **Application**

95. When Lynn tells her husband, "I'd really like to go out to dinner more often," instead of saying, "Our best friends go out to dinner every week," she is being _____ rather than _____.
    a. spontaneous, strategic.
    b. provisional, certain.
    c. equal, superior.
    d. empathetic, neutral.
    e. problem-oriented, controlling.
    Answer: a   **Type: M**   **Page: 342**   **Application**

INSTRUCTIONS for questions 96–100: Match each description below with the appropriate defense mechanism.

    a.   verbal aggression
    b.   compensation
    c.   rationalization
    d.   repression
    e.   regression

96. Stressing a strength in one area to cover up a perceived shortcoming in another area
    Answer: b   **Type: Matching**   **Page: 339**   **Knowledge**

97. Pretending you don't hear criticism
    Answer: d   **Type: Matching**   **Page: 339**   **Knowledge**

98. Accusing a critic of the same fault another person claims you are guilty of
    Answer: a   **Type: Matching**   **Page: 338**   **Knowledge**

99. Offering a logical but untrue explanation of your behavior
    Answer: c   **Type: Matching**   **Page: 339**   **Knowledge**

100. Playing helpless to avoid facing attack
    Answer: e   **Type: Matching**   **Page: 339**   **Knowledge**

INSTRUCTIONS for questions 101–105: Match each defense mechanism with its description.

    a.   rationalization
    b.   sarcasm
    c.   apathy
    d.   physical avoidance
    e.   displacement

101. Disguising an attack with a barbed, humorous message
    Answer: b   **Type: Matching**   **Page: 338**   **Application**

102. Acting like you don't care that you didn't get the lead in the play
    Answer: c   **Type: Matching**   **Page: 340**   **Application**

103. Snapping at your roommate after being criticized by your boss
    Answer: e   **Type: Matching**   **Page: 340**   **Application**

104. Blaming your lack of exercise on a desire to conserve your energy
    Answer: a   **Type: Matching**   **Page: 339**   **Application**

105. Steering clear of someone who points out your flaws
    Answer: d   **Type: Matching**   **Page: 339**   **Application**

INSTRUCTIONS for questions 106–110: Match the type of disconfirming response with its behavioral description.

    a. impervious
    b. tangential
    c. generalized complaining
    d. impersonal
    e. irrelevant

106. Shelley says, "Let's decide what we're doing this weekend after I get paid tomorrow," and you reply, " I'm really excited about getting an A on my test."
    Answer: e   **Type: Matching**   **Page: 332**   **Analysis**

107. Vince says, "I'm so tired," and you reply, "Boy, everybody's got problems today."
    Answer: d   **Type: Matching**   **Page: 334**   **Analysis**

108. You see Denise smile at you, but you walk past without smiling back.
    Answer: a   **Type: Matching**   **Page: 331**   **Analysis**

109. "I wish you would be more helpful."
    Answer: c   **Type: Matching**   **Page: 332**   **Analysis**

110. Gail asks how your roommate is feeling; you tell her about your own health.
    Answer: b   **Type: Matching**   **Page: 334**   **Analysis**

INSTRUCTIONS for questions 111–128: Identify each of the following statements within quotation marks as according to the clear message format.

    a. feeling
    b. behavior
    c. interpretation
    d. consequence
    e. intention

111. "Whenever we fight, both of us wind up regretting it."
    Answer: d   **Type: Matching**   **Page: 350**   **Application**

112. "I sure am grateful for your help."
    Answer: a   **Type: Matching**   **Page: 349**   **Application**

113. "I just want you to know how much this affects me."
    Answer: e   **Type: Matching**   **Page: 350**   **Application**

114. "You're smoking again after you said you were quitting."
    Answer: b   **Type: Matching**   **Page: 347**   **Application**

115. "I guess you just don't like me."
    Answer: c   **Type: Matching**   **Page: 348**   **Application**

116. "Because we were five minutes late, we couldn't be seated until intermission."
    Answer: d   **Type: Matching**   **Page: 350**   **Application**

117. "You seem pretty sure of yourself."
    Answer: c   **Type: Matching**   **Page: 348**   **Application**

118. "I'm uncomfortable about that."
    Answer: a   **Type: Matching**   **Page: 349**   **Application**

119. "I'd like to know whether you are angry.   "
    Answer: e   **Type: Matching**   **Page: 350**   **Application**

120. "It seems to me that you're just trying to set me against her."
    Answer: c   **Type: Matching**   **Page: 348**   **Application**

121. "I'm glad you're coming."
    Answer: a   **Type: Matching**   **Page: 349**   **Application**

122. "Gene didn't call at the usual time."
    Answer: b   **Type: Matching**   **Page: 347**   **Application**

123. "You shouldn't expect me to help you out again.."
    Answer: e   **Type: Matching**   **Page: 350**   **Application**

124. "You must be mad at me."
    Answer: c   **Type: Matching**   **Page: 348**   **Application**

125. "I'm really burned up about that bill."
    Answer: a   **Type: Matching**   **Page: 349**   **Application**

126. "When you didn't call to say you would be late, I became worried.   "
    Answer: d   **Type: Matching**   **Page: 350**   **Application**

127. "Ever since you said that I was wrong, I've been afraid to ask your opinion."
    Answer: d   **Type: Matching**   **Page: 350**   **Application**

128. "Something must be bothering you.."
    Answer: c   **Type: Matching**   **Page: 348**   **Application**

129. Describe two of your important relationships in terms of communication climate. What factors contribute to the overall climate in each relationship? Describe confirming and disconfirming behaviors for each relationship that led you to your overall assessment.
    Answer: **Type: E**   **Pages: 329–334**   **Analysis**

130. How do defensive behaviors work in the sphere of work relationships? Given your knowledge of Gibb's categories, what advice would you give to a manager?
    Answer: **Type: E**   **Pages: 340–345**   **Application**

131. Pick the two defense mechanisms you most commonly use. For each, describe (a) a recent incident when you used it, (b) the part of your self-concept you were protecting, and (c) the consequences of your defensiveness. If you haven't used defense mechanisms recently, answer this question with defense mechanisms you have used in the past. Be specific.
    Answer: **Type: E**   **Pages: 337–340**   **Synthesis**

132. Describe an important relationship in which you are involved in terms of a positive or negative "spiral" of behavior. Indicate how behaviors over the past six months (or any defined segment of time) have tended to "beget" similar behaviors in your relationship. Comment on the future direction of your spiral.

Answer: **Type: E**   **Pages: 334–337**   **Evaluation**

133. Imagine the following scene: Your instructor (we'll call him Dr. Roberts) angrily thrusts your research paper back at you saying, "This paper is not only late, it is full of errors." Write a response to Dr. Roberts that demonstrates three different ways to respond using Chapter Ten's strategies for handling criticism non-defensively.

Answer: **Type: E**   **Pages: 353–359**   **Application**

134. Define cognitive dissonance. Give five examples from your life that illustrate this concept in action. Label any defensive behaviors you use to cope with cognitive dissonance.

Answer: **Type: E**   **Pages: 337–340**   **Synthesis**

135. Use the Clear Message Format to respond to one of two situations described below, identifying each of the five parts of the message.
A friend of yours is in the habit of borrowing your belongings and doesn't return them to you without you having to ask for them back several times. Now your friend is returning a sweater of yours and there's a stain on it.
One of your friends has been especially supportive lately, has called often, spent time getting you out socially and even prepared dinner for you to help you get through a difficult time.

Answer: **Type: E**   **Pages: 346–351**   **Application**

136. Describe confirming and disconfirming communication. List the various types of confirming and disconfirming messages and provide examples for three of them.

Answer: **Type: E**   **Pages: 330–334**   **Comprehension**

137. Consider this saying, "I can be right or I can be happy." Discuss this in terms of defensiveness/nondefensive concepts from the text, as well as any pertinent Gibb climate components.

Answer: **Type: E**   **Pages: 337–359**   **Synthesis**

CHAPTER 11
MANAGING INTERPERSONAL CONFLICTS

1. Research has shown that strong marriages manage conflict in constructive ways.
   Answer: T   **Type: T**   **Page: 369**   **Knowledge**

2. Destructive fights often start because the initiator confronts a partner who isn't ready for a confrontation.
   Answer: T   **Type: T**   **Page: 388**   **Knowledge**

3. Interdependence must exist between two parties in order for a conflict to exist.
   Answer: T   **Type: T**   **Page: 367**   **Knowledge**

4. A conflict can exist only when both parties are aware of a disagreement.
   Answer: T   **Type: T**   **Page: 367**   **Knowledge**

5. One key to the win-win approach to conflict resolution is to look for the single best solution at the beginning of your conversation.
   Answer: F   **Type: T**   **Page: 390**   **Comprehension**

6. The text says that "counting to ten" applies to win-win problem solving.
   Answer: T   **Type: T**   **Page: 387**   **Analysis**

7. As long as one person in the relationship is aware of the disagreement, a conflict exists.
   Answer: F   **Type: T**   **Page: 367**   **Knowledge**

8. The win-win approach to conflict resolution requires parties to reach a solution through compromise.
   Answer: F   **Type: T**   **Page: 376**   **Knowledge**

9. With enough skill you should be able to use win-win problem solving successfully in almost any conflict.
   Answer: F   **Type: T**   **Page: 377**   **Knowledge**

10. When people express hostility in obscure ways, "passive aggression" occurs.
    Answer: T   **Type: T**   **Page: 374**   **Knowledge**

11. A full-fledged conflict will not occur unless the individuals involved try to prevent one another from achieving their goals.
    Answer: T   **Type: T**   **Page: 368**   **Comprehension**

12. Direct aggression is described as physical attacks and swearing, but does not include teasing or nonverbal gestures.
    Answer: F   **Type: T**   **Page: 374**   **Knowledge**

13. Gender is the most important variable in determining conflict style.
    Answer: F   **Type: T**   **Page: 384**   **Knowledge**

14. The situation at hand and the behavior of the other person in the conflict are more powerful determinants of a person's conflict style than gender.
    Answer: T   **Type: T**   **Page: 384**   **Knowledge**

15. Some scholars assert that conflict style is often determined simply by a person's biological makeup.
    Answer: T   **Type: T**   **Page: 386**   **Knowledge**

16. A conflict can exist even if the parties in conflict are not dependent on each other.
    Answer: F   **Type: T**   **Page: 367**   **Knowledge**

17. College students who kept diaries of their relationships reported that they took part in about 10 arguments per week.
    Answer: F   **Type: T**   **Page: 368**   **Knowledge**

18. Avoidance is never an effective conflict style to choose.
    Answer: F   **Type: T**   **Page: 372**   **Knowledge**

19. An avoiding conflict style reflects the belief that there is no good way to resolve the conflict at hand.
    Answer: T   **Type: T**   **Page: 370**   **Knowledge**

20. In high-context, collectivist countries, avoidance and accommodation are considered positive, appropriate ways to handle conflict.
    Answer: T   **Type: T**   **Page: 372**   **Comprehension**

21. Even when accommodation is a genuine act of kindness, it is not considered an acceptable style because the accommodator is showing a lack of regard for him/herself.
    Answer: F   **Type: T**   **Page: 372**   **Comprehension**

22. Compromise is considered a win-win conflict style because each person gets at least some of what they want.
    Answer: F   **Type: T**   **Page: 376**   **Knowledge**

23. What conflict style to choose should be determined by the style you are most comfortable using.
    Answer: F   **Type: T**   **Pages: 377–378**   **Comprehension**

24. Collaboration is considered the single "best" way to resolve a conflict.
    Answer: F   **Type: T**   **Page: 377**   **Knowledge**

25. Conflict is considered relational because it is determined by the way the parties interact with each other.
    Answer: T   **Type: T**   **Page: 379**   **Knowledge**

26. In a symmetrical conflict style, the partners use different but mutually reinforcing behaviors.
    Answer: F   **Type: T**   **Page: 379**   **Knowledge**

27. A complementary conflict style can be problematic for couples, but a symmetrical one will not be.
    Answer: F   **Type: T**   **Pages: 379–380**   **Knowledge**

28. In an intimate-nonaggressive pattern, the parties avoid conflicts and each other instead of facing issues head-on.
    Answer: F   **Type: T**   **Page: 381**   **Knowledge**

29. Conflict rituals are not necessarily wrong until they become the only way relational partners handle their conflicts.
    Answer: T   **Type: T**   **Page: 383**   **Knowledge**

30. Probably the most important cultural factor in shaping attitudes toward conflict is an orientation toward individualism or collectivism.
    Answer: T   **Type: T**   **Page: 385**   **Knowledge**

31. The ethnic background of communicators is not a significant factor in their views regarding conflict.
    Answer: F   **Type: T**   **Page: 386**   **Knowledge**

32. A constructive conflict style is rarely used, due in part to people not being aware that it is a viable alternative to a competitive approach.
    Answer: T   **Type: T**   **Page: 386**   **Knowledge**

33. A win-win, collaborative approach might be beneficial, but it isn't very realistic to use due to its detail and complicated structure.
    Answer: F   **Type: T**   **Page: 394**   **Comprehension**

34. In a survey of conflict views of college men and women, women were described as being
    a. more concerned with maintaining the relationship during a conflict.
    b. more concerned with power in the conflict.
    c. more interested in the content of the conflict.
    d. more ego-involved in the conflict than men.
    e. All of these answers are correct.
    Answer: a   **Type: M**   **Page: 384**   **Comprehension**

35. Complementary and symmetrical conflict styles have been shown to produce
    a. marriages that got back together after conflict.
    b. couples who find other mates while getting divorced.
    c. a greater percentage of divorces that are settled amicably.
    d. both "good" results as well as "bad" ones.
    e. divorces that only have the facade of politeness.
    Answer: d   **Type: M**   **Page: 380**   **Comprehension**

36. Individuals in low-context cultures typically resolve conflict by
    a. avoidance.
    b. indirect communication.
    c. nonassertion.
    d. All of these answers are correct
    e. None of these answers are correct
    Answer: e   **Type: M**   **Pages: 385–386**   **Synthesis**

37. An uncontrolled, spontaneous "explosion," a "Vesuvius," is
    a. encouraged by your text as a first step to solving conflict.
    b. therapeutic when you feel it's impossible to be relational and your partner understands what you're doing.
    c. a great way of eliminating defensive behaviors by "clearing the air."
    d. one way to make sure your partner will listen to you.
    e. All of these answers are correct.
    Answer: b   **Type: M**   **Page: 395**   **Comprehension**

38. Win-win problem solving is seldom used because
    a. there is a lack of awareness of it.
    b. emotional reflexes prevent constructive solutions.
    c. it requires both persons' cooperation.
    d. win-win problem solving is actually the most used problem-solving style of all.
    e. a, b, and c are correct
    Answer: e   **Type: M**   **Pages: 386–387**   **Comprehension**

39. A person who buys a piece of new furniture, finds it damaged, and says nothing because he doesn't want to confront the retailer, is engaging in the personal conflict style of
    a. avoiding.
    b. accommodating.
    c. indirect communication.
    d. compromising.
    e. None of these answers are correct
    Answer: a   **Type: M**   **Page: 370**   **Application**

40. In order for a conflict to exist, two interdependent parties must perceive
    a. incompatible goals.
    b. scarce resources.
    c. interference from the other party in achieving their goals.
    d. a, b, and c are correct.
    e. both a and c are correct.
    Answer: d   **Type: M**   **Pages: 367–368**   **Knowledge**

41. When people deliver subtle aggressive messages involving feelings of resentment, anger, or rage that they aren't able or willing to express directly, they are engaging in what psychologist George Bach calls
    a. defense arousal.
    b. nonverbal conflict.
    c. pseudo-messages.
    d. crazymaking.
    e. one-up conflict resolution.
    Answer: d   **Type: M**   **Page: 375**   **Knowledge**

42. Conflict rituals are
   a.   inherently wrong.
   b.   the best way to solve the variety of conflicts that are part of any relationship.
   c.   almost always positive.
   d.   unacknowledged but repeating patterns of dealing with conflict.
   e.   All of these answers are correct.
   Answer: d   **Type: M**   **Page: 382**   **Comprehension**

43. The "ownership" of a problem almost always belongs to
   a.   the person who brings it up.
   b.   the person to whom the complaint is directed.
   c.   the person with the lowest amount of self-disclosure.
   d.   the person with the greatest amount of passive aggressive behavior.
   e.   the most assertive person.
   Answer: a   **Type: M**   **Pages: 387–388**   **Comprehension**

44. You and your partner's pattern of managing disagreements that repeats itself over time is called your
   a.   relational conflict style.
   b.   cognitive dissonance pattern.
   c.   harmony/disharmony pattern.
   d.   "Vesuvius."
   e.   clear message format.
   Answer: a   **Type: M**   **Page: 379**   **Knowledge**

45. In the Communication Transcript in Chapter Eleven, Chris tries to resolve a conflict with her roommate Terry over cleaning their apartment by
   a.   relying on authority as a source of power.
   b.   using the "Vesuvius" method to get Terry's attention.
   c.   appealing to their mutual self-interests.
   d.   employing "crazymaking" strategies.
   e.   None of these answers are correct
   Answer: c   **Type: M**   **Pages: 392–393**   **Comprehension**

46. All of the following are true about conflict, except
   a.   conflict is natural.
   b.   every relationship of any depth at all has conflict.
   c.   conflict can be beneficial.
   d.   people typically have similar conflict styles.
   e.   b and d
   Answer: d   **Type: M**   **Pages: 368–369**   **Synthesis**

47. Studies of different cultures and conflict reveal that
   a.   assertiveness is valued worldwide.
   b.   North Americans avoid confrontation more than other cultures studied.
   c.   individualistic cultures are less assertive than collective ones.
   d.   the assertiveness appropriate in North America would be rude and insensitive in collectivist cultures.
   e.   All of these answers are correct are true.
   Answer: d   **Type: M**   **Page: 385**   **Comprehension**

48. One of the best methods to use to describe your problem and needs to a partner during conflict resolution is
    a. paraphrasing.
    b. perception checking.
    c. the clear message format
    d. high-level abstractions.
    e. emotional description.

    Answer: c   **Type: M**   **Page: 389**   **Knowledge**

49. Rhonda complains to Collin that she's tired of their weekend routine. Irritated, Collin snaps back that he's tired of her complaining. Their conflict pattern reflects which of the following conflict styles?
    a. complementary
    b. symmetrical
    c. tangential
    d. conditional
    e. None of these answers are correct

    Answer: b   **Type: M**   **Pages: 379–380**   **Analysis**

50. Studies of intimate and aggressive relational conflict styles find that
    a. the pattern partners choose may reveal a great deal about the kind of relationship they have chosen.
    b. the intimate-nonaggressive style fails to handle problems.
    c. intimate-aggressive partners avoid conflicts.
    d. intimacy and aggression are opposites and thus not productive topics for study.
    e. intimacy and aggression work best in symmetrical relationships.

    Answer: a   **Type: M**   **Page: 381**   **Comprehension**

51. In order to decide which conflict style you should use, you should consider
    a. the situation.
    b. the other person.
    c. your goals.
    d. the relationship.
    e. All of these answers are correct.

    Answer: e   **Type: M**   **Pages: 377–378**   **Comprehension**

52. Conflict rituals
    a. are always damaging.
    b. should be replaced with compromise.
    c. most often involve avoidance by both of the participants in the conflict.
    d. become problems when they are seen as the only way to resolve problems.
    e. are defined as ways partners use guilt and intimidation to fight dirty.

    Answer: d   **Type: M**   **Page: 383**   **Knowledge**

53. Norman and Fredrick seem to argue all the time. Coworkers describe the two as hotheads, but recognize that the two men seem to like sparring and are very close friends. Their conflict style is best described as
    a. nonintimate-aggressive.
    b. nonintimate-nonaggressive.
    c. intimate-aggressive.
    d. intimate-nonaggressive.
    Answer: c   **Type: M**   **Page: 381**   **Analysis**

54. Leah and Rachel have never gotten along. Rachel says that the best way for them to continue to work in the same office is to do their best to avoid one another. Their conflict style is best described as
    a. nonintimate-aggressive.
    b. nonintimate-nonaggressive.
    c. intimate-aggressive.
    d. intimate-nonaggressive.
    Answer: b   **Type: M**   **Page: 381**   **Analysis**

55. Despite their very different personalities, Sandra and Maureen have been able to share an office together by agreeing to disagree when a conflict comes up that might threaten their friendship. Their conflict style is best described as
    a. nonintimate-aggressive.
    b. nonintimate-nonaggressive.
    c. intimate-aggressive.
    d. intimate-nonaggressive.
    Answer: d   **Type: M**   **Page: 381**   **Analysis**

56. At which step in the win-win, collaborative process would you utilize the clear message format?
    a. Identify your problem and unmet needs.
    b. Negotiate a solution.
    c. Make a date.
    d. Describe your problem and needs.
    e. Consider your partner's point of view.
    Answer: d   **Type: M**   **Page: 389**   **Knowledge**

57. At which step in the win-win, collaborative process would brainstorming be appropriate?
    a. Identify your problem and unmet needs.
    b. Negotiate a solution.
    c. Make a date.
    d. Describe your problem and needs.
    e. Consider your partner's point of view.
    Answer: b   **Type: M**   **Page: 390**   **Knowledge**

58. Of the following statements, which most accurately describes the part gender plays in conflict style?
    a. Gender is less important in determining conflict style than the behavior of the other person in the conflict.
    b. Research indicates that the stereotype of women as passive is nearly 90% accurate.
    c. There are virtually no discernible differences between the conflict styles of men and women
    d. When actual behaviors are observed, women are more likely to withdraw from discussion issues than men are.
    e. All of these answers are correct.
    Answer: a   **Type: M**   **Page: 384**   **Knowledge**

59. When unhappy couples argue, they
    a. use evaluative "you" language.
    b. ignore each other's nonverbal relational messages.
    c. have minimal empathy for the other.
    d. are not problem-oriented.
    e. All of these answers are correct .
    Answer: e   **Type: M**   **Page: 369**   **Knowledge**

60. The habitual approach you take when your needs appear incompatible with what another wants is called your
    a. conflict ritual.
    b. conflict style.
    c. passive aggression.
    d. conflict manner.
    e. crazymaking.
    Answer: b   **Type: M**   **Page: 369**   **Knowledge**

61. When John steered clear of Kathy after they had an argument, he was using what style of conflict?
    a. accommodating
    b. compromising
    c. avoiding
    d. passive aggression
    e. crazymaking
    Answer: c   **Type: M**   **Page: 370**   **Application**

62. The conflict style where one has a low concern for him/herself and a high concern for others is called
    a. avoiding.
    b. collaborating.
    c. compromising.
    d. competing
    e. accommodating.
    Answer: e   **Type: M**   **Page: 372**   **Knowledge**

63. Sue wanted to see a movie with her friends Friday night, but ended up at a bar since that's where most of the girls wanted to go. Sue used what conflict style in this situation?
    a. avoiding
    b. collaborating
    c. compromising
    d. competing
    e. accommodating
    Answer: e   **Type: M**   **Page: 372**   **Knowledge**

64. The distinguishing characteristic in win-lose problem solving is
    a. passivity.
    b. power.
    c. aggression.
    d. discussion.
    e. assertiveness.
    Answer: b   **Type: M**   **Page: 373**   **Knowledge**

65. Sue and John argue and John storms out of the house. Sue calls John asking for forgiveness. He returns and they reconcile. Soon they fight again with John once again leaving. This is an example of a(n)
    a. complementary style.
    b. symmetrical style.
    c. conflict ritual.
    d. avoiding style.
    e. win-lose.
    Answer: c   **Type: M**   **Page: 382**   **Application**

66. Of the following, what is not a step in negotiating a solution in the collaborative conflict style approach?
    a. Identify and define the conflict.
    b. Generate 3 or 4 possible solutions.
    c. Evaluate the alternative solutions.
    d. Decide on the best solution.
    e. All of these answers are steps.
    Answer: e   **Type: M**   **Page: 390**   **Knowledge**

67. A competing/win-lose conflict style
    a. involves high concern for self and low concern for others.
    b. can sometimes enhance a relationship.
    c. has a distinguishing characteristic of power.
    d. occurs when people perceive a situation as being an "either-or" one.
    e. All of these answers are correct.
    Answer: e   **Type: M**   **Pages: 372–373**   **Knowledge**

68. Avoiding is sometimes an appropriate style to choose when
    a. the issue is temporary or minor.
    b. speaking up might cause physical harm.
    c. the relationship isn't worth the effort.
    d. a and b are correct.
    e. All of these answers are correct.
    Answer: e   **Type: M**   **Page: 372**   **Knowledge**

69. All of the following are types of direct aggression except
    a. teasing.
    b. character attacks.
    c. threats.
    d. shoving.
    e. nonverbal emblems.
    Answer: d   **Type: M**   **Page: 374**   **Knowledge**

70. What plays a significant role in the effectiveness of the accommodating conflict style?
    a. goodwill
    b. motivation
    c. skill
    d. intelligence
    e. None of these answers are correct
    Answer: b   **Type: M**   **Page: 372**   **Knowledge**

INSTRUCTIONS for questions 71–75: Match each of the following crazymakers with its description.
    a.   mind reader
    b.   crisis tickler
    c.   guilt maker
    d.   pseudoaccommodator
    e.   avoider

71. When this person's partner brings up a problem, she pretends to be busy with the laundry.
    Answer: e   **Type: Matching**   **Page: 375**   **Comprehension**

72. This person pretends to give in and then continues to act in the same way.
    Answer: d   **Type: Matching**   **Page: 375**   **Comprehension**

73. This person handles conflict by trying to make her partner feel responsible for causing her discomfort.
    Answer: c   **Type: Matching**   **Page: 375**   **Comprehension**

74. This person almost brings what's bothering him to the surface, but never quite comes out and expresses himself.
    Answer: b   **Type: Matching**   **Page: 375**   **Comprehension**

75. Instead of expressing her feelings honestly, this person explains what her partner "really" means or what's "really wrong."
    Answer: a   **Type: Matching**   **Page: 375**   **Comprehension**

INSTRUCTIONS for questions 76–80: Match each of the following crazymakers with its description.
    a.   joker
    b.   withholder
    c.   gunnysacker
    d.   trivial tyrannizer
    e.   trapper

76. James tells Sarah he wants her advice, and when she offers it, he becomes very angry and accuses her of trying to tell him what to do.
    Answer: e   **Type: Matching**   **Page: 375**   **Analysis**

77. Elaine deliberately cranks up the volume on her music, knowing that it irritates her mother.
    Answer: d   **Type: Matching**   **Page: 375**   **Analysis**

78. Jeffrey kept all his frustrations to himself and then when his sister asked him to run an errand for him he erupted, telling her all the ways he felt she had imposed upon him in the past two weeks.
    Answer: c   **Type: Matching**   **Page: 375**   **Analysis**

79. Renee refused to speak to Henry for two days.
    Answer: b   **Type: Matching**   **Page: 375**   **Analysis**

80. Thomas laughed off his business partner's comments that he was shirking some of his work responsibilities by saying, "And who got out of the wrong side of the bed today?"
    Answer: a   **Type: Matching**   **Page: 375**   **Analysis**

81. Explain a current conflict you are having with a friend or loved one. Apply the win-win method to arrive at a solution using all six steps as though you were speaking to your partner.
    Answer: **Type: E**   **Pages: 386–391**   **Synthesis**

82. Your text states that compromise hardly deserves the positive image it seems to carry. Describe a time when you compromised to settle a conflict. Did your experience present a more negative or more positive outcome? What is your view of compromise as a conflict resolution outcome?
    Answer: **Type: E**   **Page: 376**   **Evaluation**

83. In a short essay, defend or refute the following statement: "Conflict is a destructive behavior."
    Answer: **Type: E**   **Pages: 368–370**   **Evaluation**

84. Imagine a conflict which seems unable to be solved. What have you learned about interpersonal communication that might enable you to work toward a resolution of the conflict?
    Answer: **Type: E**   **Pages: 368–369, 386–395**   **Evaluation**

85. Pick the two crazymakers you use most often. For each, describe the circumstances in which the crazymaker is used, the function which the crazymaker serves, the consequences of using the crazymaker, and any alternative behavior which would be more constructive.
    Answer: **Type: E**   **Page: 375**   **Evaluation**

86. "In order for there to be winners, there have to be losers." Discuss this statement by examining an interpersonal conflict in which you have been involved.
    Answer: **Type: E**   **Pages: 386–391**   **Synthesis**

87. Define the term conflict as described in your text. Explain in detail each element of the definition.
    Answer: **Type: E**   **Pages: 367–368**   **Analysis**

88. Examine the differences between men and women in how they approach conflict. Include research findings as well as your own personal experiences in your discussion.
    Answer: **Type: E**   **Pages: 383–384**   **Evaluation**